TOEFL 실전모의고사

시원스쿨 LAB

ETS 토플 공식 파트너
TOEFL 실전모의고사

초판 1쇄 발행 2025년 12월 4일

지은이 시원스쿨어학연구소
펴낸곳 (주)에스제이더블유인터내셔널
펴낸이 양홍걸 이시원

홈페이지 www.siwonschool.com
주소 서울시 영등포구 영신로 166 시원스쿨
교재 구입 문의 02)2014-8151
고객센터 02)6409-0878

ISBN 979-11-7550-049-5 13740
Number 1-110505-26269920-09

이 책은 저작권법에 따라 보호받는 저작물이므로 무단복제와 무단전재를 금합니다. 이 책 내용의 전부 또는 일부를 이용하려면 반드시 저작권자와 ㈜에스제이더블유인터내셔널의 서면 동의를 받아야 합니다.

머리말

미국 ETS(Educational Testing Service)는 2026년 1월 21일부터 TOEFL iBT 시험을 전면 개정한다고 공식 발표했습니다. 1964년 첫 시행 이후, TOEFL은 전 세계 수험생들이 영어 실력을 입증하기 위한 가장 권위 있는 국제 영어 시험으로 자리매김해 왔습니다. 그러나 그동안 시험이 상위권 대학, 특히 미국 명문대 입학 기준에 초점을 두고 있다는 지적도 꾸준히 제기되어 왔습니다. 이에 따라 ETS는 보다 폭넓은 수준의 대학에서 요구하는 현실적 영어 능력을 평가하고, 수험생에게는 더 간결하고 효율적인 시험 경험을 제공하기 위해 시험 구조와 문항 유형을 대대적으로 개편하기로 결정했습니다.

개정 TOEFL의 주요 변화는 다음과 같습니다.

❶ Reading(읽기)과 Listening(듣기) 영역은 다단계 적응형(multistage adaptive) 형식으로 바뀌어, 응시자의 실력에 따라 시험 난이도가 실시간으로 조정됩니다. 또한, 특정 전공 지식이나 배경지식이 필요한 지문은 축소되고, 캠퍼스 생활, 이메일, 공지문, 웹사이트 등 실제적이고 현대적인 상황을 반영한 내용이 추가됩니다.

❷ Writing(쓰기)과 Speaking(말하기) 영역 또한 큰 폭의 변화를 맞습니다. 기존의 통합형(integrated) 과제는 모두 폐지되며, 준비 시간 없이 바로 응답해야 하는 짧은 문항 중심으로 구성됩니다. 특히 Writing 영역에서는 2023년에 도입된 토론형 과제가 유지되는 한편, 문장 만들기 및 이메일 쓰기 등 실용적인 과제가 새롭게 추가됩니다.

❸ 시험 결과 발표 기간은 기존의 5일 내외에서 72시간 이내로 단축되며, 점수 체계 또한 기존의 0-120점 방식에서 CEFR(the Common European Framework of Reference for Languages 유럽공통참조기준) 연동 1-6 밴드(0.5 단위) 체계로 전환됩니다.

❹ 형식은 간소화되었지만, TOEFL의 핵심 철학인 실력 기반 평가 원칙은 더욱 강화됩니다. 난이도 조정 시스템을 통해 수험자의 실제 언어 능력이 보다 정밀하게 측정되며, 고득점을 위해서는 '운'이 아닌 정확하고 탄탄한 영어 실력이 요구됩니다.

이 책은 개정된 TOEFL의 새로운 방향성을 충실히 반영하여 구성되었으며, TOEFL iBT 실전 모의고사 3회분을 제공합니다. ETS 토플 공식 파트너인 시원스쿨은 신뢰도 높은 콘텐츠를 신속하고 정확하게 제공함으로써, 수험생들이 시험 변화로 인한 혼란을 최소화하고 효과적으로 대비할 수 있도록 하였습니다.

이 책이 변화하는 시험에 효과적으로 대비하고, 자신의 영어 실력을 정확히 진단하며 한 단계 성장할 수 있는 든든한 길잡이가 되길 바랍니다.

시원스쿨어학연구소

목차

- 머리말　03
- 목차　04
- 개정 TOEFL에 대한 모든 것　06

TEST 1

1. Reading Module 1　11
2. Reading Module 2　21
3. Listening Module 1　28
4. Listening Module 2　41
5. Writing　48
6. Speaking　55

TEST 2

1. Reading Module 1　67
2. Reading Module 2　77
3. Listening Module 1　84
4. Listening Module 2　97
5. Writing　104
6. Speaking　111

TEST 3

1. Reading Module 1　123
2. Reading Module 2　136
3. Listening Module 1　142
4. Listening Module 2　151
5. Writing　158
6. Speaking　165

Answers

1. TEST 1 2
2. TEST 2 32
3. TEST 3 63

온라인 부록

1. 토플 필수 어휘 1000 (PDF)
2. Answers (PDF)
3. 음원 (MP3)

* lab.siwonschool.com 접속 ▶ 교재/MP3 탭 클릭 ▶ 해당 도서 검색 ▶ 다운로드

개정 TOEFL에 대한 모든 것

2026년 1월 21일부터 시행되는 개정 TOEFL iBT는 다음과 같은 특징을 갖고 있습니다.

1 두 개의 모듈과 더미 문항이 출제되는 Reading과 Listening

Reading 영역은 두 개의 모듈(세트)로 구성되어 있습니다. 먼저 첫 번째 모듈을 모두 풀면, 두 번째 모듈이 자동으로 제시되며, 이때 두 번째 모듈의 난이도는 수험자의 첫 번째 모듈 성적에 따라 조정됩니다.

Listening 영역 또한 Reading과 동일하게 두 개의 모듈로 구성되며, 응시자의 실력 수준에 따라 두 번째 모듈의 난이도가 달라집니다.

또한, 각 모듈에는 2023년 7월 개정 이후 한동안 제외되었던 더미(dummy) 문항이 다시 포함됩니다. 더미 문항은 점수 산정에 반영되지 않는 문항으로, 실제 시험 중에는 어느 문항이, 몇 문항이 더미인지 구별하기 어렵습니다. 따라서 수험자는 모든 문항을 실제 시험 문항이라 생각하고 성실히 응시해야 합니다.

2 Writing과 Speaking 시험 순서 변경

개정 이전에는 Listening 영역이 종료된 직후 Speaking 영역이 바로 이어지는 구조였습니다. 이로 인해 Listening을 늦게 마치는 수험생들은 시험장 내에서 다른 수험생들의 Speaking 답변 소리에 방해를 받아 집중하기 어려운 불편함을 겪기도 했습니다.

이러한 문제를 개선하기 위해 개정된 TOEFL에서는 Listening 영역이 끝난 뒤 Writing 영역이 이어지도록 시험 순서가 조정되었습니다. 이로써 수험생들은 보다 조용하고 안정적인 환경에서 시험을 치를 수 있게 되었습니다.

3 학문적 내용은 감소하고 실생활 기반 내용은 증가

개정 TOEFL은 실생활과 밀접한 상황에서의 영어 사용 능력을 중점적으로 평가합니다. 기존 시험이 비교적 장문의 학문적 지문으로 구성되었던 것과 달리, 개정 시험에서는 대학 생활이나 일상 속에서 실제로 마주할 수 있는 상황을 다룬 짧고 실용적인 내용이 주를 이룹니다.

특히, 기존 Writing 및 Speaking 영역에 출제되던 통합형 과제(Integrated Task)는 긴 학술적 주제를 바탕으로 한 지문과 강의 내용을 정리한 뒤 답변을 작성해야 했기 때문에, 노트테이킹이 필수적이었습니다. 그러나 개정 TOEFL 에서는 이러한 형식이 사라지고, 실생활과 밀접하게 연관된 짧고 실용적인 문항으로 대체되었습니다. 수험자는 별도의 준비 시간 없이 즉시 응답해야 하는 형태의 과제를 통해 실제 영어 사용 능력을 평가받게 됩니다.

주요 변화	개정 전	개정 후
점수 체계	• 0-120점	• CEFR 연동 1-6 밴드(0.5 단위)
점수 발표	• 약 5일 이후	• 72시간 이후
Reading (읽기 영역)	• 600-700 단어의 학술적 지문 읽기	• 단어 완성하기(Complete the Words) • 실용문 읽기(Read in Daily Life) • 200-300 단어의 학술적 지문 읽기 (Read an Academic Passage)
Listening (듣기 영역)	• 긴 대화 및 강의 듣기	• 듣고 적절한 응답 고르기 (Listen and Choose a Response) • 대화 듣기 (Listen to a Conversation) • 공지 듣기 (Listen to an Announcement) • 강연 듣기 (Listen to an Academic Talk)
Writing (쓰기 영역)	• 학술적 지문과 강의를 요약하는 통합형 과제(Integrated Task) • 학술적 토론을 위한 글쓰기 (Write for an Academic Discussion)	• 문장 만들기(Build a Sentence) • 이메일 쓰기(Write an Email) • 학술적 토론을 위한 글쓰기 (Write for an Academic Discussion)
Speaking (말하기 영역)	• 질문에 대한 나의 의견을 답변하는 독립형 과제(Independent Task) • 짧은 지문, 대화 또는 강의를 요약하는 통합형 과제 (Integrated Task)	• 듣고 따라 말하기(Listen and Repeat) • 면접 보기(Take an Interview)

TEST 1

실전모의고사 유의 사항

실제 시험과 동일한 환경에서 연습하기 위해 다음 사항을 반드시 지켜 주세요.

1 Reading – Listening – Writing – Speaking 순서로 한 번에 진행
중간에 휴식 없이 네 영역을 연속으로 풀며 실제 시험 흐름에
익숙해집니다.

2 Listening은 음원을 먼저 듣기
문제를 미리 읽지 말고, 반드시 음원을 모두 들은 후에 문제를 풉니다.
실제 시험과 동일한 조건으로 문제를 푸는 것이 중요합니다.

3 Listening과 Speaking 음원은 한 번만 듣기
반복 청취는 금지하며, 한 번의 청취로 내용을 이해하고 답변하는 훈련을
합니다.

4 노트테이킹 도구 준비하기
백지와 연필을 준비해 Listening 영역에서 필요한 내용을 간단히
메모하며 문제를 풉니다.

5 시간을 재며 Writing과 Speaking 문제 풀기
각 영역의 제한 시간 내에 답안을 작성하거나 말하기 연습을 진행해 실제
시험 감각을 익힙니다.

Answers p.2

READING

TOEFL iBT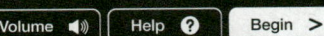

Reading Section

In the reading section, you will answer 35-48 questions to demonstrate how well you understand academic and non-academic texts in English. There are three types of tasks.

Type of Task	Description
Complete the Words	Fill in the missing letters in a paragraph.
Read in Daily Life	Answer questions about everyday reading materials.
Read an Academic Passage	Answer questions about academic passages.

Module 1

TOEFL iBT

Reading | Questions **1-10** of 20

Fill in the missing letters in the paragraph.

Music is a universal element of human culture, influencing both emotions and social connections. As melo_ _ _ _ and rhyth_ _ spread, th_ _ inspire creativ_ _ _ , preserve tradi_ _ _ _ _ _ , and con_ _ _ _ communities ac_ _ _ _ generations. Some coun_ _ _ _ _ are kn_ _ _ for class_ _ _ _ compositions or folk heritage, while others embrace modern genres that reshape cultural identity and daily life. No matter the genre, music remains vital for expression and understanding across cultures worldwide.

TOEFL iBT

Reading | Question **11** of 20

Read an email.

Subject: Low Storage Space

Dear Ms. Hazel,

We are notifying you that your account is running low on storage space. If no action is taken by May 5, some messaging features may stop working properly. You can increase storage space by deleting old files. Thank you for your attention to this matter.

Best regards,
Jack Keating

What is the main purpose of the email?

(A) To provide a notification
(B) To offer a new service
(C) To verify an account
(D) To report a technical issue

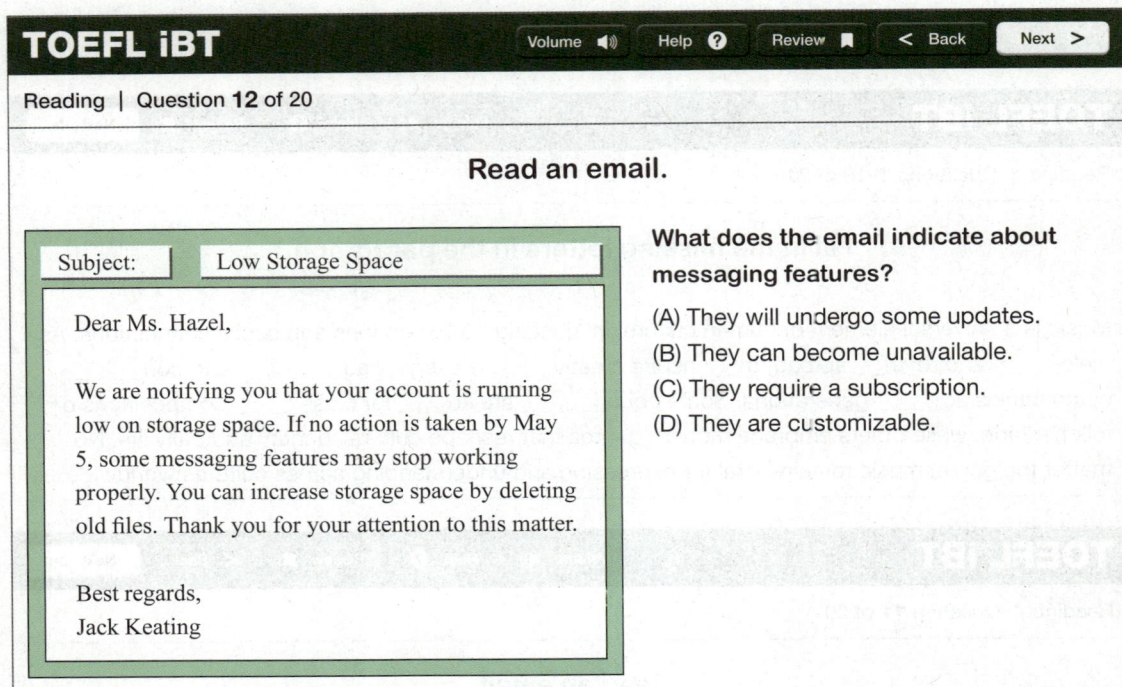

Read an email.

Subject: Fire Safety Inspection

The next fire safety inspection in our building is scheduled for June 21 from 10 A.M. to 4 P.M. This inspection will be carried out by certified fire safety professionals.

During this time, sprinklers, smoke detectors, fire alarms, fire extinguishers, and emergency exits will be tested. If you are on site, you may hear loud alarms and experience temporary restrictions in hallways or stairwells. Residential units and office spaces will not be accessed by inspectors directly.

Please remember: Fire safety inspections are conducted regularly to meet building safety codes. Willful damage or theft of fire equipment, such as tampering with smoke detectors or removing fire extinguishers, is strictly prohibited and can constitute a criminal offense.

If you have questions or need assistance, please contact Building Management. Inspection findings will be posted on the community bulletin board and emailed to everyone within a few days. We appreciate your cooperation in helping maintain a safe living and working environment.

The email is most likely sent to
(A) local fire station workers
(B) residents and office tenants
(C) the company that constructed the building
(D) people who are interested in leasing the apartment

Read an email.

Subject: Fire Safety Inspection

The next fire safety inspection in our building is scheduled for June 21 from 10 A.M. to 4 P.M. This inspection will be carried out by certified fire safety professionals.

During this time, sprinklers, smoke detectors, fire alarms, fire extinguishers, and emergency exits will be tested. If you are on site, you may hear loud alarms and experience temporary restrictions in hallways or stairwells. Residential units and office spaces will not be accessed by inspectors directly.

Please remember: Fire safety inspections are conducted regularly to meet building safety codes. Willful damage or theft of fire equipment, such as tampering with smoke detectors or removing fire extinguishers, is strictly prohibited and can constitute a criminal offense.

If you have questions or need assistance, please contact Building Management. Inspection findings will be posted on the community bulletin board and emailed to everyone within a few days. We appreciate your cooperation in helping maintain a safe living and working environment.

What can be inferred about the building's fire equipment?

(A) It is protected by law.
(B) It may require some new upgrades.
(C) It is inspected by property managers.
(D) Several smoke detectors have malfunctioned recently.

Read an email.

Subject: Fire Safety Inspection

The next fire safety inspection in our building is scheduled for June 21 from 10 A.M. to 4 P.M. This inspection will be carried out by certified fire safety professionals.

During this time, sprinklers, smoke detectors, fire alarms, fire extinguishers, and emergency exits will be tested. If you are on site, you may hear loud alarms and experience temporary restrictions in hallways or stairwells. Residential units and office spaces will not be accessed by inspectors directly.

Please remember: Fire safety inspections are conducted regularly to meet building safety codes. Willful damage or theft of fire equipment, such as tampering with smoke detectors or removing fire extinguishers, is strictly prohibited and can constitute a criminal offense.

If you have questions or need assistance, please contact Building Management. Inspection findings will be posted on the community bulletin board and emailed to everyone within a few days. We appreciate your cooperation in helping maintain a safe living and working environment.

The receiver of the email will be notified of

(A) changes in the schedule of the June 21 inspection
(B) new guidelines for fire safety from the city
(C) the results of the June 21 inspection
(D) the fees for building maintenance

The Role of Seaweed

Seaweed provides vital benefits to both marine ecosystems and human societies, serving as a source of food, oxygen, and essential nutrients. Unlike land plants, seaweed lacks true roots and leaves. It instead absorbs minerals and carbon dioxide directly from the seawater. This ability allows it to grow in environments where other plants cannot survive. By reducing the erosion of shorelines, producing oxygen, and forming the base of many marine food webs, seaweed is crucial for the health of marine ecosystems.

One fascinating group of seaweeds is kelp, which can form vast underwater forests stretching for miles. These towering structures create shelter for fish, invertebrates, and even marine mammals such as sea otters. In return, many of these species contribute organic matter back into the ecosystem, reinforcing the kelp forest's vitality. This dynamic partnership not only supports biodiversity but also helps buffer coastlines against strong waves and storms.

Not all aspects of seaweed are positive. Some invasive seaweed species spread aggressively, crowding out native plants and altering local ecosystems. For example, the introduction of Caulerpa taxifolia has disrupted coastal habitats in parts of the Mediterranean. By studying the diverse roles of seaweed, researchers can better manage its harmful impacts while also utilizing its potential for food, medicine, biofuel, and climate solutions.

According to the passage, seaweed is beneficial in terms of

(A) generating essential nutrients in coastal areas
(B) absorbing oxygen from the seawater
(C) acting as a primary consumer in marine food webs
(D) protecting shorelines using its dense roots

The Role of Seaweed

Seaweed provides vital benefits to both marine ecosystems and human societies, serving as a source of food, oxygen, and essential nutrients. Unlike land plants, seaweed lacks true roots and leaves. It instead absorbs minerals and carbon dioxide directly from the seawater. This ability allows it to grow in environments where other plants cannot survive. By reducing the erosion of shorelines, producing oxygen, and forming the base of many marine food webs, seaweed is **crucial** for the health of marine ecosystems.

One fascinating group of seaweeds is kelp, which can form vast underwater forests stretching for miles. These towering structures create shelter for fish, invertebrates, and even marine mammals such as sea otters. In return, many of these species contribute organic matter back into the ecosystem, reinforcing the kelp forest's vitality. This dynamic partnership not only supports biodiversity but also helps buffer coastlines against strong waves and storms.

Not all aspects of seaweed are positive. Some invasive seaweed species spread aggressively, crowding out native plants and altering local ecosystems. For example, the introduction of Caulerpa taxifolia has disrupted coastal habitats in parts of the Mediterranean. By studying the diverse roles of seaweed, researchers can better manage its harmful impacts while also utilizing its potential for food, medicine, biofuel, and climate solutions.

The word "crucial" in the passage is closest in meaning to

(A) necessary
(B) active
(C) fresh
(D) sturdy

The Role of Seaweed

Seaweed provides vital benefits to both marine ecosystems and human societies, serving as a source of food, oxygen, and essential nutrients. Unlike land plants, seaweed lacks true roots and leaves. It instead absorbs minerals and carbon dioxide directly from the seawater. This ability allows it to grow in environments where other plants cannot survive. By reducing the erosion of shorelines, producing oxygen, and forming the base of many marine food webs, seaweed is crucial for the health of marine ecosystems.

One fascinating group of seaweeds is kelp, which can form vast underwater forests stretching for miles. These towering structures create shelter for fish, invertebrates, and even marine mammals such as sea otters. In return, many of these species contribute organic matter back into the ecosystem, reinforcing the kelp forest's vitality. This dynamic partnership not only supports biodiversity but also helps buffer coastlines against strong waves and storms.

Not all aspects of seaweed are positive. Some invasive seaweed species spread aggressively, crowding out native plants and altering local ecosystems. For example, the introduction of Caulerpa taxifolia has disrupted coastal habitats in parts of the Mediterranean. By studying the diverse roles of seaweed, researchers can better manage its harmful impacts while also utilizing its potential for food, medicine, biofuel, and climate solutions.

Which of the following is NOT mentioned in the passage as a function of seaweed?

(A) Playing a role in oxygen production
(B) Transferring nutrients into the ocean through its roots
(C) Providing shelter for fish and sea mammals
(D) Preventing the deterioration of shorelines

The Role of Seaweed

Seaweed provides vital benefits to both marine ecosystems and human societies, serving as a source of food, oxygen, and essential nutrients. Unlike land plants, seaweed lacks true roots and leaves. It instead absorbs minerals and carbon dioxide directly from the seawater. This ability allows it to grow in environments where other plants cannot survive. By reducing the erosion of shorelines, producing oxygen, and forming the base of many marine food webs, seaweed is crucial for the health of marine ecosystems.

One fascinating group of seaweeds is kelp, which can form vast underwater forests stretching for miles. These towering structures create shelter for fish, invertebrates, and even marine mammals such as sea otters. In return, many of these species contribute organic matter back into the ecosystem, reinforcing the kelp forest's vitality. This dynamic partnership not only supports biodiversity but also helps buffer coastlines against strong waves and storms.

Not all aspects of seaweed are positive. Some invasive seaweed species spread aggressively, crowding out native plants and altering local ecosystems. For example, the introduction of Caulerpa taxifolia has disrupted coastal habitats in parts of the Mediterranean. By studying the diverse roles of seaweed, researchers can better manage its harmful impacts while also utilizing its potential for food, medicine, biofuel, and climate solutions.

What can be inferred about kelp?

(A) It grows in mostly sunny environments.
(B) Its forests can sometimes rise to heights above sea level.
(C) It safeguards other organisms from dangerous conditions.
(D) It blocks rainstorms from forming above the ocean.

The Role of Seaweed

Seaweed provides vital benefits to both marine ecosystems and human societies, serving as a source of food, oxygen, and essential nutrients. Unlike land plants, seaweed lacks true roots and leaves. It instead absorbs minerals and carbon dioxide directly from the seawater. This ability allows it to grow in environments where other plants cannot survive. By reducing the erosion of shorelines, producing oxygen, and forming the base of many marine food webs, seaweed is crucial for the health of marine ecosystems.

One fascinating group of seaweeds is kelp, which can form vast underwater forests stretching for miles. These towering structures create shelter for fish, invertebrates, and even marine mammals such as sea otters. In return, many of these species contribute organic matter back into the ecosystem, reinforcing the kelp forest's vitality. This dynamic partnership not only supports biodiversity but also helps buffer coastlines against strong waves and storms.

Not all aspects of seaweed are positive. Some invasive seaweed species spread aggressively, crowding out native plants and altering local ecosystems. For example, the introduction of Caulerpa taxifolia has disrupted coastal habitats in parts of the Mediterranean. By studying the diverse roles of seaweed, researchers can better manage its harmful impacts while also utilizing its potential for food, medicine, biofuel, and climate solutions.

What can be inferred about the diverse roles of seaweed?

(A) This diversity makes seaweed a threat to some areas of the Mediterranean Sea.
(B) This diversity may result in several practical uses in the future.
(C) This diversity will require management and cooperation from nations all around the world.
(D) This diversity is related to the evolution of other types of marine plants.

Module 2

TOEFL iBT

Reading | Questions **1-10** of 15

Fill in the missing letters in the paragraph.

Footage captured by submarines has shown us that strange creatures thrive in the deepest parts of the ocean. People te_ _ to bel_ _ _ _ that su_ _ extreme environ_ _ _ _ _ are ju_ _ barren zon_ _ . In rea_ _ _ _ , research h_ _ clearly sh_ _ _ _ that li_ _ is abundant there. Scientists have recorded more species near hydrothermal vents than in any other deep-ocean habitat. These ecosystems sustain unique food chains and reveal clues about life's origins.

Bioremediation

Environmental science explores how human societies manage and respond to pollution. Industrial and urban areas often struggle with contaminated soil and water. Historically, clean-up efforts relied on chemical treatments or excavation, which could be expensive and disruptive. These methods removed pollutants but often damaged ecosystems and required constant maintenance to prevent recontamination.

In recent years, bioremediation has emerged as an alternative. Bioremediation is a process that uses living organisms, such as bacteria, fungi, or plants, to break down or absorb pollutants. Bioremediation can restore contaminated sites while preserving ecological functions, supporting soil health, and even encouraging the return of wildlife. By using natural means, this approach can rehabilitate environments in ways that are less disruptive than traditional methods.

Economic and technological factors influence the adoption of bioremediation. Advances in monitoring tools and engineering microorganisms have improved the efficiency of clean-up projects, making it a cost-effective solution for many industrial sites. Governments and private companies are increasingly investing in bioremediation, recognizing its potential to meet environmental regulations and community expectations.

However, bioremediation is not without limitations. It can be slower than chemical methods and may not be effective for all types of pollutants. Some organisms used in cleanup may require careful management to prevent unintended ecological impacts. Despite these considerations, bioremediation represents a promising and sustainable approach to environmental restoration, demonstrating how science can harness natural processes to address human-caused problems.

What is suggested in the passage about bioremediation?

(A) It removes pollutants at a faster rate than traditional methods.
(B) It minimizes the need for monitoring tools and engineering technology.
(C) It helps to restore contaminated land while preserving ecological functions.
(D) It uses chemical treatments to prevent recontamination.

Bioremediation

Environmental science explores how human societies manage and respond to pollution. Industrial and urban areas often struggle with contaminated soil and water. Historically, clean-up efforts relied on chemical treatments or excavation, which could be expensive and disruptive. These methods removed pollutants but often damaged ecosystems and required constant maintenance to prevent recontamination.

In recent years, bioremediation has emerged as an alternative. Bioremediation is a process that uses living organisms, such as bacteria, fungi, or plants, to break down or absorb pollutants. Bioremediation can restore contaminated sites while preserving ecological functions, supporting soil health, and even encouraging the return of wildlife. By using natural means, this approach can rehabilitate environments in ways that are less disruptive than traditional methods.

Economic and technological factors influence the adoption of bioremediation. Advances in monitoring tools and engineering microorganisms have improved the efficiency of clean-up projects, making it a cost-effective solution for many industrial sites. Governments and private companies are increasingly investing in bioremediation, recognizing its potential to meet environmental regulations and community expectations.

However, bioremediation is not without limitations. It can be slower than chemical methods and may not be effective for all types of pollutants. Some organisms used in cleanup may require careful management to prevent unintended ecological impacts. Despite these considerations, bioremediation represents a promising and sustainable approach to environmental restoration, demonstrating how science can harness natural processes to address human-caused problems.

What does the passage mention as a benefit of bioremediation?

(A) Higher growth rates of fungi
(B) Restoration of animal populations
(C) Reduced levels of water wastage
(D) Protection of important bacteria in soil

Bioremediation

Environmental science explores how human societies manage and respond to pollution. Industrial and urban areas often struggle with contaminated soil and water. Historically, clean-up efforts relied on chemical treatments or excavation, which could be expensive and disruptive. These methods removed pollutants but often damaged ecosystems and required constant maintenance to prevent recontamination.

In recent years, bioremediation has emerged as an alternative. Bioremediation is a process that uses living organisms, such as bacteria, fungi, or plants, to break down or absorb pollutants. Bioremediation can restore contaminated sites while preserving ecological functions, supporting soil health, and even encouraging the return of wildlife. By using natural means, this approach can rehabilitate environments in ways that are less disruptive than traditional methods.

Economic and technological factors influence the adoption of bioremediation. Advances in monitoring tools and engineering microorganisms have improved the efficiency of clean-up projects, making it a cost-effective solution for many industrial sites. Governments and private companies are increasingly investing in bioremediation, recognizing its potential to meet environmental regulations and community expectations.

However, bioremediation is not without limitations. It can be slower than chemical methods and may not be effective for all types of pollutants. Some organisms used in cleanup may require careful management to prevent unintended ecological impacts. Despite these considerations, bioremediation represents a promising and sustainable approach to environmental restoration, demonstrating how science can harness natural processes to address human-caused problems.

The word "harness" at the end of the passage is closest in meaning to

(A) attach
(B) tackle
(C) utilize
(D) occupy

Bioremediation

Environmental science explores how human societies manage and respond to pollution. Industrial and urban areas often struggle with contaminated soil and water. Historically, clean-up efforts relied on chemical treatments or excavation, which could be expensive and disruptive. These methods removed pollutants but often damaged ecosystems and required constant maintenance to prevent recontamination.

In recent years, bioremediation has emerged as an alternative. Bioremediation is a process that uses living organisms, such as bacteria, fungi, or plants, to break down or absorb pollutants. Bioremediation can restore contaminated sites while preserving ecological functions, supporting soil health, and even encouraging the return of wildlife. By using natural means, this approach can rehabilitate environments in ways that are less disruptive than traditional methods.

Economic and technological factors influence the adoption of bioremediation. Advances in monitoring tools and engineering microorganisms have improved the efficiency of clean-up projects, making it a cost-effective solution for many industrial sites. Governments and private companies are increasingly investing in bioremediation, recognizing its potential to meet environmental regulations and community expectations.

However, bioremediation is not without limitations. It can be slower than chemical methods and may not be effective for all types of pollutants. Some organisms used in cleanup may require careful management to prevent unintended ecological impacts. Despite these considerations, bioremediation represents a promising and sustainable approach to environmental restoration, demonstrating how science can harness natural processes to address human-caused problems.

Why does the author mention governments and private companies?

(A) To highlight the organizations that use bioremediation the most
(B) To encourage readers to follow the examples set by both entities
(C) To indicate that environmental regulations are very important
(D) To underscore the considerable potential of bioremediation

Bioremediation

Environmental science explores how human societies manage and respond to pollution. Industrial and urban areas often struggle with contaminated soil and water. Historically, clean-up efforts relied on chemical treatments or excavation, which could be expensive and disruptive. These methods removed pollutants but often damaged ecosystems and required constant maintenance to prevent recontamination.

In recent years, bioremediation has emerged as an alternative. Bioremediation is a process that uses living organisms, such as bacteria, fungi, or plants, to break down or absorb pollutants. Bioremediation can restore contaminated sites while preserving ecological functions, supporting soil health, and even encouraging the return of wildlife. By using natural means, this approach can rehabilitate environments in ways that are less disruptive than traditional methods.

Economic and technological factors influence the adoption of bioremediation. Advances in monitoring tools and engineering microorganisms have improved the efficiency of clean-up projects, making it a cost-effective solution for many industrial sites. Governments and private companies are increasingly investing in bioremediation, recognizing its potential to meet environmental regulations and community expectations.

However, bioremediation is not without limitations. It can be slower than chemical methods and may not be effective for all types of pollutants. Some organisms used in cleanup may require careful management to prevent unintended ecological impacts. Despite these considerations, bioremediation represents a promising and sustainable approach to environmental restoration, demonstrating how science can harness natural processes to address human-caused problems.

What is the relationship between paragraphs 3 and 4?

(A) Paragraph 4 provides an answer to a question posed in paragraph 3.
(B) Paragraph 4 introduces some drawbacks to the advantages presented in paragraph 3.
(C) Paragraph 4 explains the various technologies introduced in paragraph 3.
(D) Paragraph 4 discusses a solution for an issue mentioned in paragraph 3.

LISTENING

TOEFL iBT Volume   Begin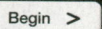

Listening Section

In the listening section, you will answer 35 to 45 questions to demonstrate how well you understand spoken English. There are three types of tasks.

Type of Task	Description
Listen and Choose a Response	Select the best response to the question or statement.
Conversations	Answer questions about short conversations.
Announcements and Academic Talks	Answer questions about announcements and academic talks.

You WILL NOT be able to return to previous questions.

Module 1

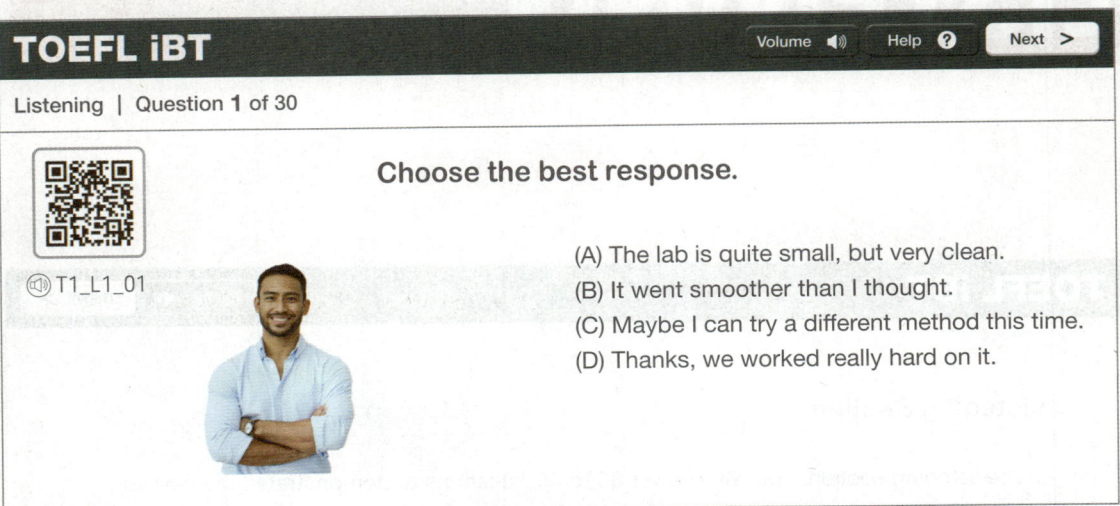

Choose the best response.

(A) The lab is quite small, but very clean.
(B) It went smoother than I thought.
(C) Maybe I can try a different method this time.
(D) Thanks, we worked really hard on it.

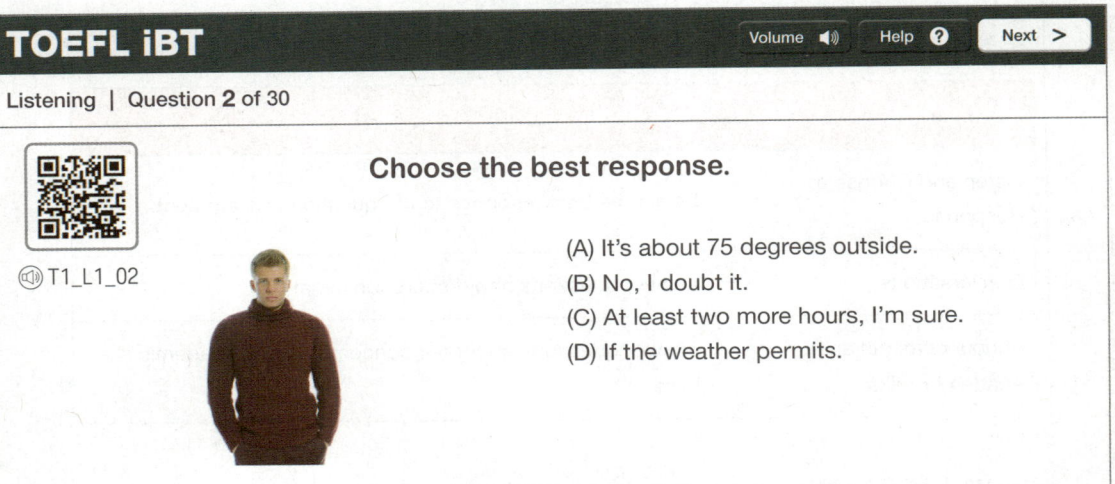

Choose the best response.

(A) It's about 75 degrees outside.
(B) No, I doubt it.
(C) At least two more hours, I'm sure.
(D) If the weather permits.

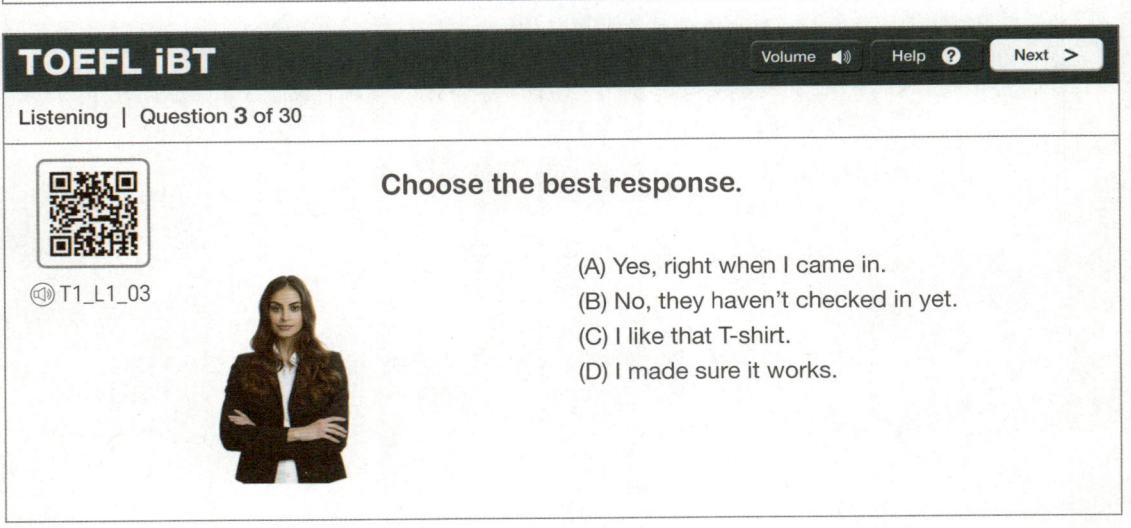

Choose the best response.

(A) Yes, right when I came in.
(B) No, they haven't checked in yet.
(C) I like that T-shirt.
(D) I made sure it works.

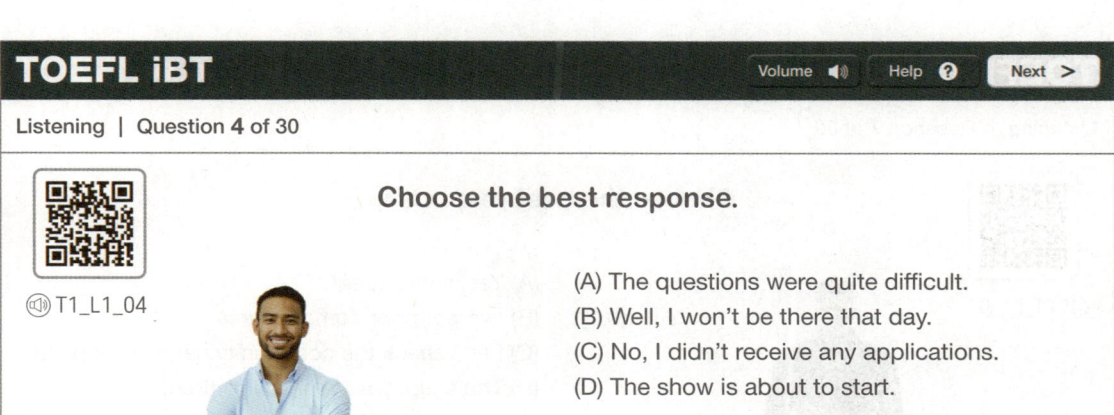

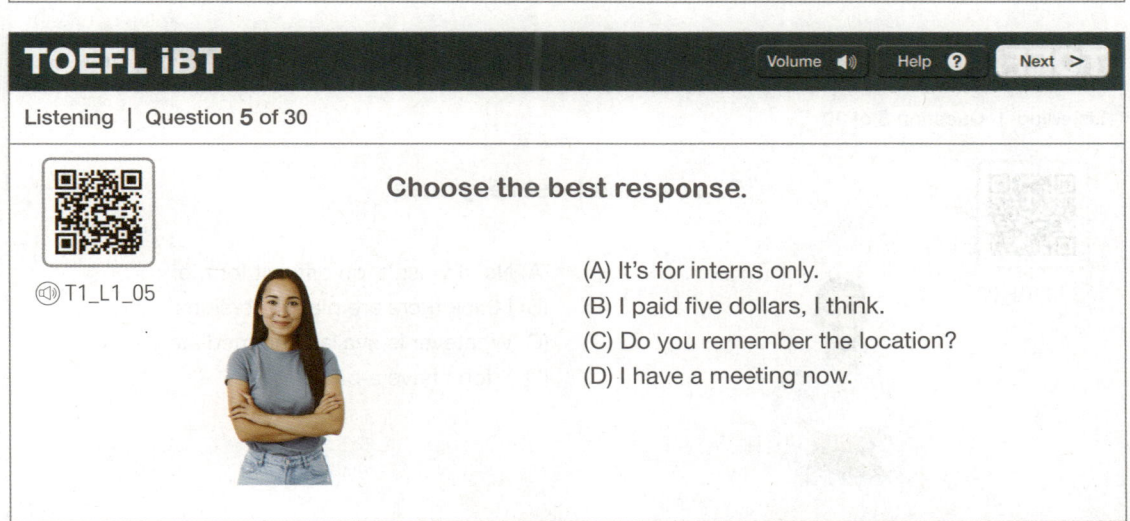

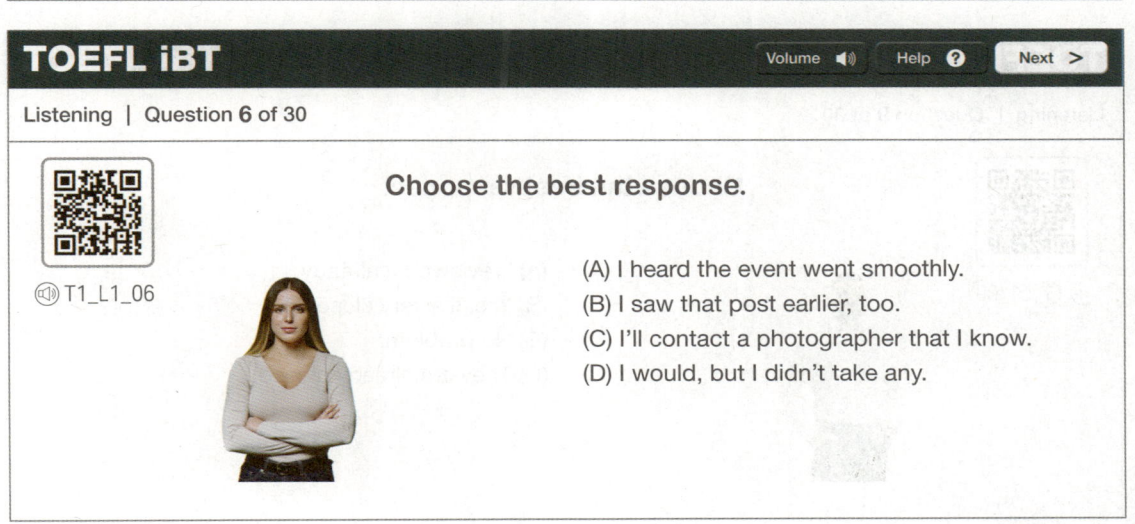

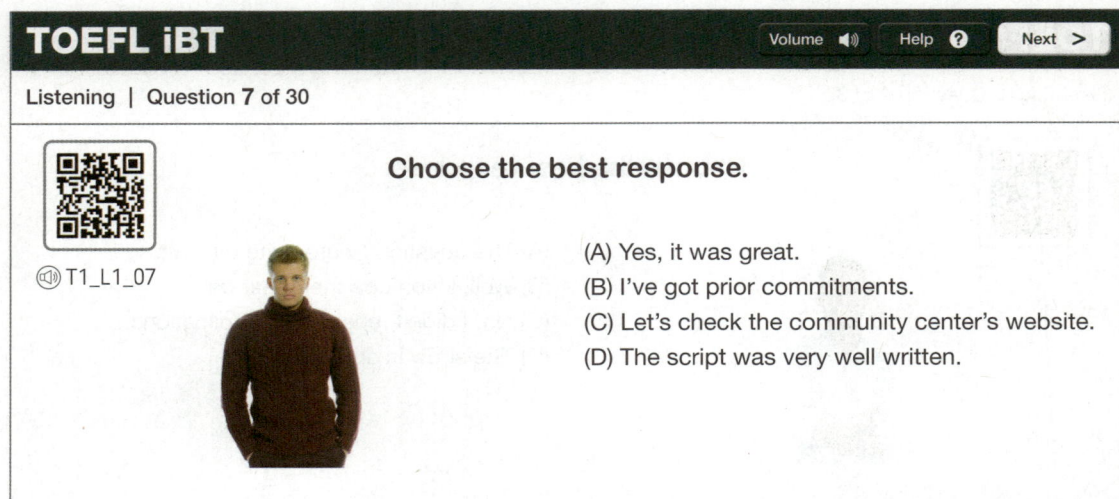

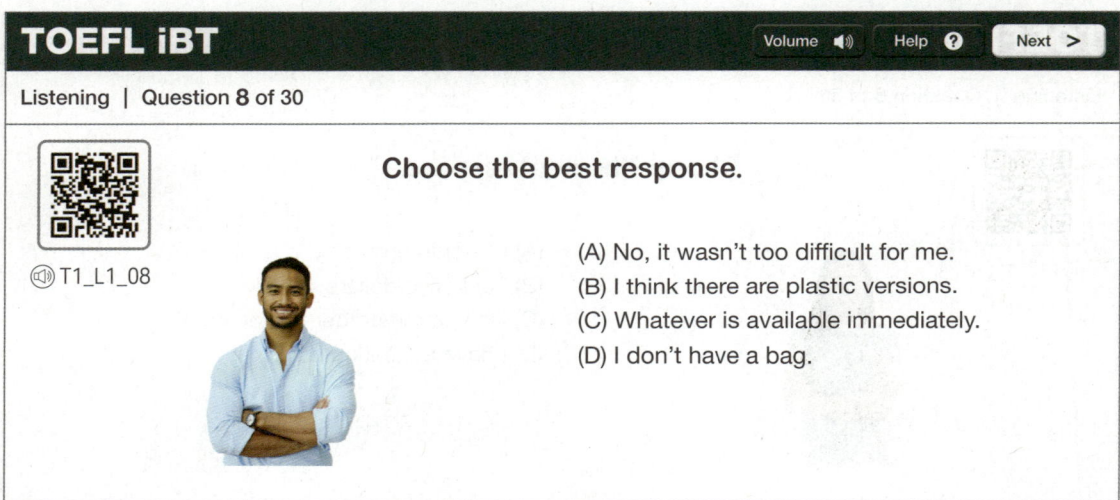

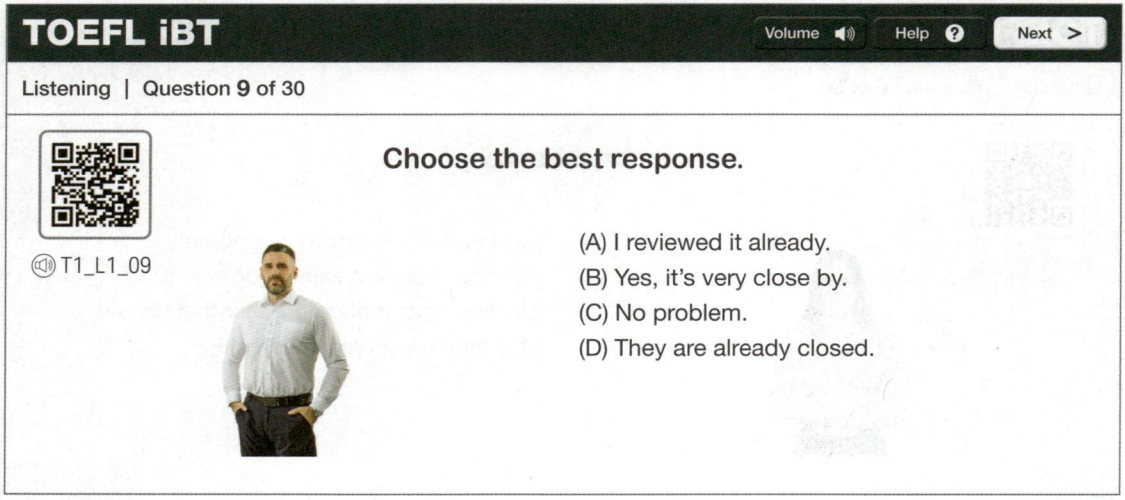

TOEFL iBT

Listening | Question 10 of 30

T1_L1_10

Choose the best response.

(A) The third-floor office lounge.
(B) Vicky is in charge of that.
(C) A new agent.
(D) Mason gave the opening remarks.

TOEFL iBT

Listening | Question 11 of 30

T1_L1_11

Choose the best response.

(A) We can try calling a taxi.
(B) Yes, she picked it up.
(C) I don't have a driver's license.
(D) He takes the bus every day.

TOEFL iBT

Listening | Question 12 of 30

T1_L1_12

Choose the best response.

(A) It includes free shipping.
(B) The distribution center is on First Avenue.
(C) I'll take care of it after lunch.
(D) I'll submit a reimbursement request.

Listen to a conversation.

T1_L1_1314

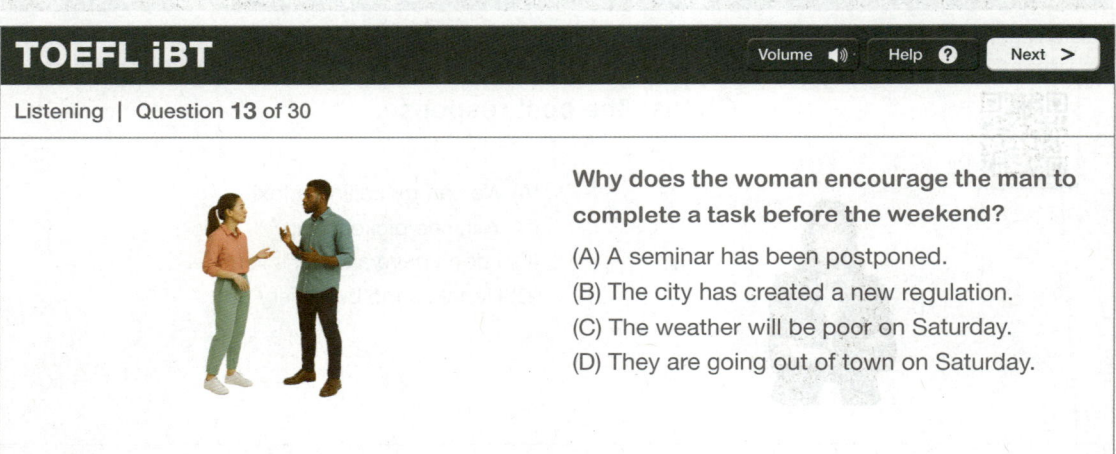

Why does the woman encourage the man to complete a task before the weekend?

(A) A seminar has been postponed.
(B) The city has created a new regulation.
(C) The weather will be poor on Saturday.
(D) They are going out of town on Saturday.

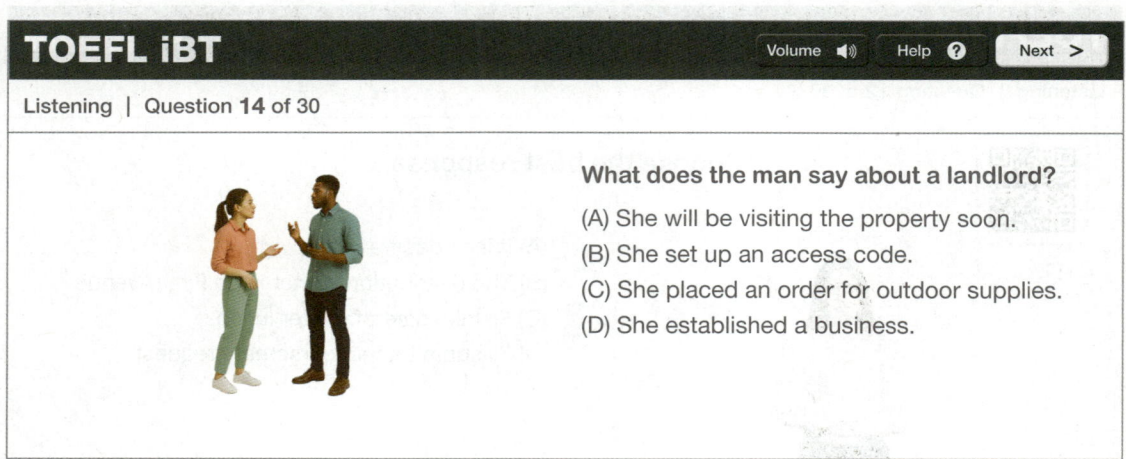

What does the man say about a landlord?

(A) She will be visiting the property soon.
(B) She set up an access code.
(C) She placed an order for outdoor supplies.
(D) She established a business.

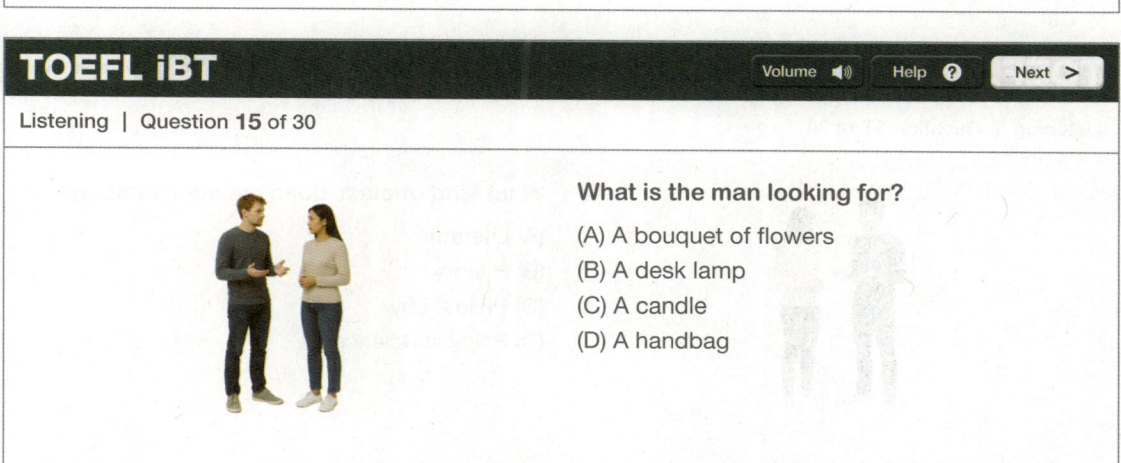

What is the man looking for?

(A) A bouquet of flowers
(B) A desk lamp
(C) A candle
(D) A handbag

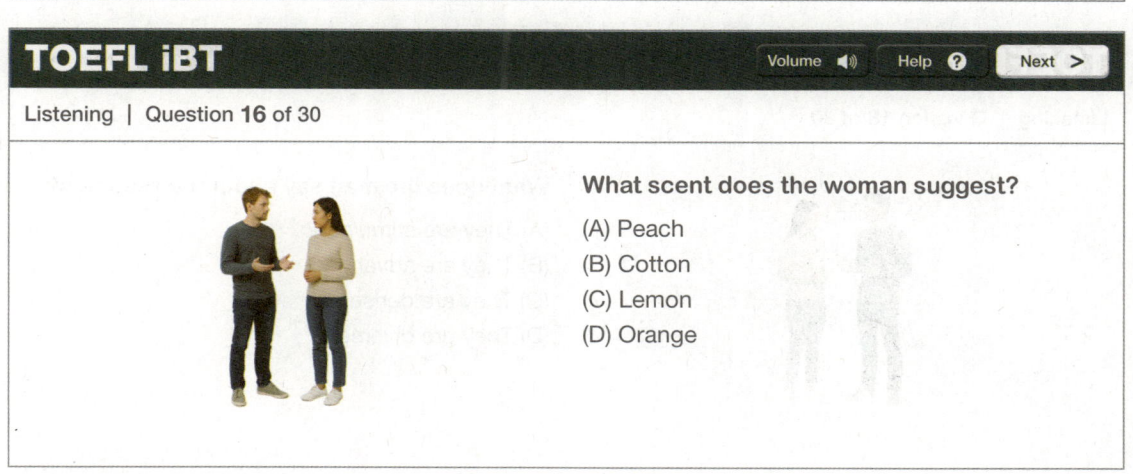

What scent does the woman suggest?

(A) Peach
(B) Cotton
(C) Lemon
(D) Orange

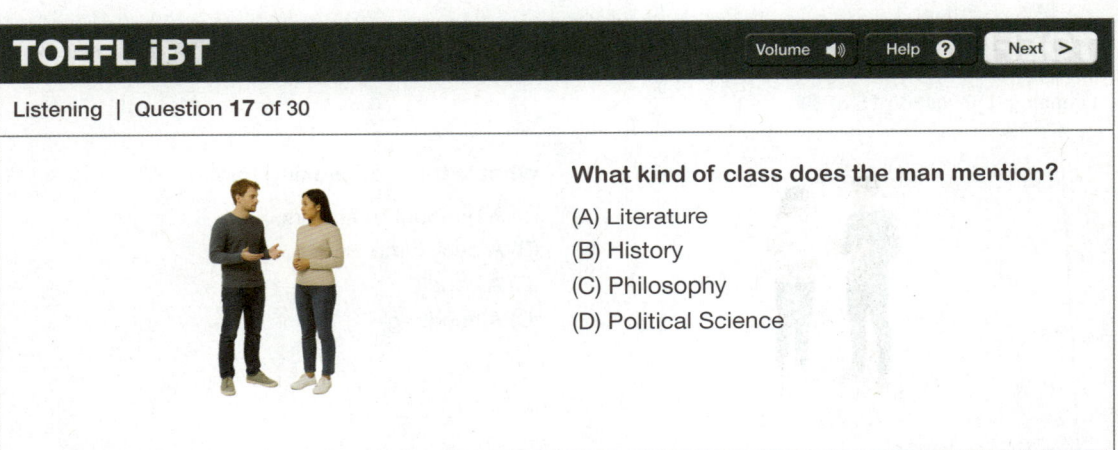

What kind of class does the man mention?

(A) Literature
(B) History
(C) Philosophy
(D) Political Science

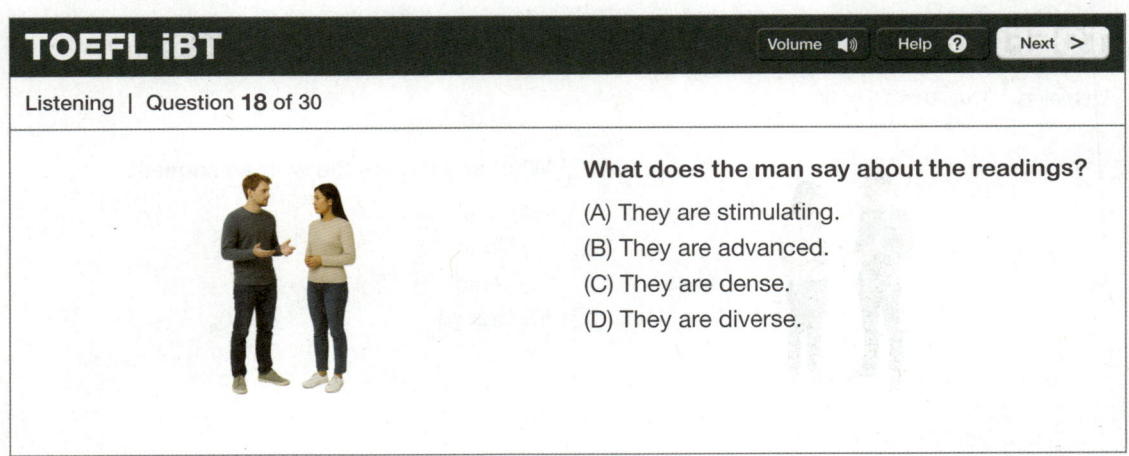

What does the man say about the readings?

(A) They are stimulating.
(B) They are advanced.
(C) They are dense.
(D) They are diverse.

TOEFL iBT

Listening | Questions **19-20** of 30

Listen to an announcement at a university club meeting.

🔊 T1_L1_1920

TOEFL iBT

Volume 🔊 | Help ❓ | Next >

Listening | Question **19** of 30

What is the main topic of the announcement?

(A) A talent show
(B) A supervising professor
(C) A special panel event
(D) A member recruitment process

TOEFL iBT

Volume 🔊 | Help ❓ | Next >

Listening | Question **20** of 30

What are students encouraged to do?

(A) Create a speech
(B) Submit a suggestion
(C) Invite their parents
(D) Pay a club fee

Listen to an announcement at a university club meeting.

T1_L1_2122

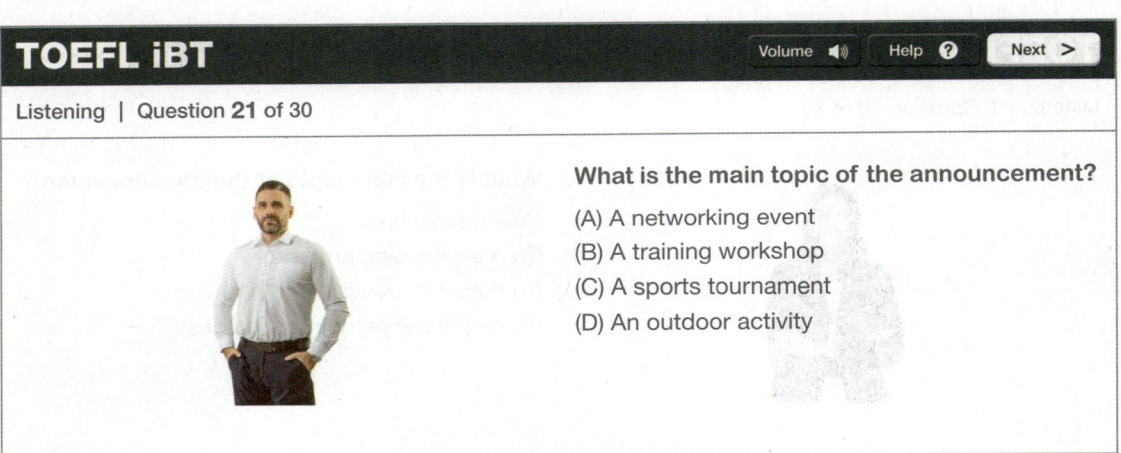

What is the main topic of the announcement?

(A) A networking event
(B) A training workshop
(C) A sports tournament
(D) An outdoor activity

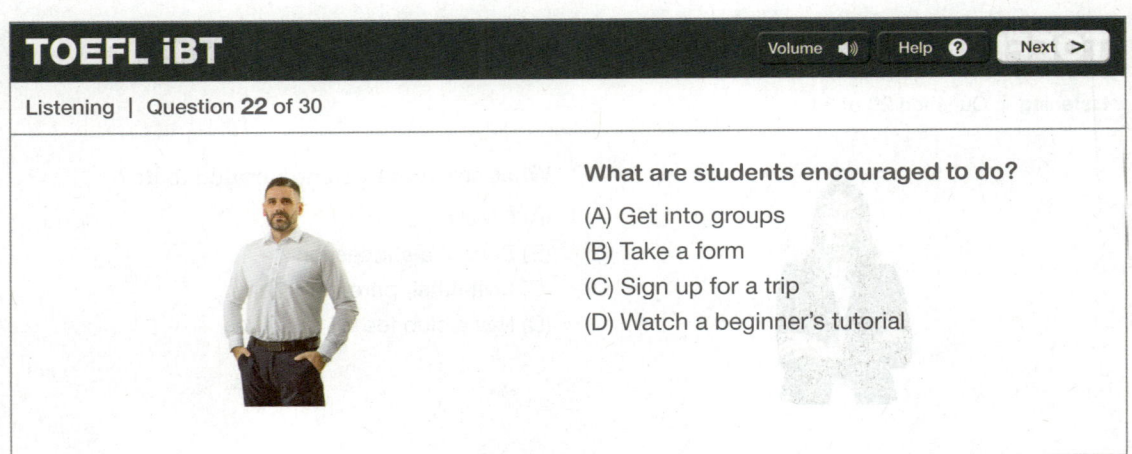

What are students encouraged to do?

(A) Get into groups
(B) Take a form
(C) Sign up for a trip
(D) Watch a beginner's tutorial

TOEFL iBT

Listening | Questions 23-24 of 30

Listen to an announcement at a campus event.

T1_L1_2324

TOEFL iBT

Listening | Question 23 of 30

What is the main topic of the announcement?

(A) An upcoming career fair
(B) A new student orientation
(C) A lecture series
(D) A public speaking contest

TOEFL iBT

Listening | Question 24 of 30

What does the speaker hope the listeners will do?

(A) Talk to some employers
(B) Visit a booth
(C) Receive a gift
(D) Buy a ticket

TOEFL iBT

Listening | Questions 25-26 of 30

Listen to an announcement at a university event.

T1_L1_2526

TOEFL iBT

Listening | Question 25 of 30

What is the main topic of the announcement?

(A) An anniversary celebration
(B) A seasonal music festival
(C) A local parade
(D) A new movie screening

TOEFL iBT

Listening | Question 26 of 30

What does the speaker hope the listeners will do?

(A) Participate in a performance
(B) Enter the raffle
(C) Bring their friends
(D) Attend the festival

TOEFL iBT

Listening | Questions 27-30 of 30

Listen to a talk in a history class.

T1_L1_2730

TOEFL iBT

Listening | Question 27 of 30

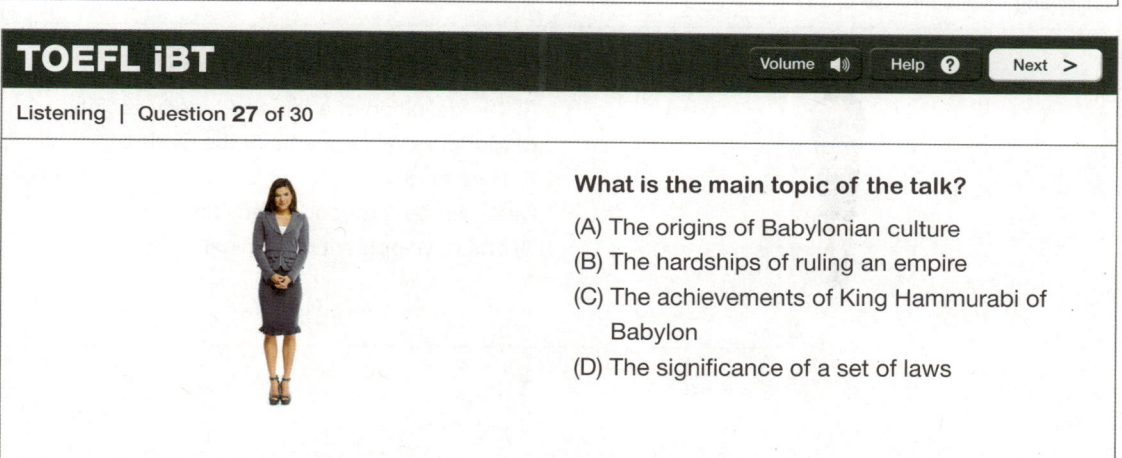

What is the main topic of the talk?

(A) The origins of Babylonian culture
(B) The hardships of ruling an empire
(C) The achievements of King Hammurabi of Babylon
(D) The significance of a set of laws

TOEFL iBT

Listening | Question 28 of 30

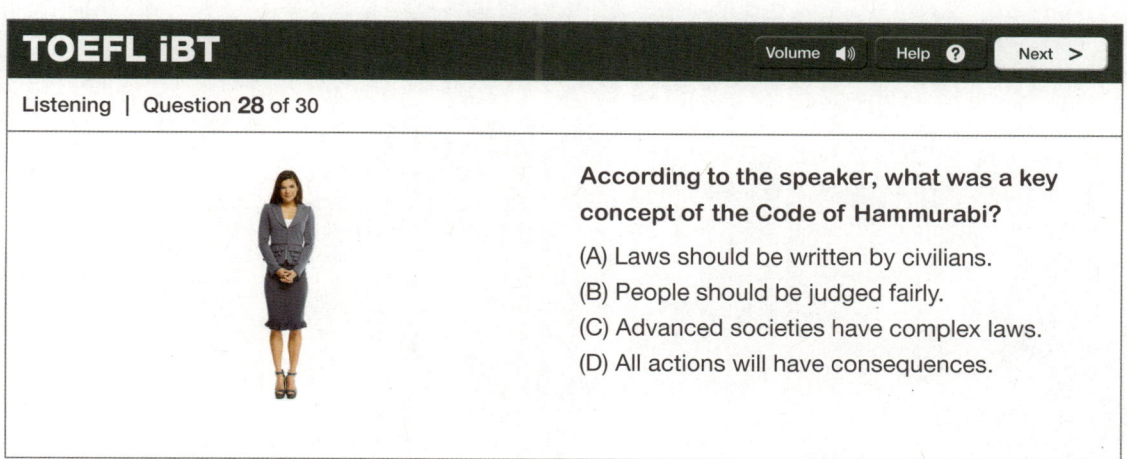

According to the speaker, what was a key concept of the Code of Hammurabi?

(A) Laws should be written by civilians.
(B) People should be judged fairly.
(C) Advanced societies have complex laws.
(D) All actions will have consequences.

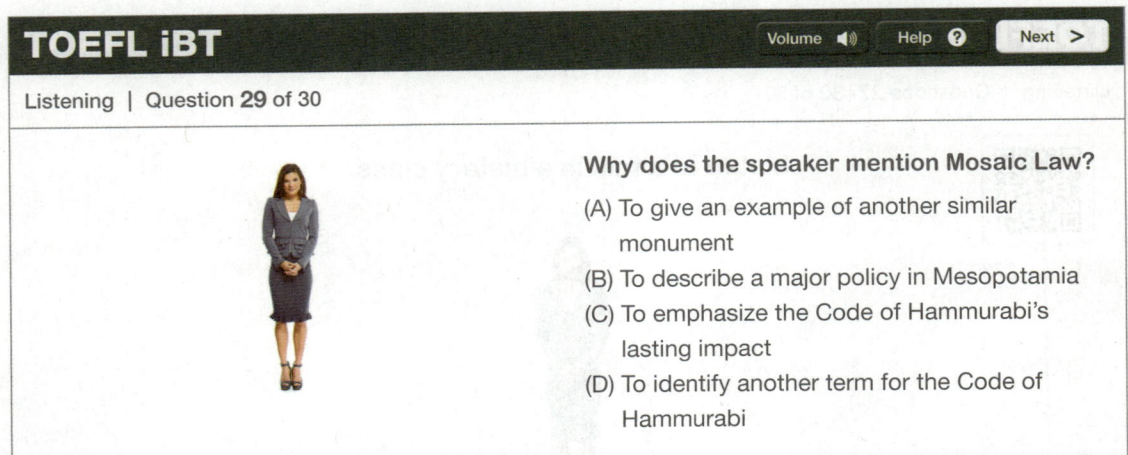

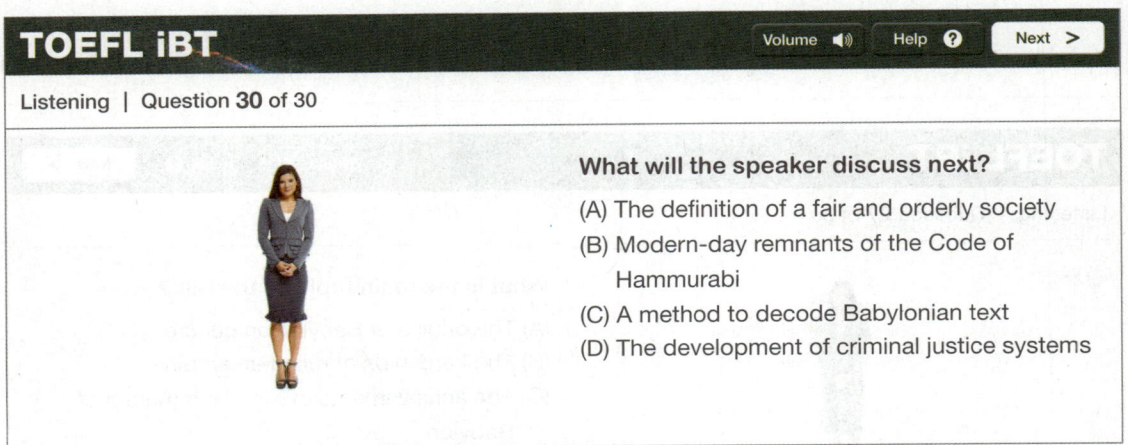

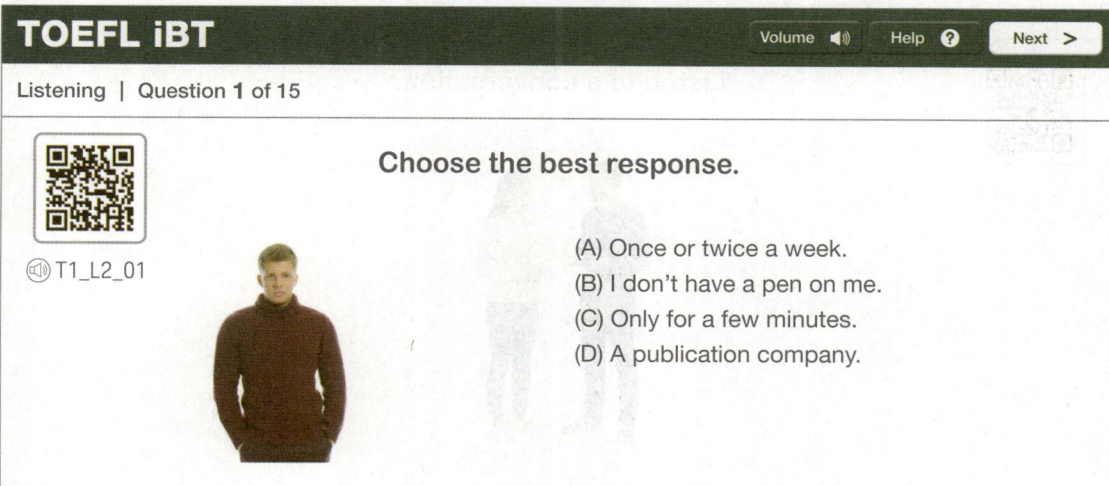

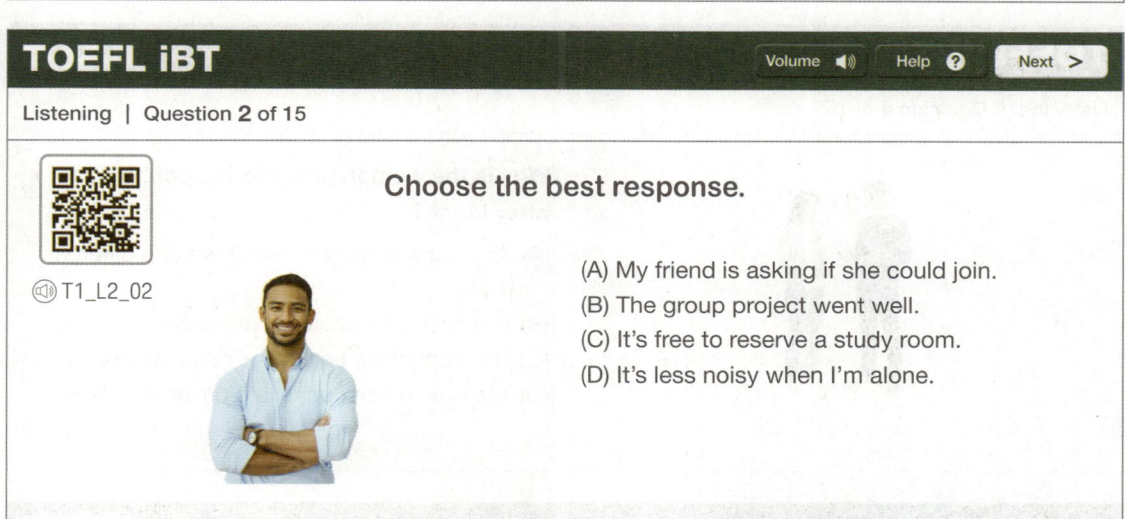

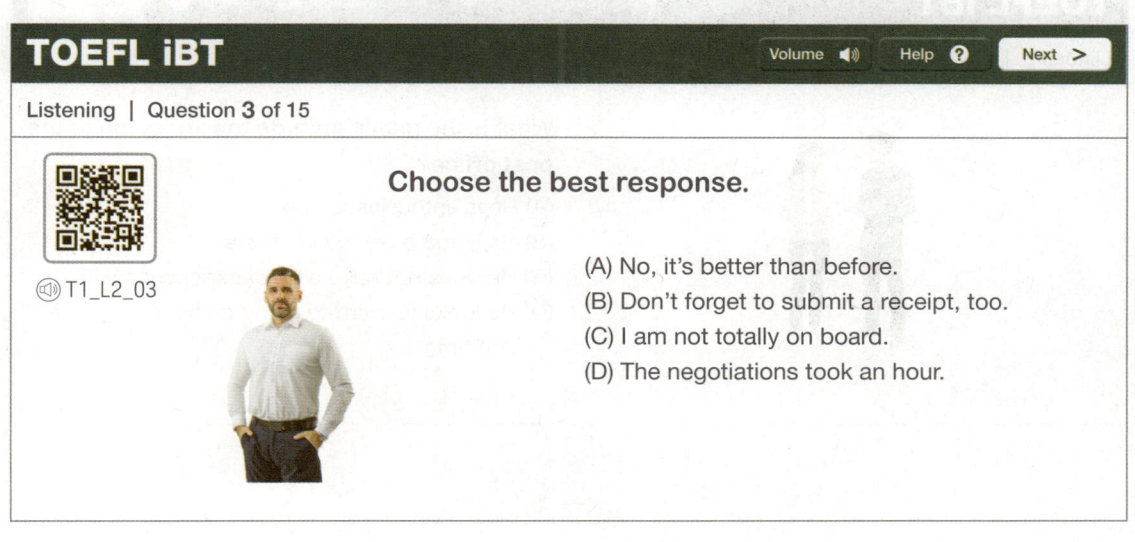

Listen to a conversation.

T1_L2_0405

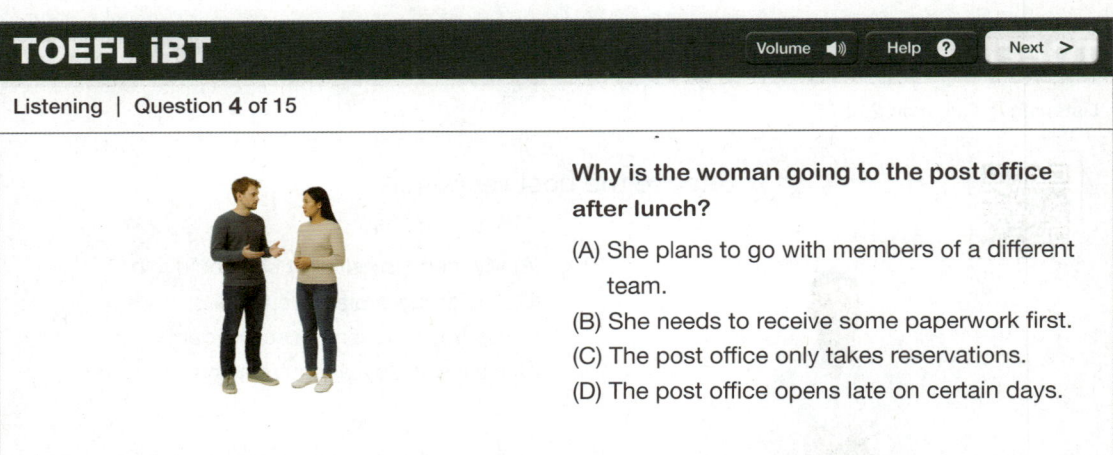

Listening | Question 4 of 15

Why is the woman going to the post office after lunch?

(A) She plans to go with members of a different team.
(B) She needs to receive some paperwork first.
(C) The post office only takes reservations.
(D) The post office opens late on certain days.

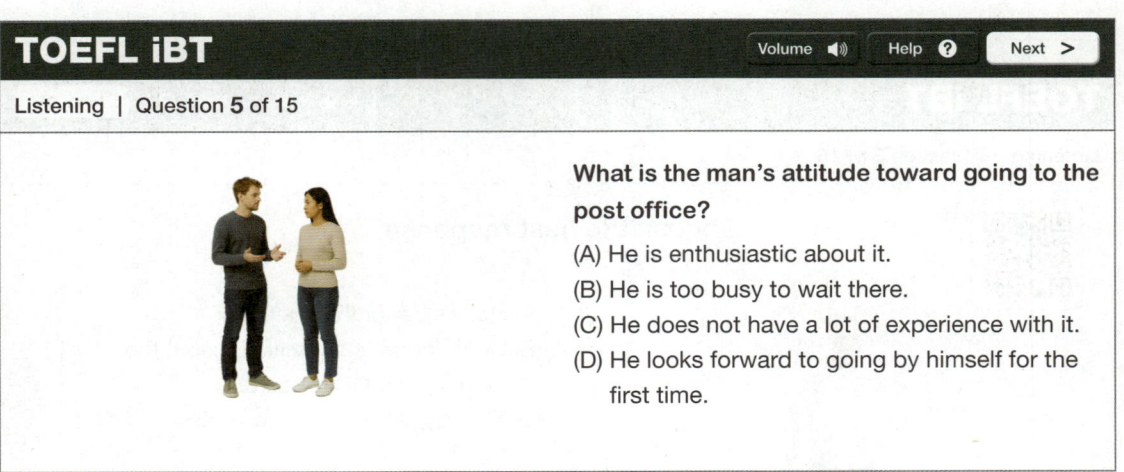

Listening | Question 5 of 15

What is the man's attitude toward going to the post office?

(A) He is enthusiastic about it.
(B) He is too busy to wait there.
(C) He does not have a lot of experience with it.
(D) He looks forward to going by himself for the first time.

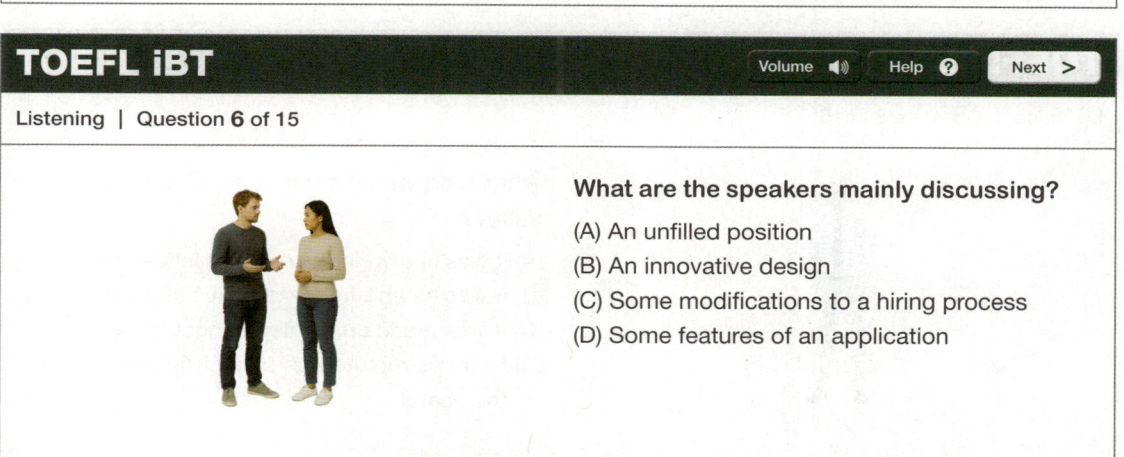

What are the speakers mainly discussing?

(A) An unfilled position
(B) An innovative design
(C) Some modifications to a hiring process
(D) Some features of an application

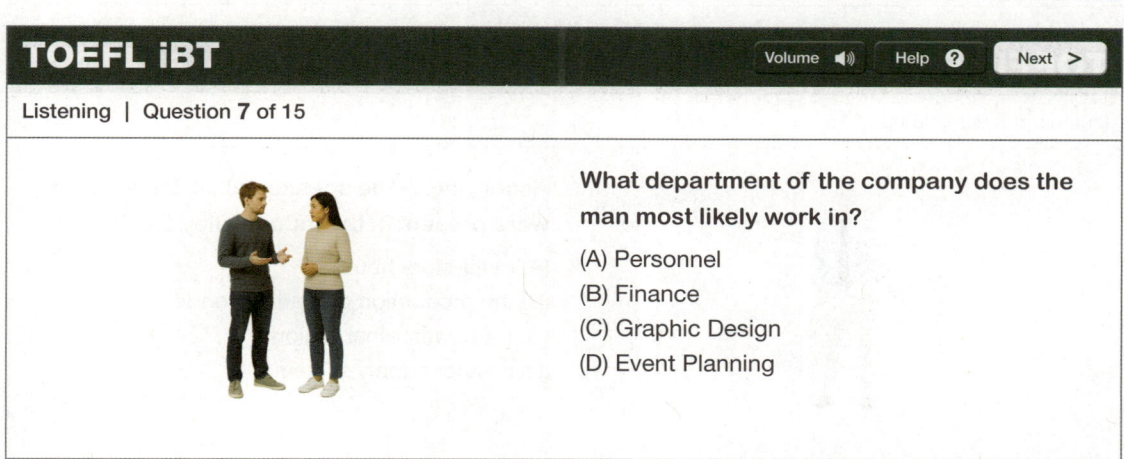

What department of the company does the man most likely work in?

(A) Personnel
(B) Finance
(C) Graphic Design
(D) Event Planning

TOEFL iBT

Listening | Questions **8-11** of 15

Listen to a talk in a history class.

T1_L2_0811

TOEFL iBT

Listening | Question **8** of 15

What is an important feature of the Indus Valley?

(A) It was known for its rich and fertile farmland.
(B) It was established by a native tribe from India.
(C) It was made up of interconnected cities.
(D) Its infrastructure was strongly influenced by the ocean.

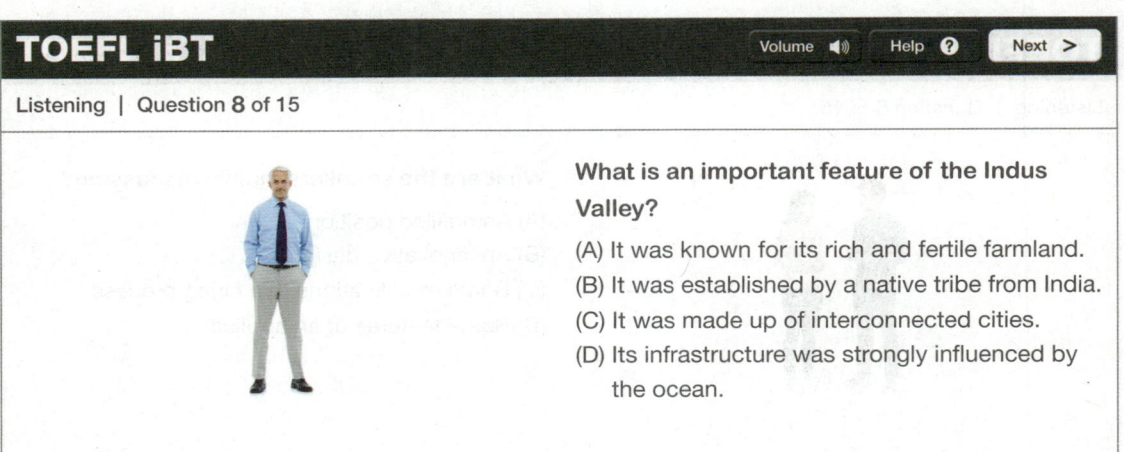

TOEFL iBT

Listening | Question **9** of 15

According to the speaker, all of the following were present in the Indus Valley EXCEPT

(A) multi-story housing
(B) the production of crafted goods
(C) trade with other regions
(D) a water supply system

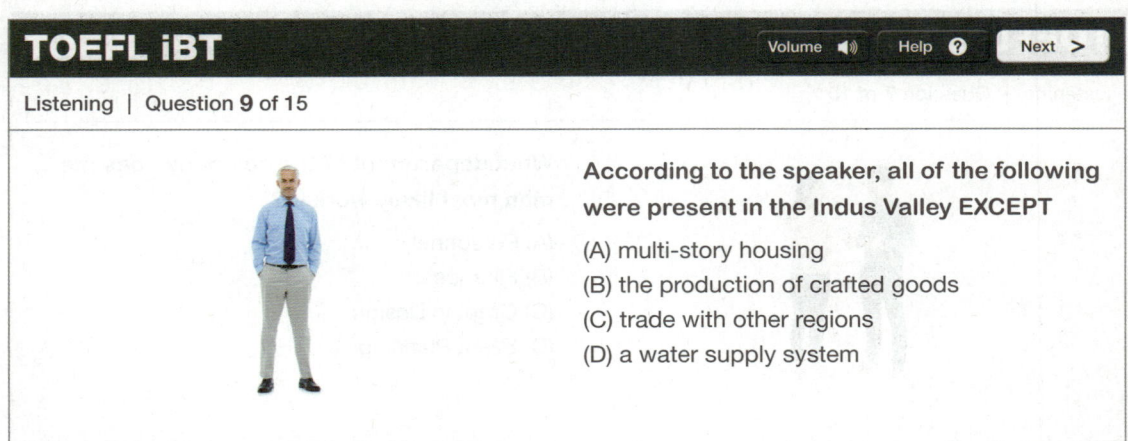

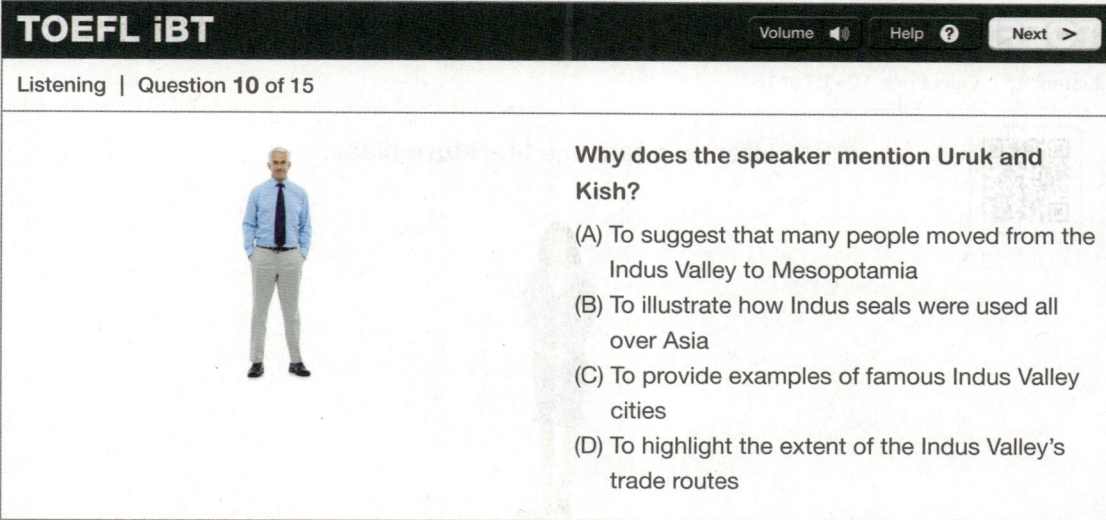

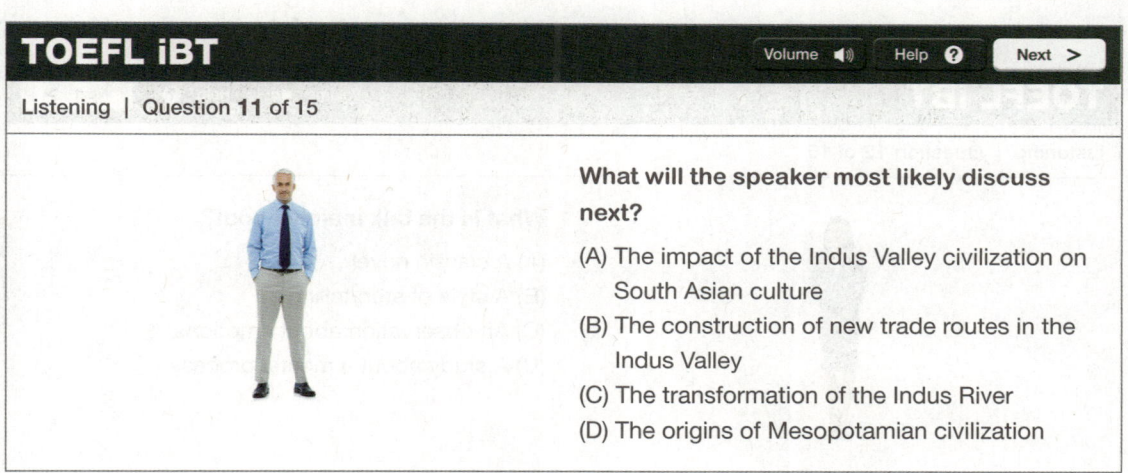

TOEFL iBT

Listening | Questions 12-15 of 15

Listen to a talk in a literature class.

T1_L2_1215

TOEFL iBT

Listening | Question 12 of 15

What is the talk mainly about?

(A) A classic novel
(B) A style of storytelling
(C) An observation about emotions
(D) A study about a mental process

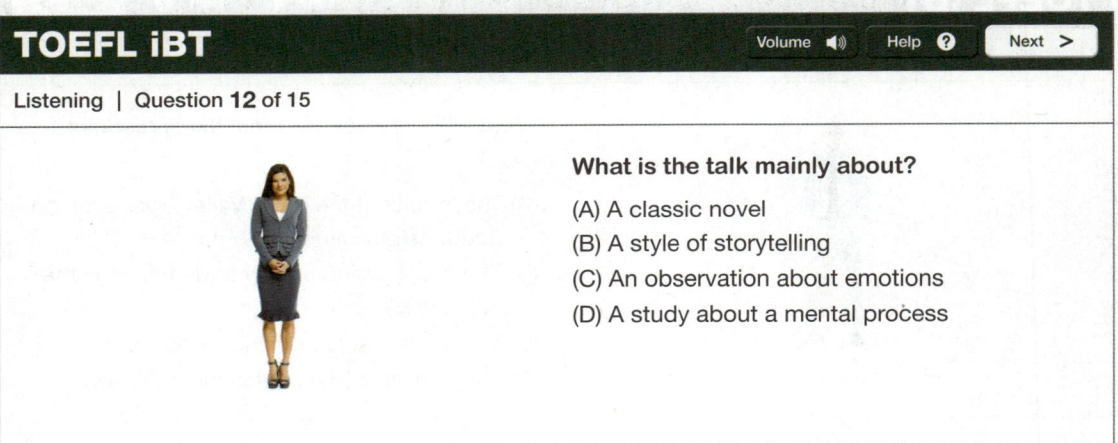

TOEFL iBT

Listening | Question 13 of 15

Why does the speaker mention the inner thoughts of the characters in a novel?

(A) To emphasize how important childhood memories are in the novel
(B) To point out the main theme of the novel
(C) To depict how continuous streams of ideas are presented in the novel
(D) To indicate that London is the primary setting of the novel

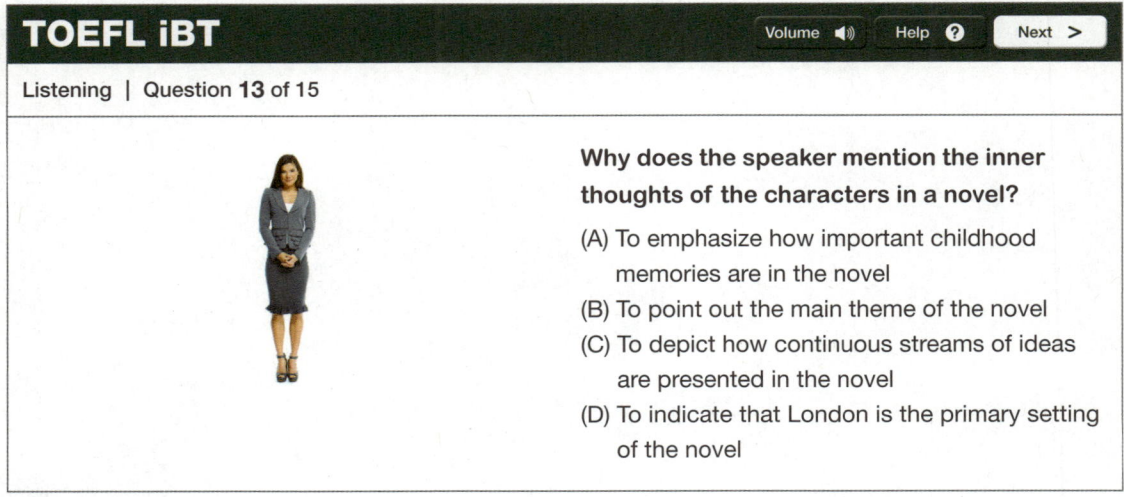

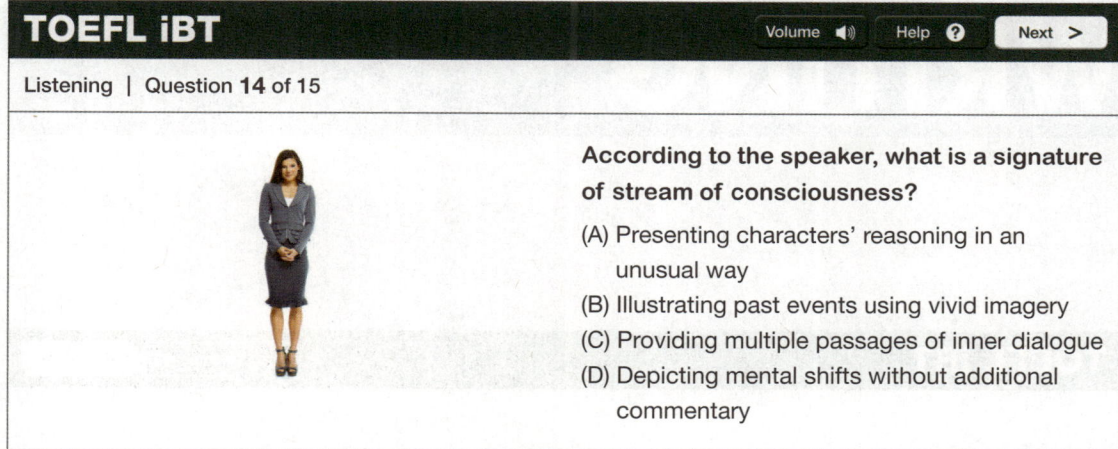

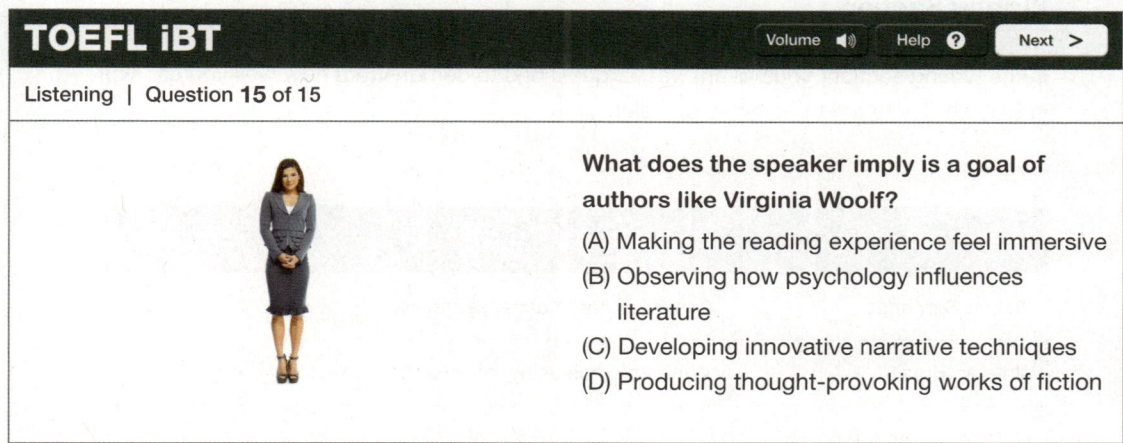

WRITING

TOEFL iBT

Writing Section

In the writing section, you will answer 12 questions to demonstrate how well you can write in English. There are three types of tasks.

Type of Task	Description
Build a Sentence	Create a grammatical sentence.
Write an Email	Write an email using information provided.
Write for an Academic Discussion	Participate in an online discussion.

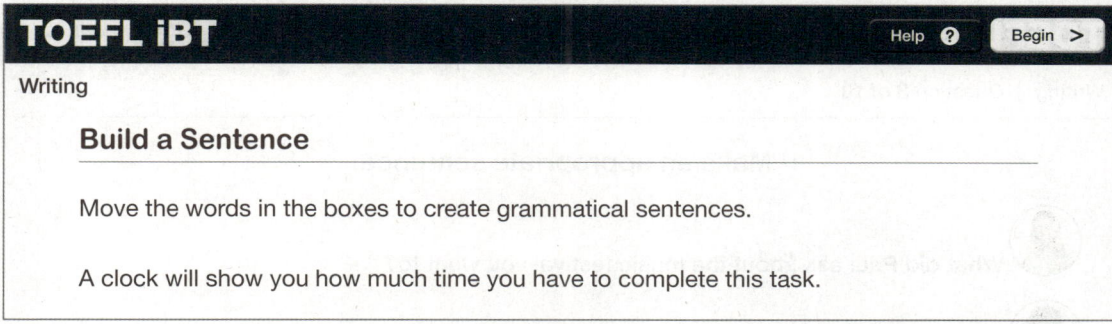

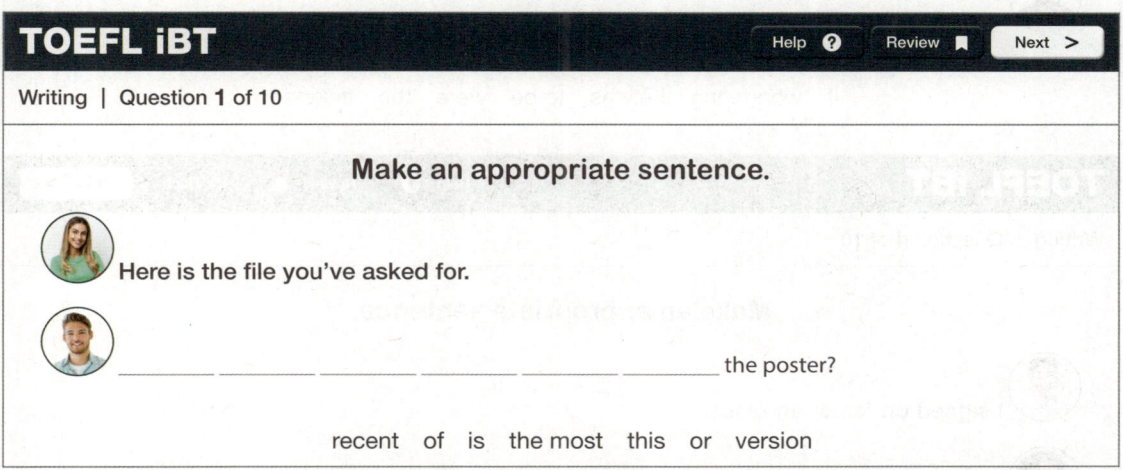

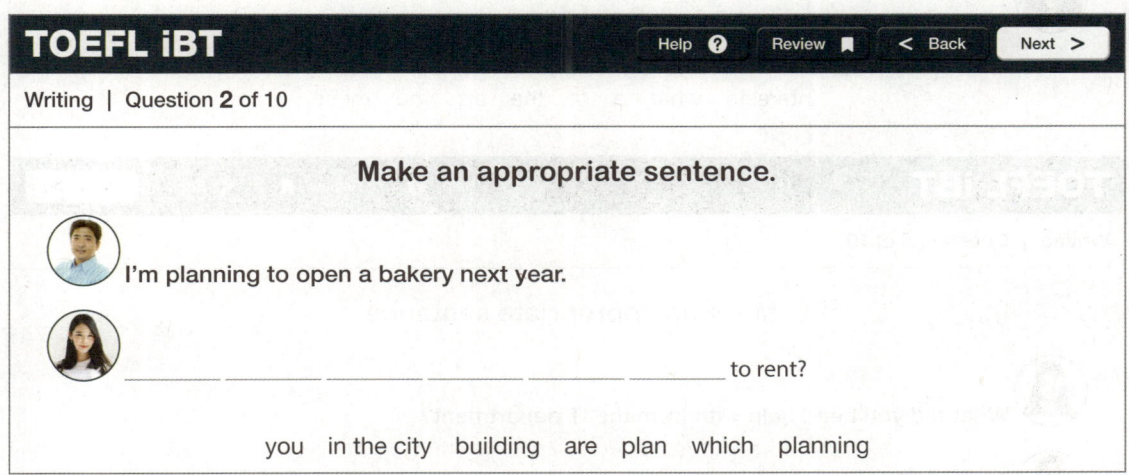

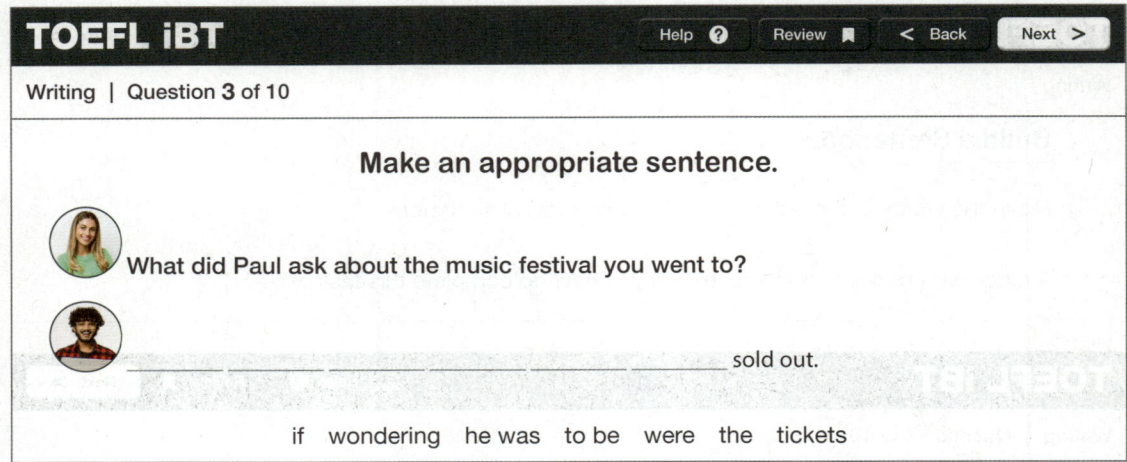

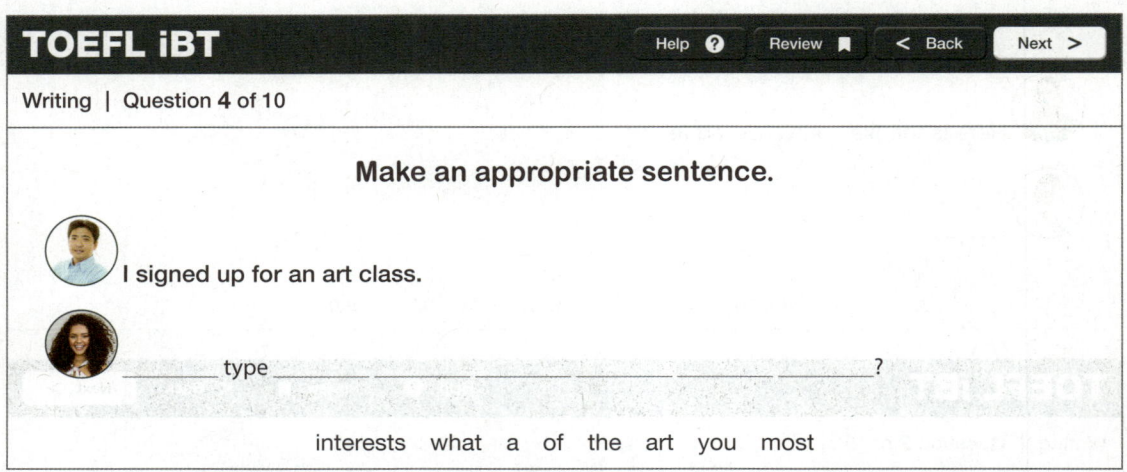

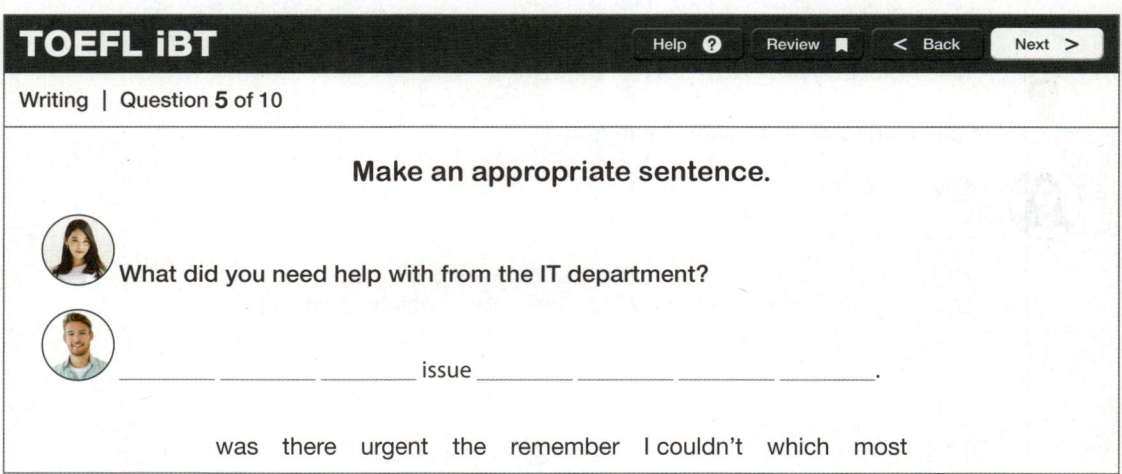

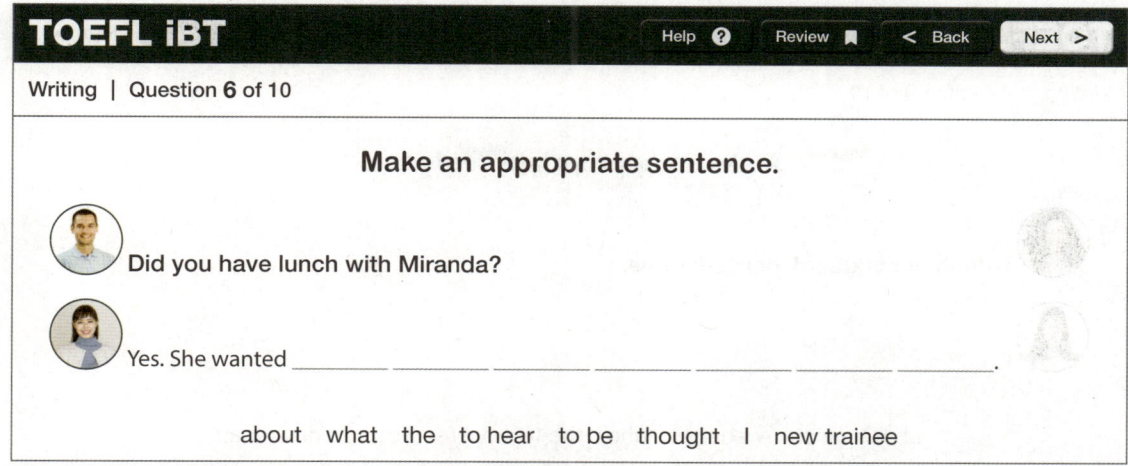

Make an appropriate sentence.

Did you have lunch with Miranda?

Yes. She wanted _____.

about   what   the   to hear   to be   thought   I   new trainee

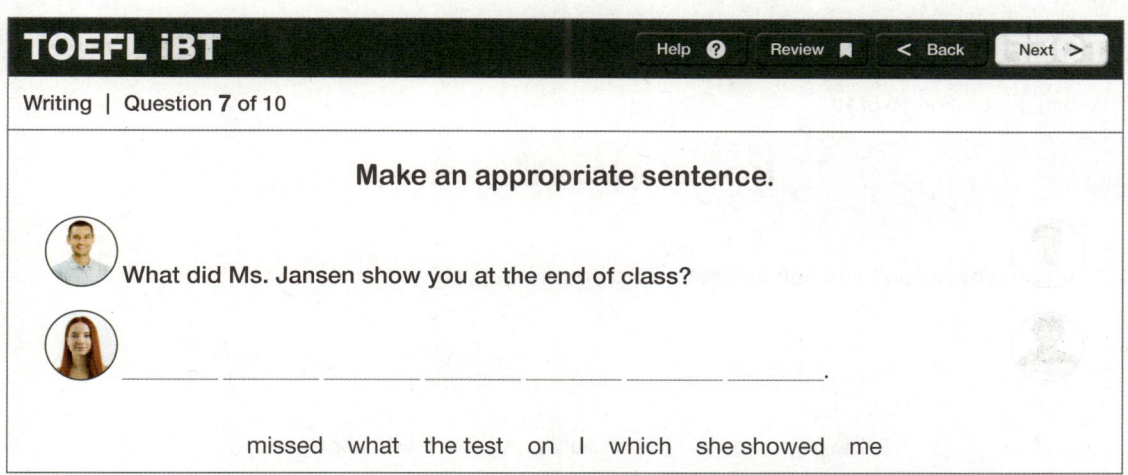

Make an appropriate sentence.

What did Ms. Jansen show you at the end of class?

_____.

missed   what   the test   on   I   which   she showed   me

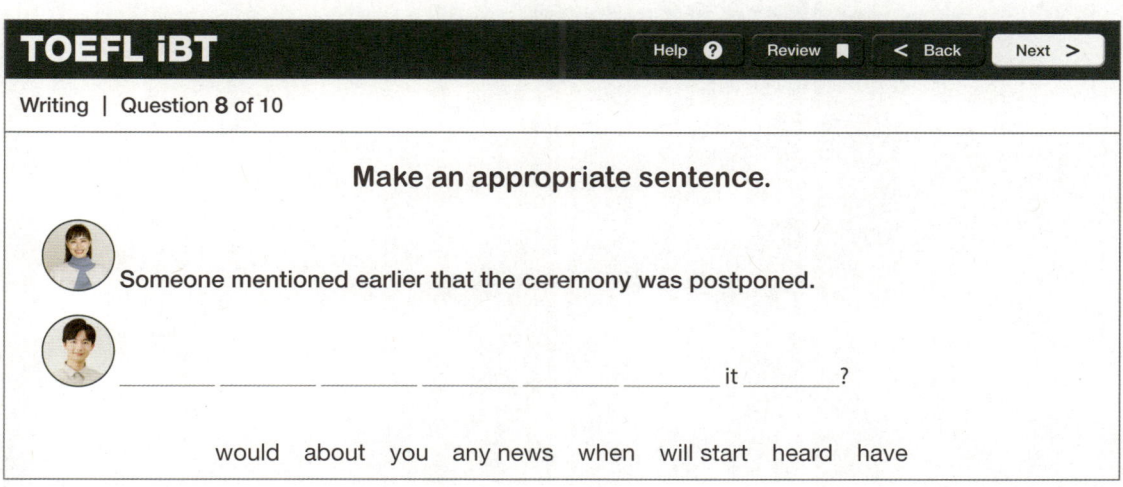

Make an appropriate sentence.

Someone mentioned earlier that the ceremony was postponed.

_____ _____ _____ _____ _____ _____ it _____?

would   about   you   any news   when   will start   heard   have

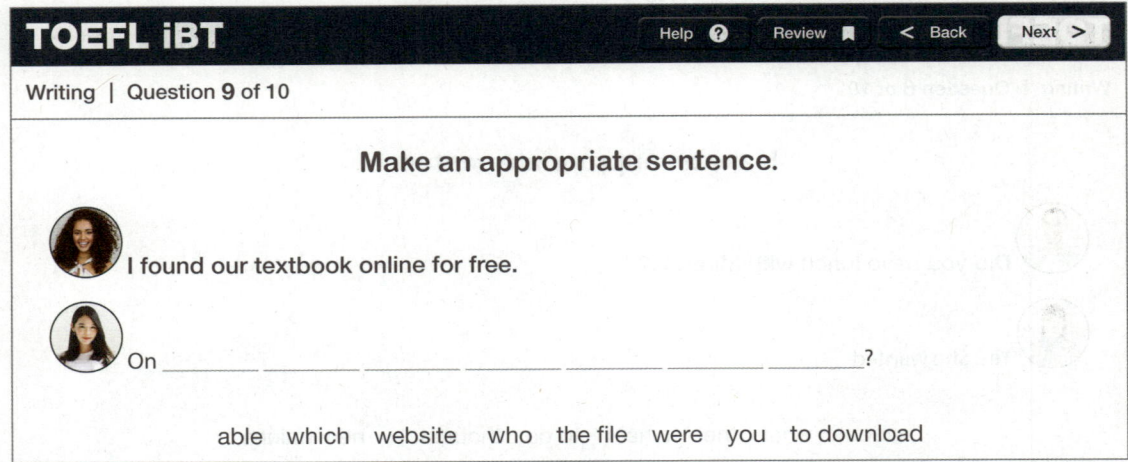

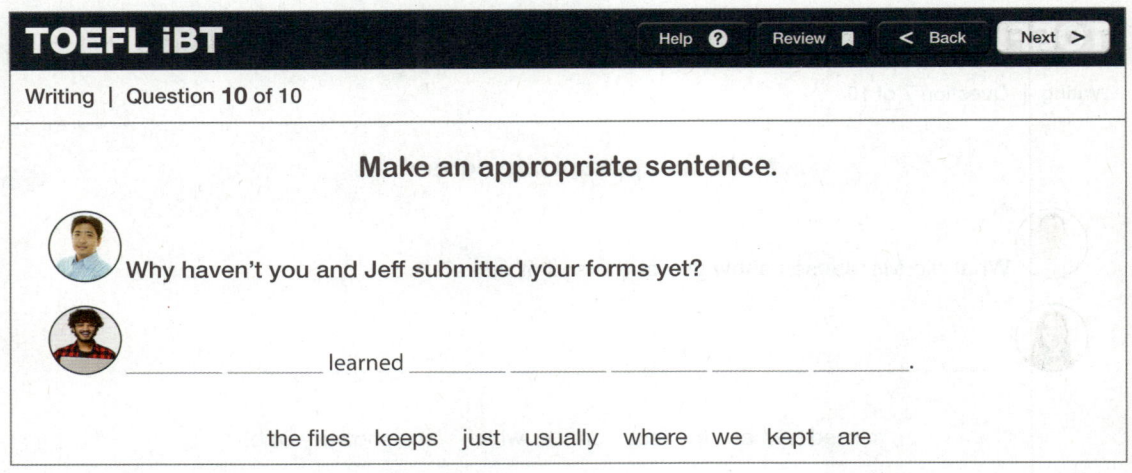

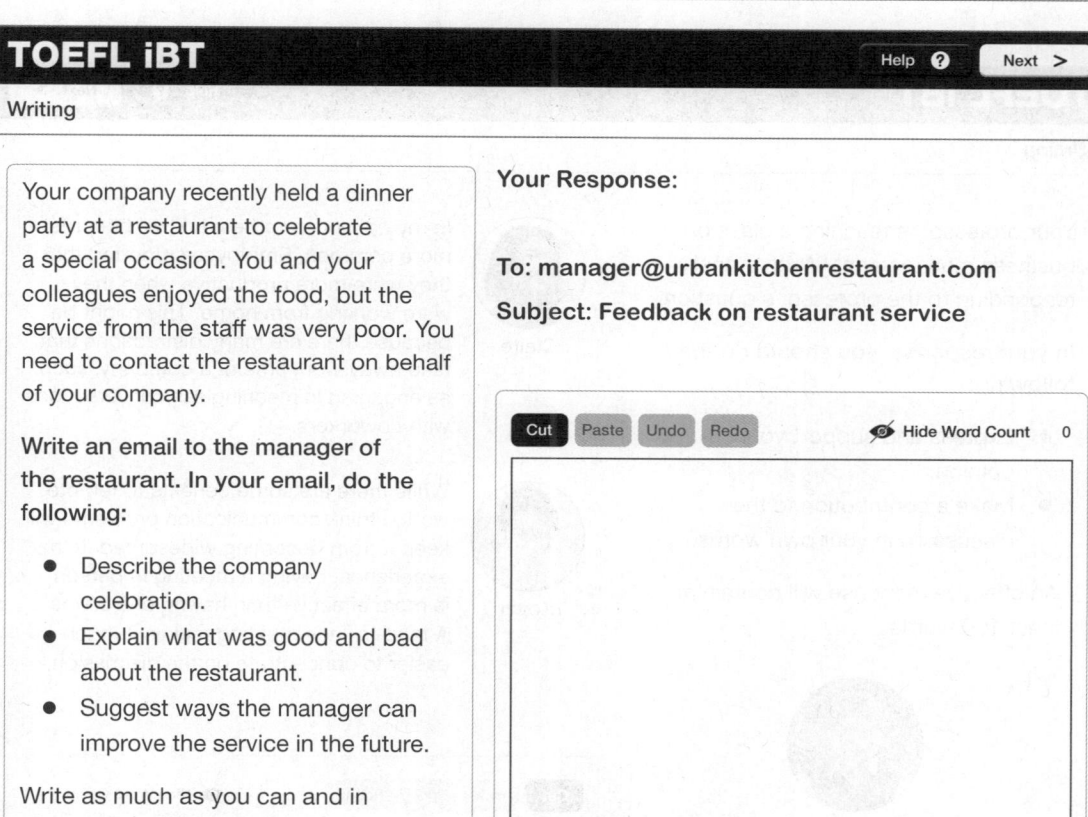

TOEFL iBT

Writing

Write an Email

You will read some information and use the information to write an email.

You will have 7 minutes to write the email.

TOEFL iBT

Writing

Your company recently held a dinner party at a restaurant to celebrate a special occasion. You and your colleagues enjoyed the food, but the service from the staff was very poor. You need to contact the restaurant on behalf of your company.

Write an email to the manager of the restaurant. In your email, do the following:

- Describe the company celebration.
- Explain what was good and bad about the restaurant.
- Suggest ways the manager can improve the service in the future.

Write as much as you can and in complete sentences.

Your Response:

To: manager@urbankitchenrestaurant.com
Subject: Feedback on restaurant service

TOEFL iBT

Help Begin >

Writing

Write for an Academic Discussion

A professor has posted a question about a topic and students have responded with their thoughts and ideas. Make a contribution to the discussion.

You will have 10 minutes to write.

TOEFL iBT

Help Next >

Writing

Your professor is teaching a class on business management. Write a post responding to the professor's question.

In your response, you should do the following:

- Express and support your opinion.
- Make a contribution to the discussion in your own words.

An effective response will contain at least 100 words.

Dr. Lee

For the past few classes, we have been discussing the concept of remote work. Some argue that the number of employees working from home will increase as it benefits both the company and employees. Others believe the challenges of implementing remote work will keep it from becoming a widespread practice. What are your thoughts on this issue?

Claire

In my opinion, remote work will become more common. Employees reported that they were more productive when they were working from home. This might be because there are many distractions that take away work time at a company, such as engaging in meaningless conversations with coworkers.

Kevin

While there are some benefits to remote work, I think communication problems will keep it from becoming widespread. In my experience, having a meeting in person is more effective than having one online. A face-to-face meeting makes it much easier to concentrate on the discussion.

SPEAKING

TOEFL iBT

Speaking Section

In the speaking section, you will answer 11 questions to demonstrate how well you can speak English. There are two types of tasks.

Type of Task	Description
Listen and Repeat	Listen and repeat what you heard.
Take an Interview	Answer questions from the interviewer.

TOEFL iBT

Speaking

Listen and Repeat

You will listen as someone speaks to you. Listen carefully and then repeat what you have heard. The clock will indicate how much time you have to speak.

No time for preparation will be provided.

TOEFL iBT

Speaking

You are being trained to help members at a gym. Listen to your trainer and repeat what he says.

TOEFL iBT

Speaking | Question **1** of 11

T1_S_01

Listen and repeat only once.

RESPONSE TIME
00:00:08

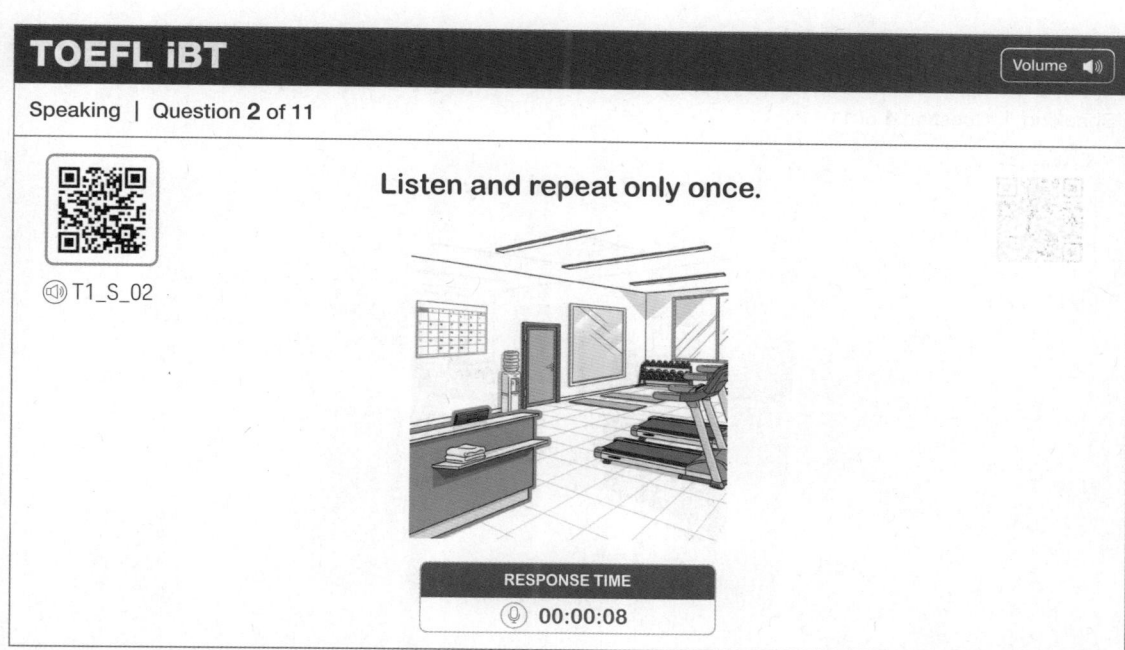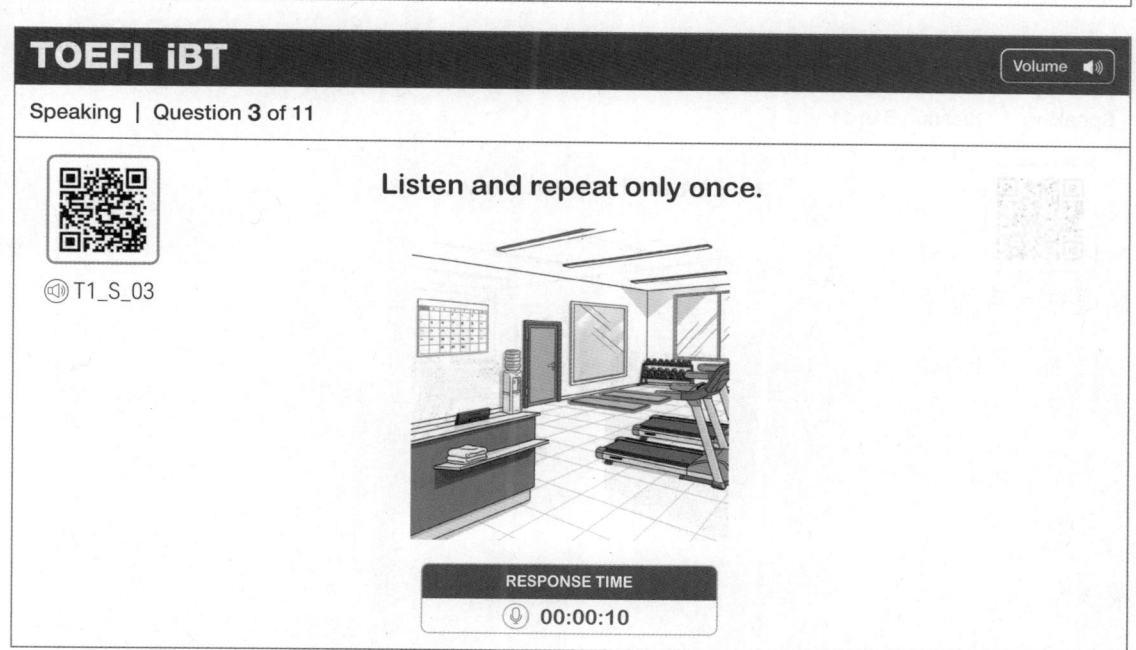

TOEFL iBT

Speaking | Question **4** of 11

T1_S_04

Listen and repeat only once.

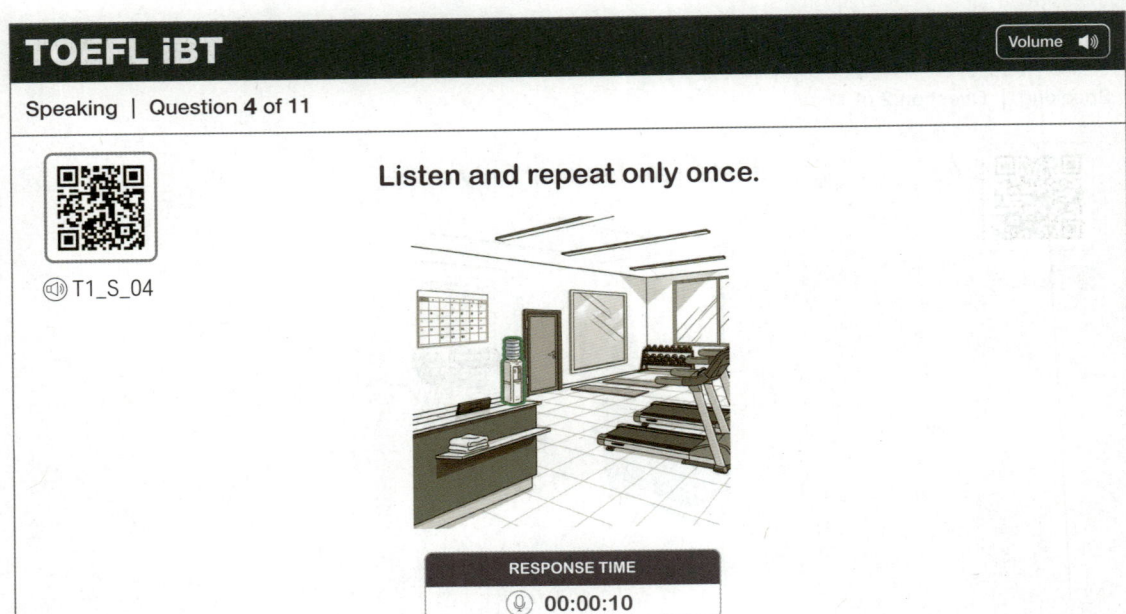

RESPONSE TIME
00:00:10

TOEFL iBT

Speaking | Question **5** of 11

T1_S_05

Listen and repeat only once.

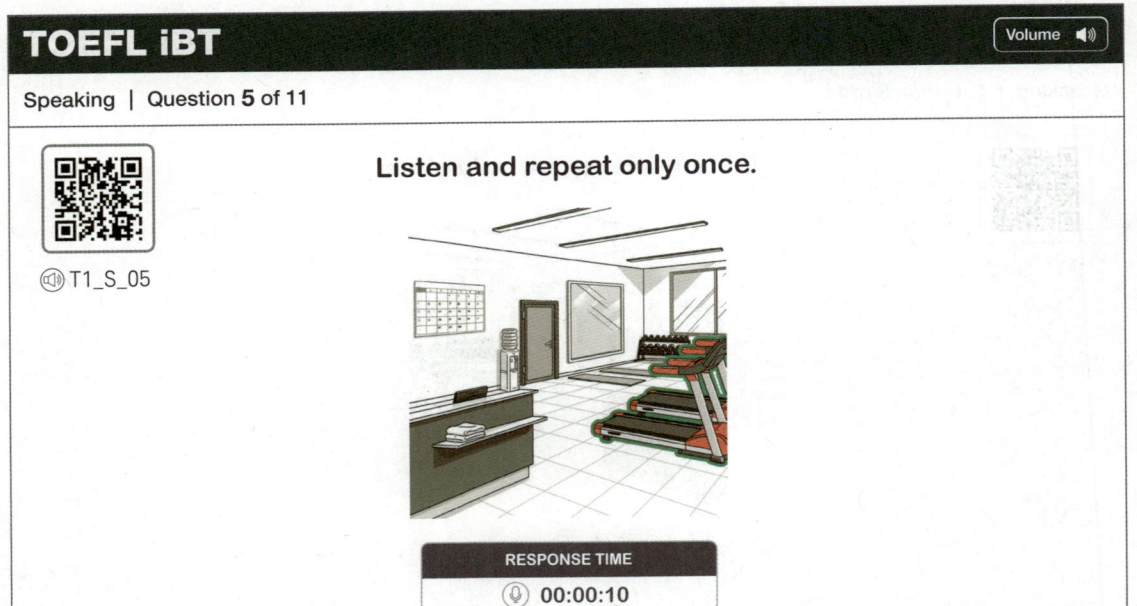

RESPONSE TIME
00:00:10

TOEFL iBT

Speaking | Question **6** of 11

T1_S_06

Listen and repeat only once.

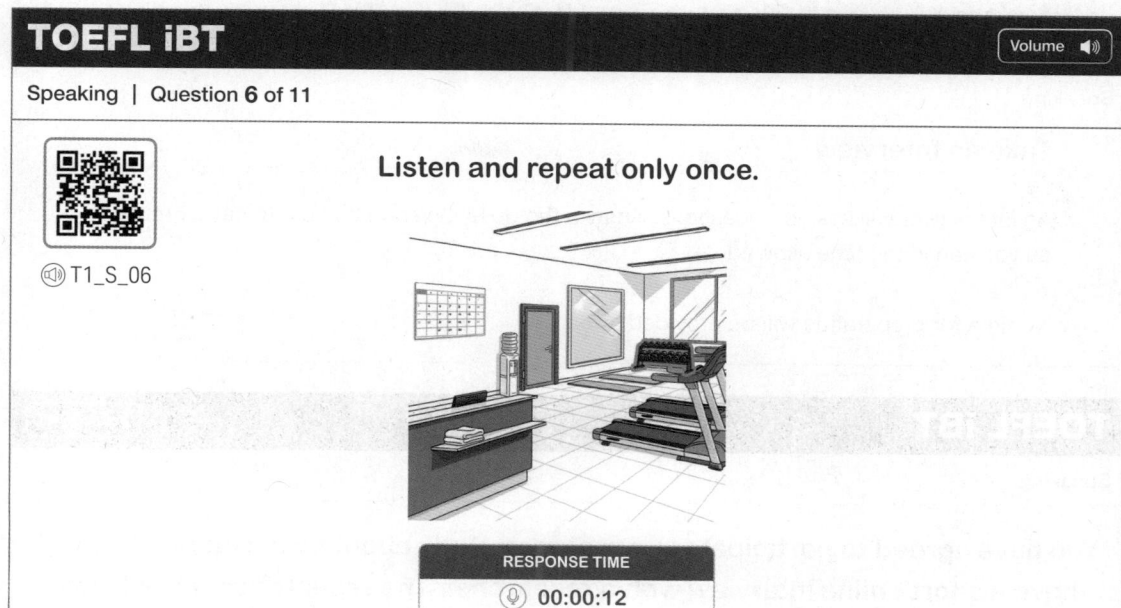

RESPONSE TIME
00:00:12

TOEFL iBT

Speaking | Question **7** of 11

T1_S_07

Listen and repeat only once.

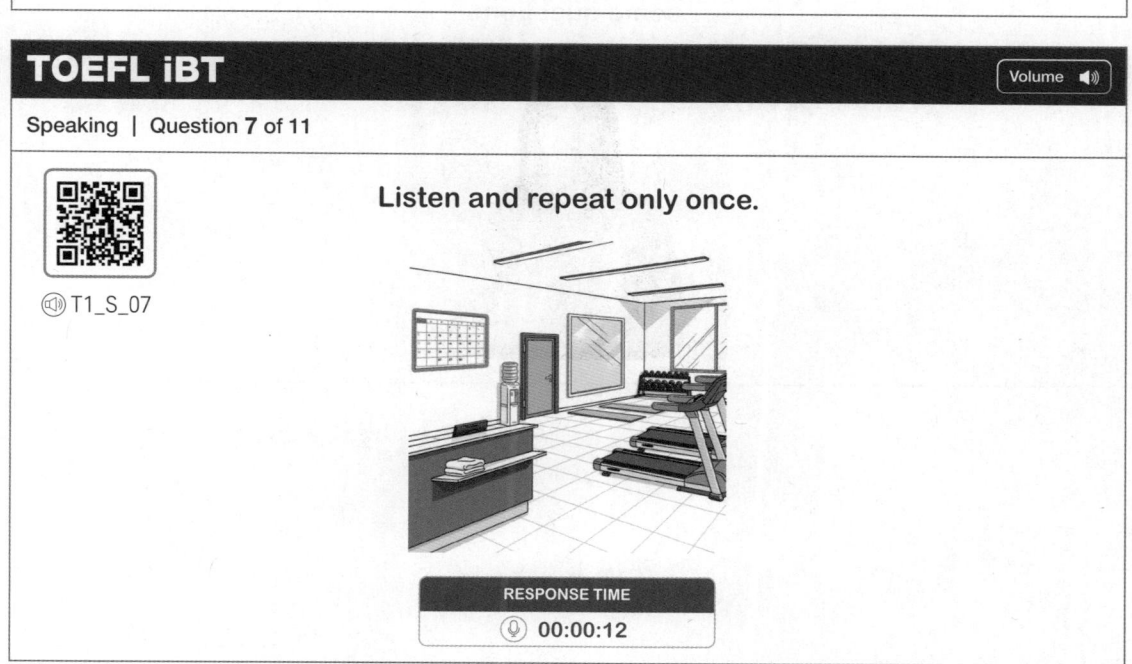

RESPONSE TIME
00:00:12

TOEFL iBT

Speaking

Take an Interview

An interviewer will ask you questions. Answer the questions and be sure to say as much as you can in the time allowed.

No time for preparation will be provided.

TOEFL iBT

Speaking

You have agreed to participate in a research study about social media. You will have a short online interview with a researcher. The researcher will ask you some questions.

TOEFL iBT

Speaking | Question **8** of 11

🔊 T1_S_08

Please answer the interviewer's questions.

RESPONSE TIME
🎙 00:00:45

TOEFL iBT

Speaking | Question **9** of 11

🔊 T1_S_09

Please answer the interviewer's questions.

RESPONSE TIME
🎙 00:00:45

TOEFL iBT

Speaking | Question **10** of 11

Please answer the interviewer's questions.

T1_S_10

RESPONSE TIME
00:00:45

TOEFL iBT

Speaking | Question **11** of 11

Please answer the interviewer's questions.

T1_S_11

RESPONSE TIME
00:00:45

TEST 2

TEST 2

⚠️ 실전모의고사 유의 사항

실제 시험과 동일한 환경에서 연습하기 위해 다음 사항을 반드시 지켜 주세요.

1. **Reading – Listening – Writing – Speaking 순서로 한 번에 진행**
   중간에 휴식 없이 네 영역을 연속으로 풀며 실제 시험 흐름에 익숙해집니다.

2. **Listening은 음원을 먼저 듣기**
   문제를 미리 읽지 말고, 반드시 음원을 모두 들은 후에 문제를 풉니다. 실제 시험과 동일한 조건으로 문제를 푸는 것이 중요합니다.

3. **Listening과 Speaking 음원은 한 번만 듣기**
   반복 청취는 금지하며, 한 번의 청취로 내용을 이해하고 답변하는 훈련을 합니다.

4. **노트테이킹 도구 준비하기**
   백지와 연필을 준비해 Listening 영역에서 필요한 내용을 간단히 메모하며 문제를 풉니다.

5. **시간을 재며 Writing과 Speaking 문제 풀기**
   각 영역의 제한 시간 내에 답안을 작성하거나 말하기 연습을 진행해 실제 시험 감각을 익힙니다.

READING

TOEFL iBT　　　　　　　　　　　　　　　　　　Volume 🔊　Help ❓　Begin >

Reading Section

In the reading section, you will answer 35-48 questions to demonstrate how well you understand academic and non-academic texts in English. There are three types of tasks.

Type of Task	Description
Complete the Words	Fill in the missing letters in a paragraph.
Read in Daily Life	Answer questions about everyday reading materials.
Read an Academic Passage	Answer questions about academic passages.

Module 1

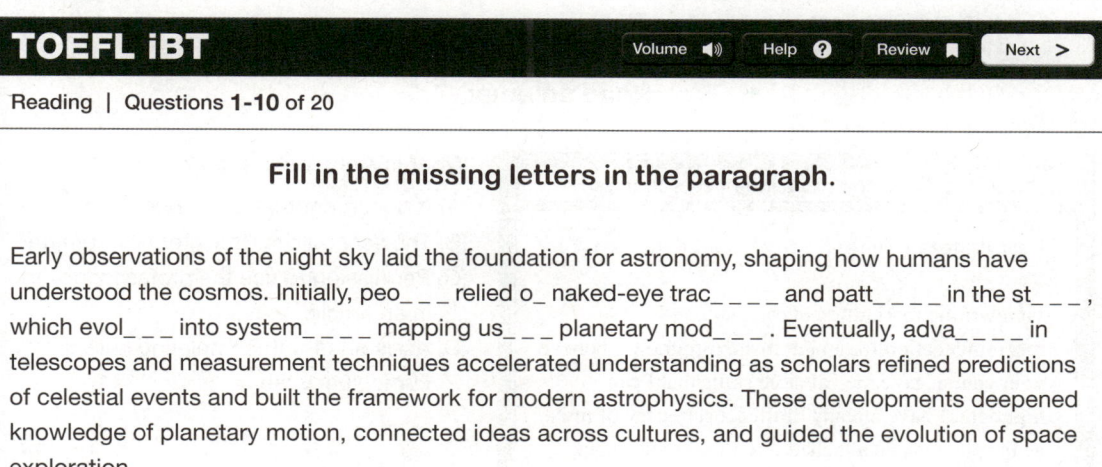

Fill in the missing letters in the paragraph.

Early observations of the night sky laid the foundation for astronomy, shaping how humans have understood the cosmos. Initially, peo_ _ _ relied o_ naked-eye trac_ _ _ _ and patt_ _ _ _ in the st_ _ _ , which evol_ _ _ into system_ _ _ _ mapping us_ _ _ planetary mod_ _ _ . Eventually, adva_ _ _ _ in telescopes and measurement techniques accelerated understanding as scholars refined predictions of celestial events and built the framework for modern astrophysics. These developments deepened knowledge of planetary motion, connected ideas across cultures, and guided the evolution of space exploration.

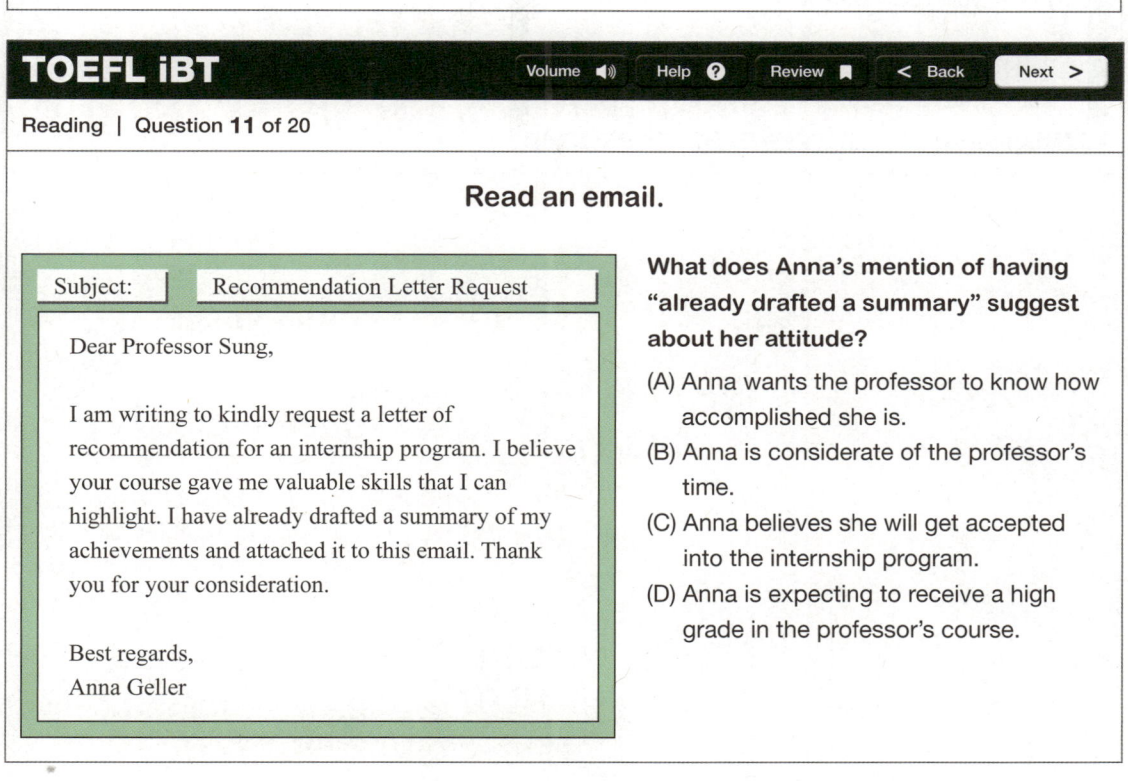

Read an email.

Subject: Recommendation Letter Request

Dear Professor Sung,

I am writing to kindly request a letter of recommendation for an internship program. I believe your course gave me valuable skills that I can highlight. I have already drafted a summary of my achievements and attached it to this email. Thank you for your consideration.

Best regards,
Anna Geller

What does Anna's mention of having "already drafted a summary" suggest about her attitude?

(A) Anna wants the professor to know how accomplished she is.
(B) Anna is considerate of the professor's time.
(C) Anna believes she will get accepted into the internship program.
(D) Anna is expecting to receive a high grade in the professor's course.

Reading Module 1

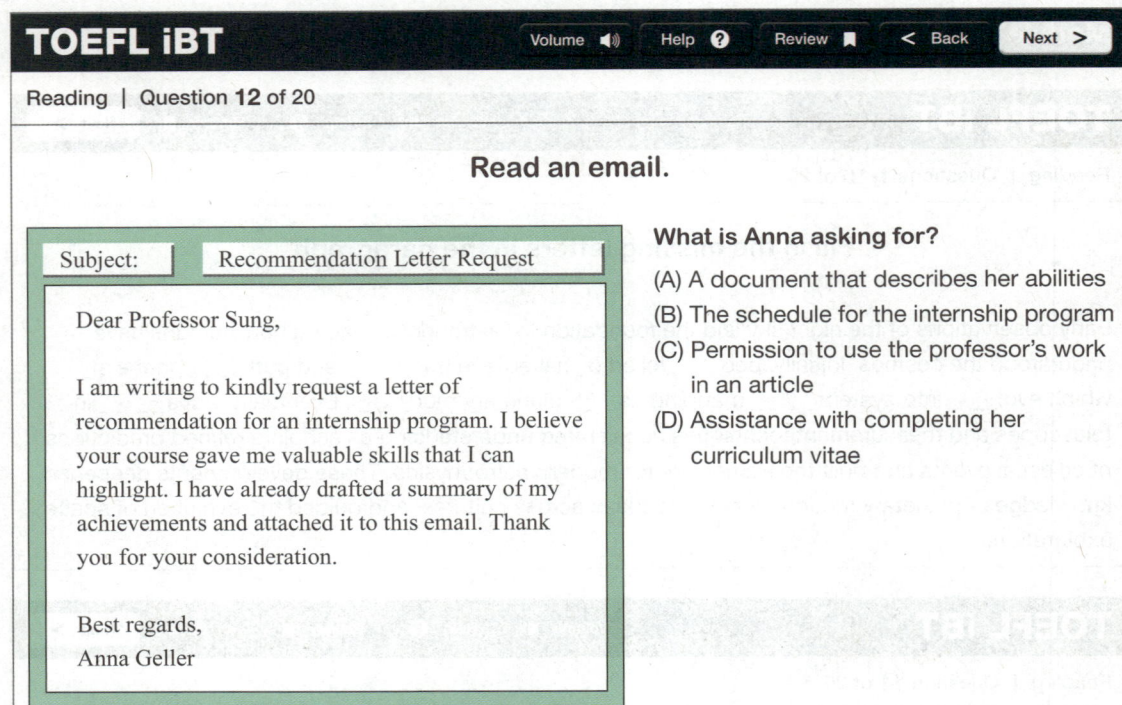

Read an email.

Subject: New Wellness Workshop Implementation – Friday, October 9

Dear Ms. Parker,

I hope you're doing well. I'm writing to let you know about a first-ever wellness workshop scheduled for Friday, October 9, from 10:00 A.M. to 12:00 P.M. This workshop is part of our employee engagement program designed to promote stress management and work-life balance.

Please note that attendance is encouraged but optional, and regular office activities will continue. We suggest that teams plan their schedules accordingly and communicate any temporary coverage needs. For individuals who have conflicting schedules, a recording of the workshop will be available afterward.

Additionally, as instructors from GC Health will be facilitating the sessions, we request that employees show them utmost respect and cordiality. Please do not forget that our staff's behavior represents our company image.

If you have any questions, contact the HR team at 555-1183.

Kind regards,
Morton Frost

What is the purpose of the workshop?

(A) To enhance teamwork skills
(B) To strengthen company culture
(C) To boost worker productivity
(D) To improve employee well-being

Read an email.

| Subject: | New Wellness Workshop Implementation – Friday, October 9 |

Dear Ms. Parker,

I hope you're doing well. I'm writing to let you know about a first-ever wellness workshop scheduled for Friday, October 9, from 10:00 A.M. to 12:00 P.M. This workshop is part of our employee engagement program designed to promote stress management and work-life balance.

Please note that attendance is encouraged but optional, and regular office activities will continue. We suggest that teams plan their schedules accordingly and communicate any temporary coverage needs. For individuals who have conflicting schedules, a recording of the workshop will be available afterward.

Additionally, as instructors from GC Health will be facilitating the sessions, we request that employees show them utmost respect and cordiality. Please do not forget that our staff's behavior represents our company image.

If you have any questions, contact the HR team at 555-1183.

Kind regards,
Morton Frost

What is indicated about the wellness workshop?

(A) It is held every other month.
(B) It requires bringing personal materials.
(C) It is not mandatory to attend.
(D) It is completely free for employees.

Read an email.

Subject: New Wellness Workshop Implementation – Friday, October 9

Dear Ms. Parker,

I hope you're doing well. I'm writing to let you know about a first-ever wellness workshop scheduled for Friday, October 9, from 10:00 A.M. to 12:00 P.M. This workshop is part of our employee engagement program designed to promote stress management and work-life balance.

Please note that attendance is encouraged but optional, and regular office activities will continue. We suggest that teams plan their schedules accordingly and communicate any temporary coverage needs. For individuals who have conflicting schedules, a recording of the workshop will be available afterward.

Additionally, as instructors from GC Health will be facilitating the sessions, we request that employees show them utmost respect and cordiality. Please do not forget that our staff's behavior represents our company image.

If you have any questions, contact the HR team at 555-1183.

Kind regards,
Morton Frost

Who will be conducting the workshop?

(A) Morton Frost
(B) The HR team
(C) Ms. Parker
(D) External educators

Buddhist Temples

Buddhist temples are sacred structures that have been built for centuries. They provide insight into the ancient spiritual practices and cultural values of Buddhist communities. Found across Asia, these temples are esteemed for their towering pagodas, intricate carvings, and golden statues of the Buddha. Angkor Wat in Cambodia and the Borobudur Temple in Indonesia are the world's most popular Buddhist sites among travelers.

Also known as monasteries, Buddhist temples serve multiple purposes. They are where monks and laypeople gather for meditation, prayer, and ceremonies. They also function as centers for teaching Buddhist philosophy and spreading moral values. Additionally, they often serve as symbols of peace, compassion, and devotion within their communities.

The construction techniques of Buddhist temples were highly advanced for their time. Builders used stone, brick, and wood, often combining them with ornate designs and detailed artwork. Some temples are decorated with murals and sculptures that narrate stories from the Buddha's life. The way in which certain temples display solar alignment, such as with sunrise or sunset, suggests that their orientation was intentionally planned. Despite variations across regions, Buddhist temples remain as landmarks of enduring cultural heritage.

The word "esteemed" in the first paragraph is closest in meaning to

(A) advanced
(B) renowned
(C) determined
(D) outdated

Buddhist Temples

Buddhist temples are sacred structures that have been built for centuries. They provide insight into the ancient spiritual practices and cultural values of Buddhist communities. Found across Asia, these temples are esteemed for their towering pagodas, intricate carvings, and golden statues of the Buddha. Angkor Wat in Cambodia and the Borobudur Temple in Indonesia are the world's most popular Buddhist sites among travelers.

Also known as monasteries, Buddhist temples serve multiple purposes. They are where monks and laypeople gather for meditation, prayer, and ceremonies. They also function as centers for teaching Buddhist philosophy and spreading moral values. Additionally, they often serve as symbols of peace, compassion, and devotion within their communities.

The construction techniques of Buddhist temples were highly advanced for their time. Builders used stone, brick, and wood, often combining them with ornate designs and detailed artwork. Some temples are decorated with murals and sculptures that narrate stories from the Buddha's life. The way in which certain temples display solar alignment, such as with sunrise or sunset, suggests that their orientation was intentionally planned. Despite variations across regions, Buddhist temples remain as landmarks of enduring cultural heritage.

What is indicated about Angkor Wat and the Borobudur Temple?

(A) They have many golden statues of Buddha.
(B) They attract the most international tourists.
(C) Their meditation rooms have been in use for centuries.
(D) Their tower structures are the tallest in the world.

Buddhist Temples

Buddhist temples are sacred structures that have been built for centuries. They provide insight into the ancient spiritual practices and cultural values of Buddhist communities. Found across Asia, these temples are esteemed for their towering pagodas, intricate carvings, and golden statues of the Buddha. Angkor Wat in Cambodia and the Borobudur Temple in Indonesia are the world's most popular Buddhist sites among travelers.

Also known as monasteries, Buddhist temples serve multiple purposes. They are where monks and laypeople gather for meditation, prayer, and ceremonies. They also function as centers for teaching Buddhist philosophy and spreading moral values. Additionally, they often serve as symbols of peace, compassion, and devotion within their communities.

The construction techniques of Buddhist temples were highly advanced for their time. Builders used stone, brick, and wood, often combining them with ornate designs and detailed artwork. Some temples are decorated with murals and sculptures that narrate stories from the Buddha's life. The way in which certain temples display solar alignment, such as with sunrise or sunset, suggests that their orientation was intentionally planned. Despite variations across regions, Buddhist temples remain as landmarks of enduring cultural heritage.

All of the following are true about Buddhist temples EXCEPT

(A) They serve as symbols of peace, compassion, and devotion.
(B) They operate as teaching centers.
(C) They are decorated with ornate designs.
(D) They are mainly used for public ceremonies.

Buddhist Temples

Buddhist temples are sacred structures that have been built for centuries. They provide insight into the ancient spiritual practices and cultural values of Buddhist communities. Found across Asia, these temples are esteemed for their towering pagodas, intricate carvings, and golden statues of the Buddha. Angkor Wat in Cambodia and the Borobudur Temple in Indonesia are the world's most popular Buddhist sites among travelers.

Also known as monasteries, Buddhist temples serve multiple purposes. They are where monks and laypeople gather for meditation, prayer, and ceremonies. They also function as centers for teaching Buddhist philosophy and spreading moral values. Additionally, they often serve as symbols of peace, compassion, and devotion within their communities.

The construction techniques of Buddhist temples were highly advanced for their time. Builders used stone, brick, and wood, often combining them with ornate designs and detailed artwork. Some temples are decorated with murals and sculptures that narrate stories from the Buddha's life. The way in which certain temples display solar alignment, such as with sunrise or sunset, suggests that their orientation was intentionally planned. Despite variations across regions, Buddhist temples remain as landmarks of enduring cultural heritage.

What is the relationship between paragraphs 2 and 3?

(A) Paragraph 3 describes the moral values mentioned in paragraph 2.
(B) Paragraph 3 offers a solution to the challenges listed in paragraph 2.
(C) Paragraph 3 discusses how Buddhist temples were designed while paragraph 2 discusses the functions their facilities provide.
(D) Paragraph 3 talks about a type of Buddhist architecture that is newer than the Buddhist structures discussed in paragraph 2.

Buddhist Temples

Buddhist temples are sacred structures that have been built for centuries. They provide insight into the ancient spiritual practices and cultural values of Buddhist communities. Found across Asia, these temples are esteemed for their towering pagodas, intricate carvings, and golden statues of the Buddha. Angkor Wat in Cambodia and the Borobudur Temple in Indonesia are the world's most popular Buddhist sites among travelers.

Also known as monasteries, Buddhist temples serve multiple purposes. They are where monks and laypeople gather for meditation, prayer, and ceremonies. They also function as centers for teaching Buddhist philosophy and spreading moral values. Additionally, they often serve as symbols of peace, compassion, and devotion within their communities.

The construction techniques of Buddhist temples were highly advanced for their time. Builders used stone, brick, and wood, often combining them with ornate designs and detailed artwork. Some temples are decorated with murals and sculptures that narrate stories from the Buddha's life. The way in which certain temples display solar alignment, such as with sunrise or sunset, suggests that their orientation was intentionally planned. Despite variations across regions, Buddhist temples remain as landmarks of enduring cultural heritage.

Why does the author mention solar alignment?

(A) To explain why some Buddhist artwork is extremely valuable
(B) To indicate that some Buddhist temples were oriented deliberately
(C) To highlight an important event in Buddha's life
(D) To describe the advanced technology behind Buddhist structures

Module 2

TOEFL iBT

Reading | Questions **1-10** of 15

Fill in the missing letters in the paragraph.

Jupiter is the largest planet in the solar system, made mostly of hydrogen and helium, with swirling clouds and massive storms. Its remark_ _ _ _ strong gravitation_ _ pull aff_ _ _ _ nearby plan_ _ _ and captu_ _ _ passing come_ _ , but its ext_ _ _ _ conditions ma _ _ it uninhabit_ _ _ _ . By stud_ _ _ _ Jupiter, astronomers can understand planetary formation: for example, how gas giants form, how their magnetic fields develop, and how deep atmospheric currents create features like the Great Red Spot.

Marathon Running

Marathon running, including city races, charity events, and international competitions, is increasingly gaining recognition as a popular form of endurance sport. Long-distance races push athletes to their physical limits, providing an opportunity for personal achievement and global camaraderie. Community marathons encourage healthy lifestyles, while elite events attract top athletes from around the world. These races offer significant health and motivational benefits, such as improved cardiovascular endurance and a strong sense of accomplishment.

However, marathon running is not without its challenges. Training demands months of preparation, requiring strict schedules and lifestyle changes. Runners risk injuries from overuse, dehydration, and exhaustion, which can undermine progress. Additionally, when participating in competitions, the costs of travel and entry fees may discourage newcomers, although many still see participation as a rewarding goal.

Various key partners are working to reduce the occurrence of marathon-related injuries. For instance, trainers are designing personalized running plans with built-in recovery periods to prevent injuries. Sporting goods companies have made advances in athletic gear, such as cushioned shoes and hydration packs, which improve performance and safety. More local governments and sponsors are also supporting community races and taking steps to educate people on how to participate safely in marathons.

Which of the following is mentioned in the passage as one health benefit of marathon running?

(A) It reduces the likelihood of injuries.
(B) It boosts one's cardiorespiratory fitness.
(C) It is an easy sport to pick up.
(D) It can compel people to eat healthier foods.

Marathon Running

Marathon running, including city races, charity events, and international competitions, is increasingly gaining recognition as a popular form of endurance sport. Long-distance races push athletes to their physical limits, providing an opportunity for personal achievement and global camaraderie. Community marathons encourage healthy lifestyles, while elite events attract top athletes from around the world. These races offer significant health and motivational benefits, such as improved cardiovascular endurance and a strong sense of accomplishment.

However, marathon running is not without its challenges. Training demands months of preparation, requiring strict schedules and lifestyle changes. Runners risk injuries from overuse, dehydration, and exhaustion, which can undermine progress. Additionally, when participating in competitions, the costs of travel and entry fees may discourage newcomers, although many still see participation as a rewarding goal.

Various key partners are working to reduce the occurrence of marathon-related injuries. For instance, trainers are designing personalized running plans with built-in recovery periods to prevent injuries. Sporting goods companies have made advances in athletic gear, such as cushioned shoes and hydration packs, which improve performance and safety. More local governments and sponsors are also supporting community races and taking steps to educate people on how to participate safely in marathons.

The word "sense" in the passage is closest in meaning to

(A) awareness
(B) wisdom
(C) cleverness
(D) feeling

Marathon Running

Marathon running, including city races, charity events, and international competitions, is increasingly gaining recognition as a popular form of endurance sport. Long-distance races push athletes to their physical limits, providing an opportunity for personal achievement and global camaraderie. Community marathons encourage healthy lifestyles, while elite events attract top athletes from around the world. These races offer significant health and motivational benefits, such as improved cardiovascular endurance and a strong sense of accomplishment.

However, marathon running is not without its challenges. Training demands months of preparation, requiring strict schedules and lifestyle changes. Runners risk injuries from overuse, dehydration, and exhaustion, which can undermine progress. Additionally, when participating in competitions, the costs of travel and entry fees may discourage newcomers, although many still see participation as a rewarding goal.

Various key partners are working to reduce the occurrence of marathon-related injuries. For instance, trainers are designing personalized running plans with built-in recovery periods to prevent injuries. Sporting goods companies have made advances in athletic gear, such as cushioned shoes and hydration packs, which improve performance and safety. More local governments and sponsors are also supporting community races and taking steps to educate people on how to participate safely in marathons.

What challenge is associated with marathon running?

(A) Lower levels of stamina
(B) Limited time for sleep
(C) Expensive training fees
(D) Strict lifestyle management

Marathon Running

Marathon running, including city races, charity events, and international competitions, is increasingly gaining recognition as a popular form of endurance sport. Long-distance races push athletes to their physical limits, providing an opportunity for personal achievement and global camaraderie. Community marathons encourage healthy lifestyles, while elite events attract top athletes from around the world. These races offer significant health and motivational benefits, such as improved cardiovascular endurance and a strong sense of accomplishment.

However, marathon running is not without its challenges. Training demands months of preparation, requiring strict schedules and lifestyle changes. Runners risk injuries from overuse, dehydration, and exhaustion, which can undermine progress. Additionally, when participating in competitions, the costs of travel and entry fees may discourage newcomers, although many still see participation as a rewarding goal.

Various key partners are working to reduce the occurrence of marathon-related injuries. For instance, trainers are designing personalized running plans with built-in recovery periods to prevent injuries. Sporting goods companies have made advances in athletic gear, such as cushioned shoes and hydration packs, which improve performance and safety. More local governments and sponsors are also supporting community races and taking steps to educate people on how to participate safely in marathons.

How are trainers addressing the issue of injuries?

(A) By developing new types of athletic gear
(B) By providing tips for quick recovery
(C) By designing personalized running plans
(D) By working only with top athletes rather than newcomers

Marathon Running

Marathon running, including city races, charity events, and international competitions, is increasingly gaining recognition as a popular form of endurance sport. Long-distance races push athletes to their physical limits, providing an opportunity for personal achievement and global camaraderie. Community marathons encourage healthy lifestyles, while elite events attract top athletes from around the world. These races offer significant health and motivational benefits, such as improved cardiovascular endurance and a strong sense of accomplishment.

However, marathon running is not without its challenges. Training demands months of preparation, requiring strict schedules and lifestyle changes. Runners risk injuries from overuse, dehydration, and exhaustion, which can undermine progress. Additionally, when participating in competitions, the costs of travel and entry fees may discourage newcomers, although many still see participation as a rewarding goal.

Various key partners are working to reduce the occurrence of marathon-related injuries. For instance, trainers are designing personalized running plans with built-in recovery periods to prevent injuries. Sporting goods companies have made advances in athletic gear, such as cushioned shoes and hydration packs, which improve performance and safety. More local governments and sponsors are also supporting community races and taking steps to educate people on how to participate safely in marathons.

What is the author's purpose in mentioning key partners?

(A) To emphasize the accessibility of marathon running
(B) To demonstrate several solutions to the challenges of marathon running
(C) To identify various people and organizations active in the marathon industry
(D) To encourage individuals to participate in community marathons

LISTENING

TOEFL iBT

Listening Section

In the listening section, you will answer 35 to 45 questions to demonstrate how well you understand spoken English. There are three types of tasks.

Type of Task	Description
Listen and Choose a Response	Select the best response to the question or statement.
Conversations	Answer questions about short conversations.
Announcements and Academic Talks	Answer questions about announcements and academic talks.

You WILL NOT be able to return to previous questions.

Module 1

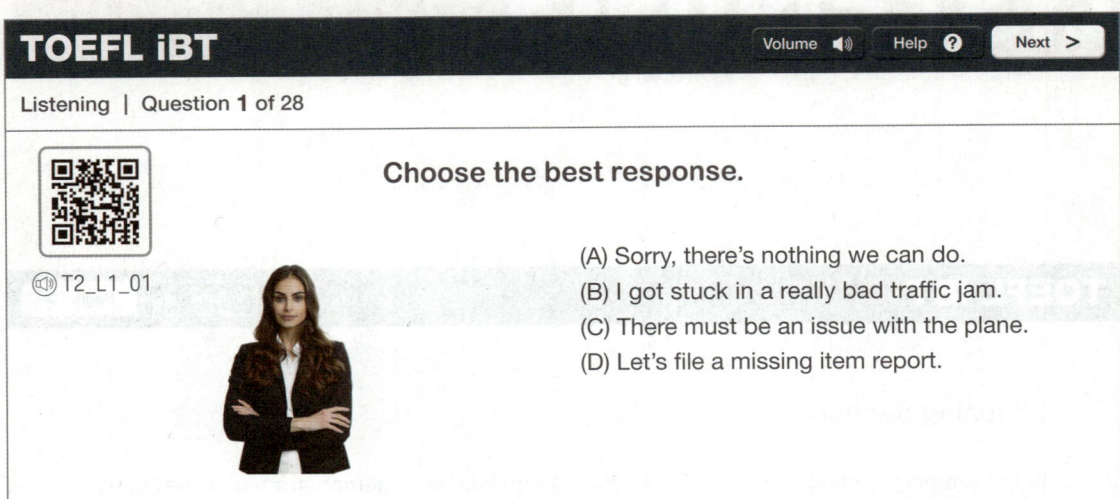

Choose the best response.

(A) Sorry, there's nothing we can do.
(B) I got stuck in a really bad traffic jam.
(C) There must be an issue with the plane.
(D) Let's file a missing item report.

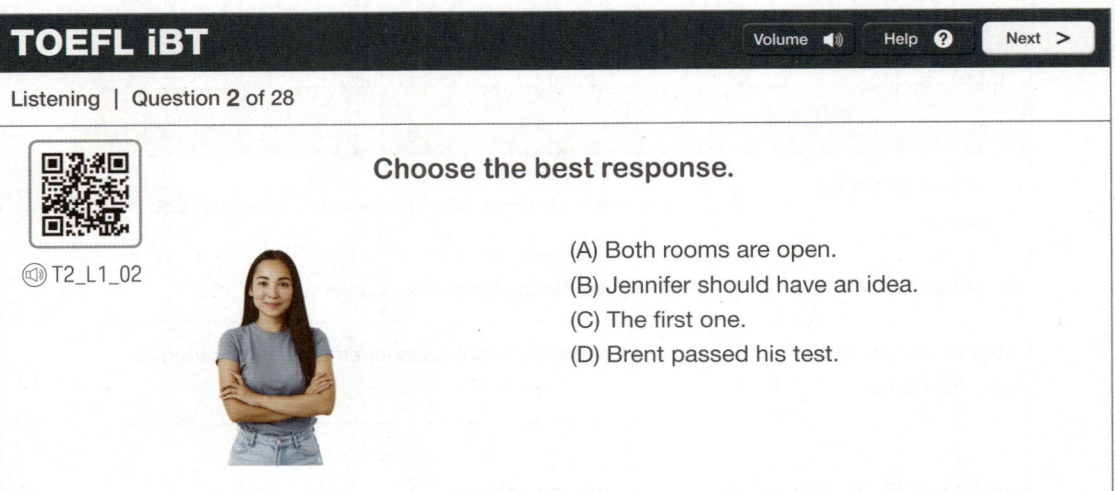

Choose the best response.

(A) Both rooms are open.
(B) Jennifer should have an idea.
(C) The first one.
(D) Brent passed his test.

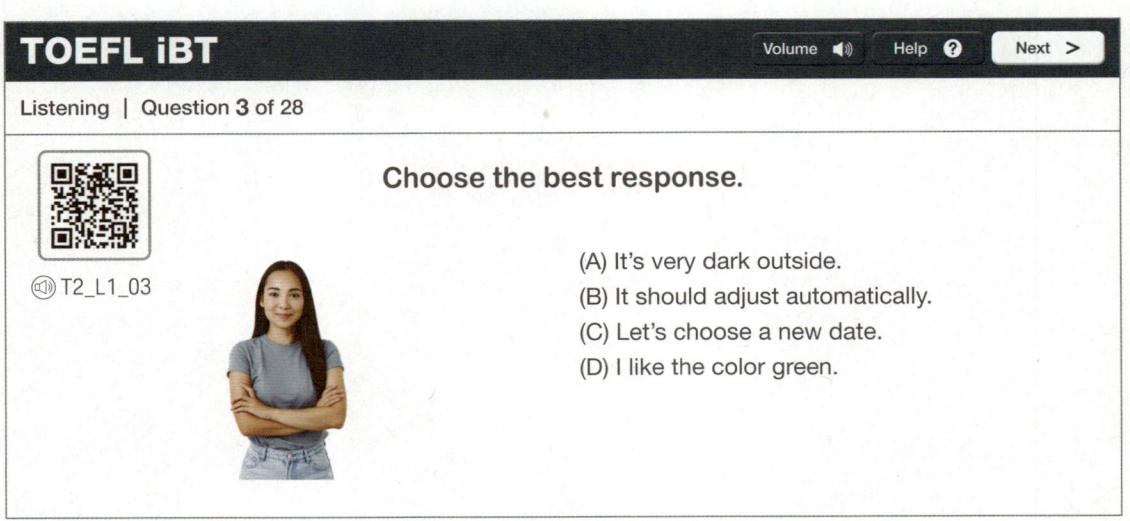

Choose the best response.

(A) It's very dark outside.
(B) It should adjust automatically.
(C) Let's choose a new date.
(D) I like the color green.

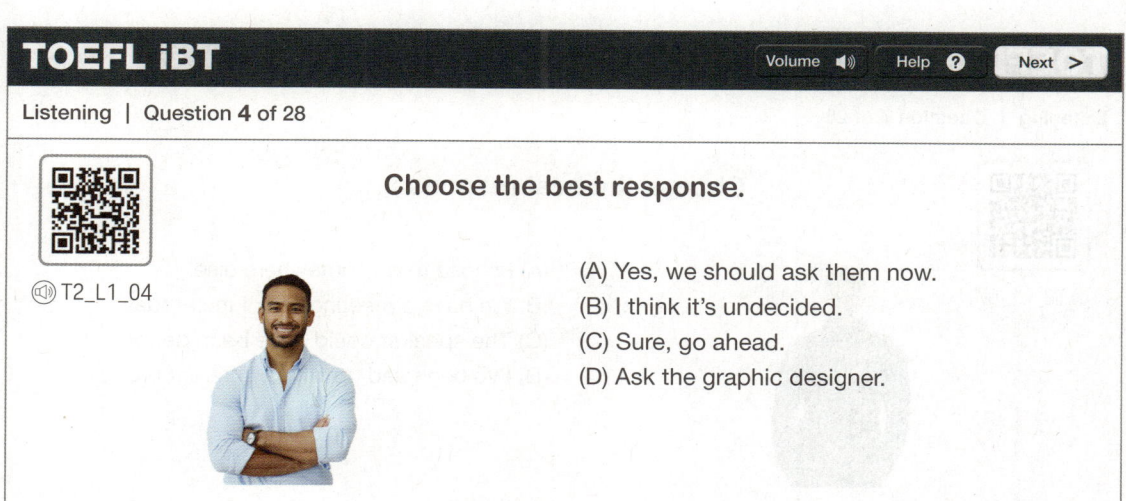

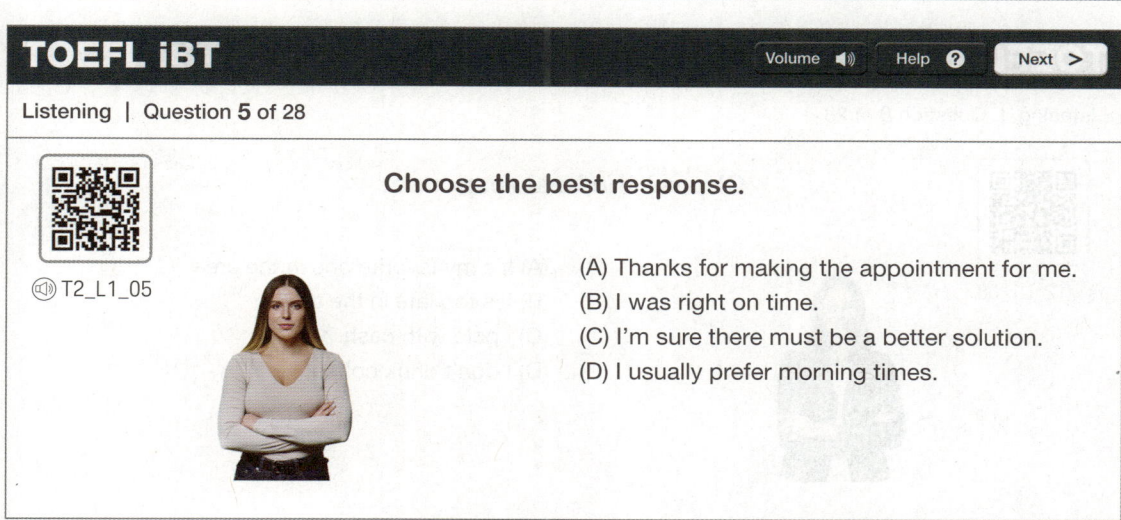

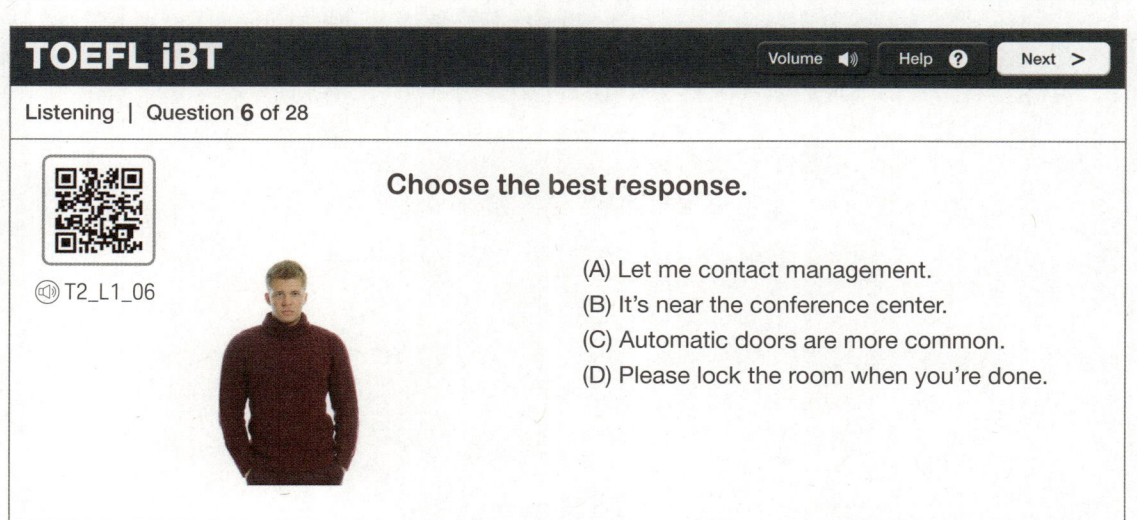

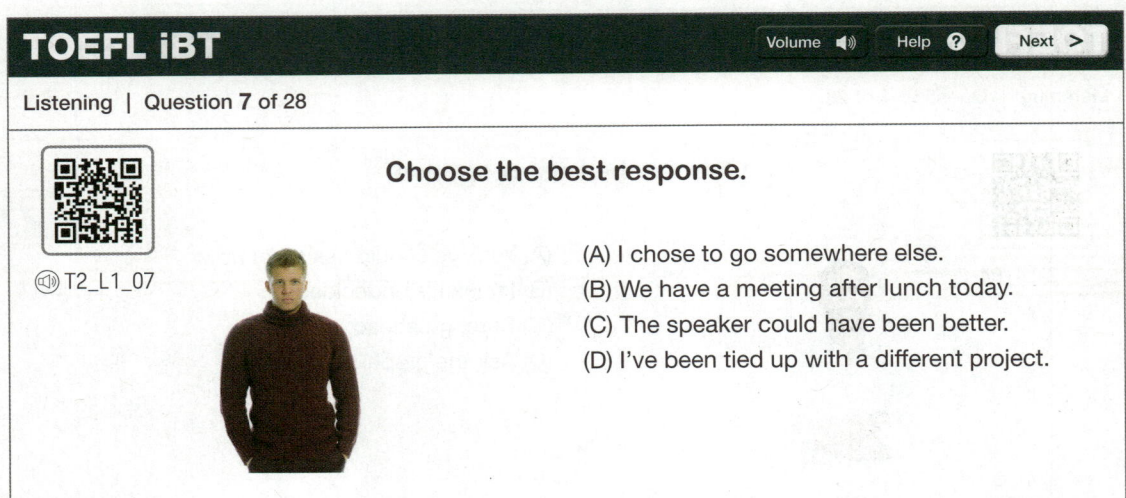

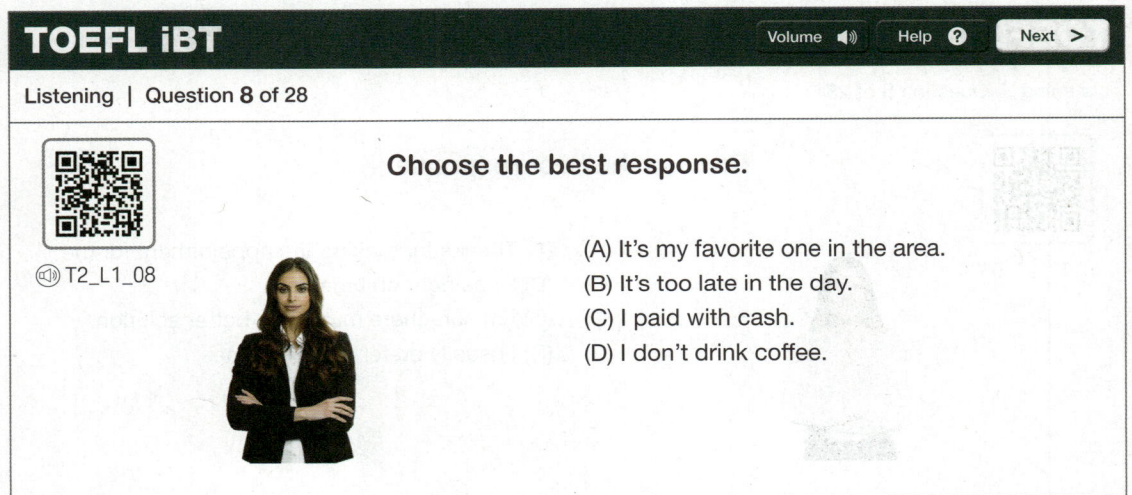

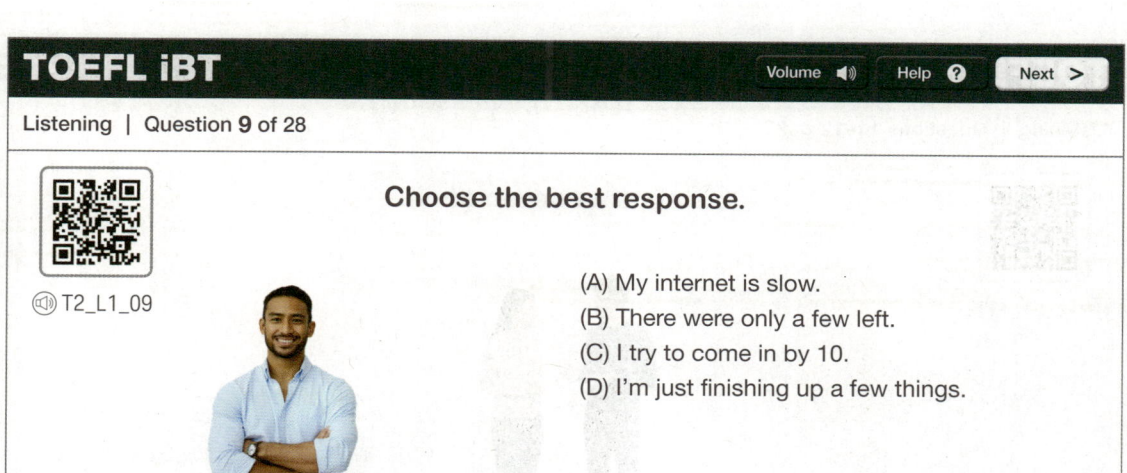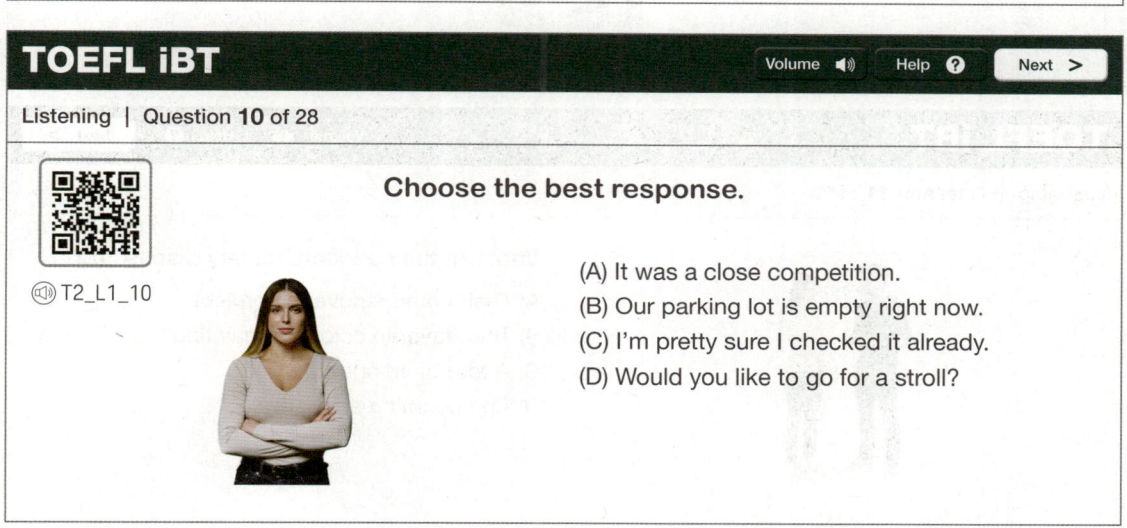

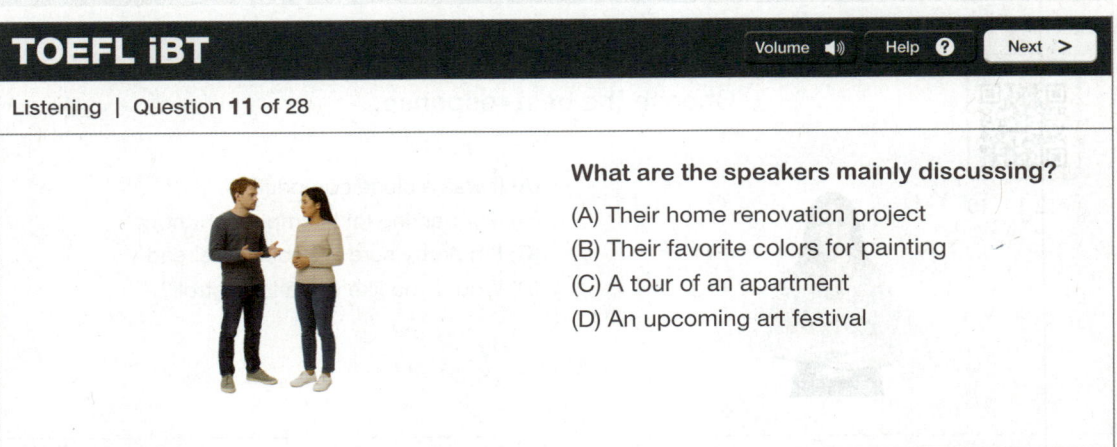

What are the speakers mainly discussing?

(A) Their home renovation project
(B) Their favorite colors for painting
(C) A tour of an apartment
(D) An upcoming art festival

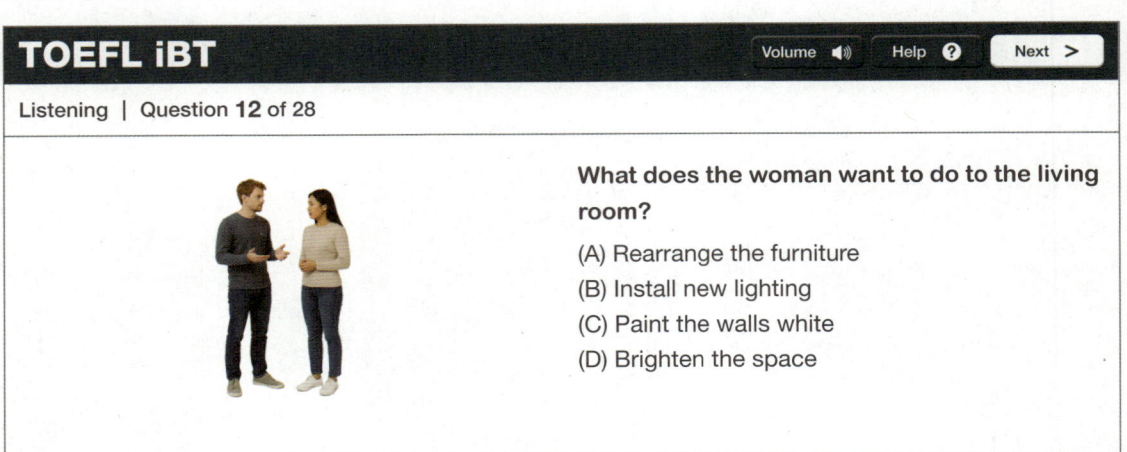

What does the woman want to do to the living room?

(A) Rearrange the furniture
(B) Install new lighting
(C) Paint the walls white
(D) Brighten the space

TOEFL iBT

Listening | Questions 13-14 of 28

T2_L1_1314

Listen to a conversation.

TOEFL iBT

Listening | Question 13 of 28

Why can't the man attend the book club?

(A) He has to give his cousin a ride.
(B) He plans to work overtime.
(C) He will be touching down in another country.
(D) He did not read the assigned novels.

TOEFL iBT

Listening | Question 14 of 28

What does the woman offer to do for the man?

(A) Record a video
(B) Take some notes
(C) Share her ideas
(D) Change a schedule

Listening Module 1   89

TOEFL iBT

Listening | Questions 15-16 of 28

Listen to a conversation.

T2_L1_1516

TOEFL iBT

Listening | Question 15 of 28

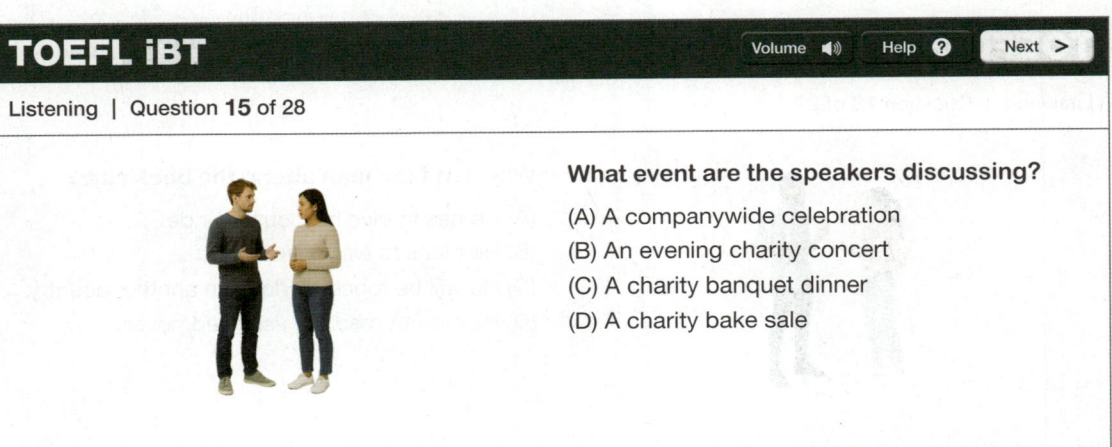

What event are the speakers discussing?

(A) A companywide celebration
(B) An evening charity concert
(C) A charity banquet dinner
(D) A charity bake sale

TOEFL iBT

Listening | Question 16 of 28

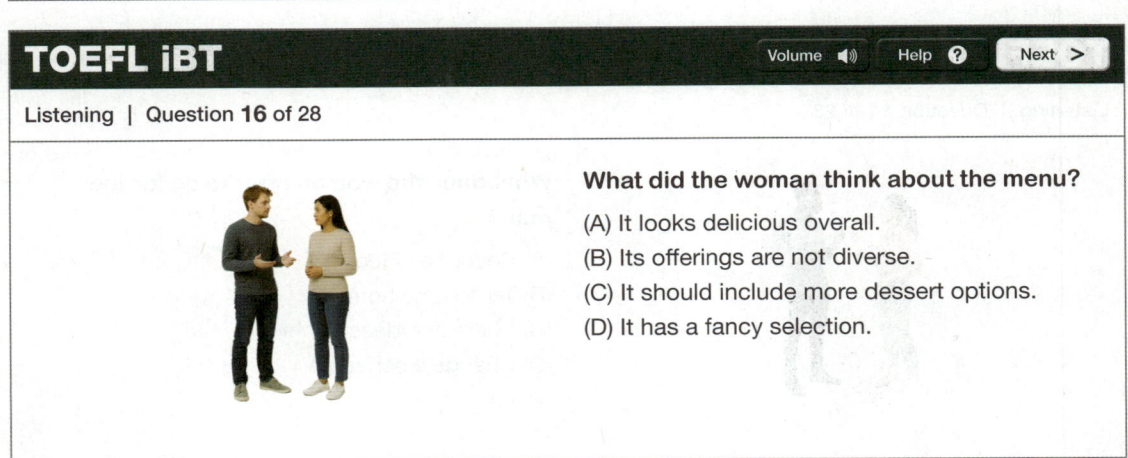

What did the woman think about the menu?

(A) It looks delicious overall.
(B) Its offerings are not diverse.
(C) It should include more dessert options.
(D) It has a fancy selection.

TOEFL iBT

Listening | Questions 17-18 of 28

Listen to an announcement on the school radio.

T2_L1_1718

TOEFL iBT

Listening | Question 17 of 28

What is the main topic of the announcement?

(A) A special one-day event at the fitness center
(B) The restoration of a damaged campus gym
(C) A sports tournament at the recreational center
(D) The launching of a new athletics team

TOEFL iBT

Listening | Question 18 of 28

What are students encouraged to do?

(A) Take a nap in the relaxation lounge
(B) Participate in group workout sessions
(C) Register for a one-day yoga class
(D) Try out some new massage chairs

TOEFL iBT

Listening | Questions 19-20 of 28

T2_L1_1920

Listen to an announcement at a university club meeting.

TOEFL iBT

Listening | Question 19 of 28

What is the main topic of the announcement?

(A) A special celebrity performance
(B) A seasonal music show
(C) A springtime gardening festival
(D) The soundtrack for a movie production

TOEFL iBT

Listening | Question 20 of 28

What are students encouraged to do?

(A) Recommend pieces to play
(B) Sign up as a volunteer
(C) Donate to the Orchestra Club
(D) Prepare an audition video

TOEFL iBT

Listening | Questions **21-24** of 28

Listen to a talk in a business class.

T2_L1_2124

TOEFL iBT

Listening | Question **21** of 28

What is the main topic of the talk?

(A) The definition of green marketing
(B) The need for sustainable growth
(C) The concept of greenwashing
(D) The development of eco-friendly materials

TOEFL iBT

Listening | Question **22** of 28

According to the talk, what is one characteristic of greenwashing?

(A) It utilizes environmentally positive language.
(B) It incorporates sustainable production methods.
(C) It establishes a neutral image of a company.
(D) It involves participating in government-led green initiatives.

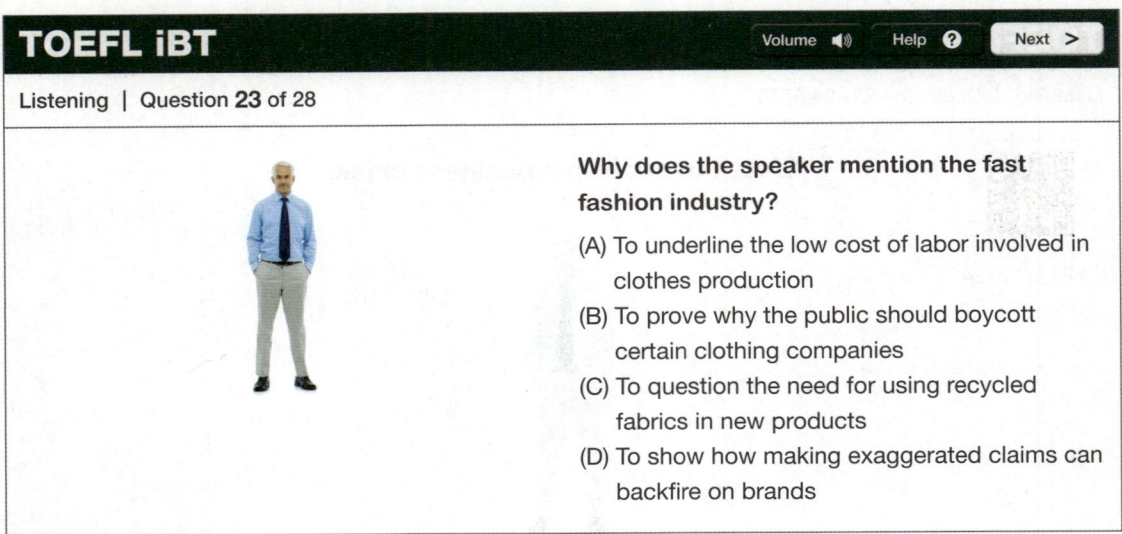

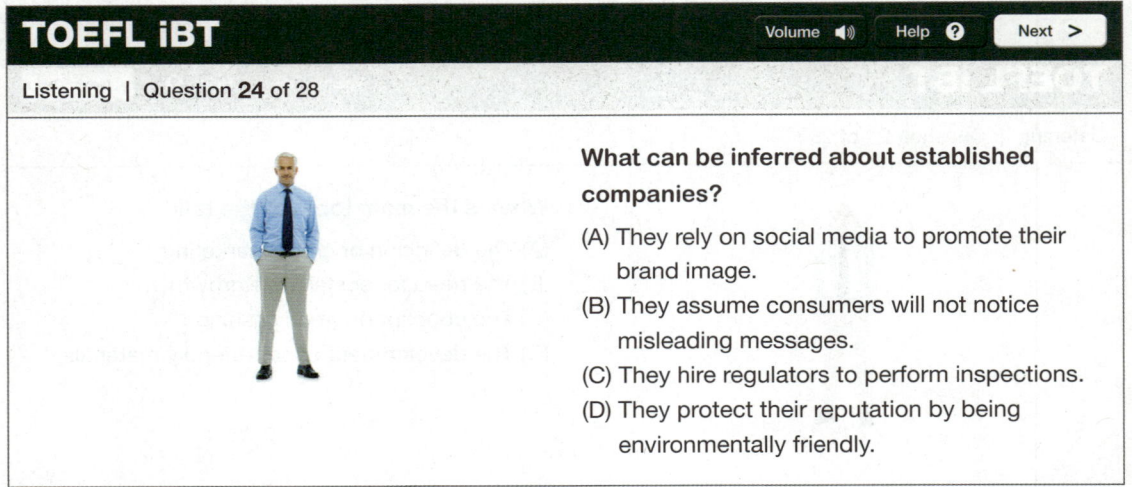

TOEFL iBT

Listening | Questions 25-28 of 28

T2_L1_2528

Listen to a talk in a psychology class.

TOEFL iBT

Listening | Question 25 of 28

What is the main topic of the talk?

(A) How people make quick judgments about others
(B) How people should facilitate dialogue when conflicts arise
(C) How people behave differently with or without an audience
(D) How to improve one's public speaking skills

TOEFL iBT

Listening | Question 26 of 28

Why does the speaker mention someone who enjoys sketching?

(A) To show the benefits of moderate peer pressure
(B) To indicate that getting nervous is a natural reaction
(C) To provide an example of social facilitation
(D) To highlight a good exercise for the brain

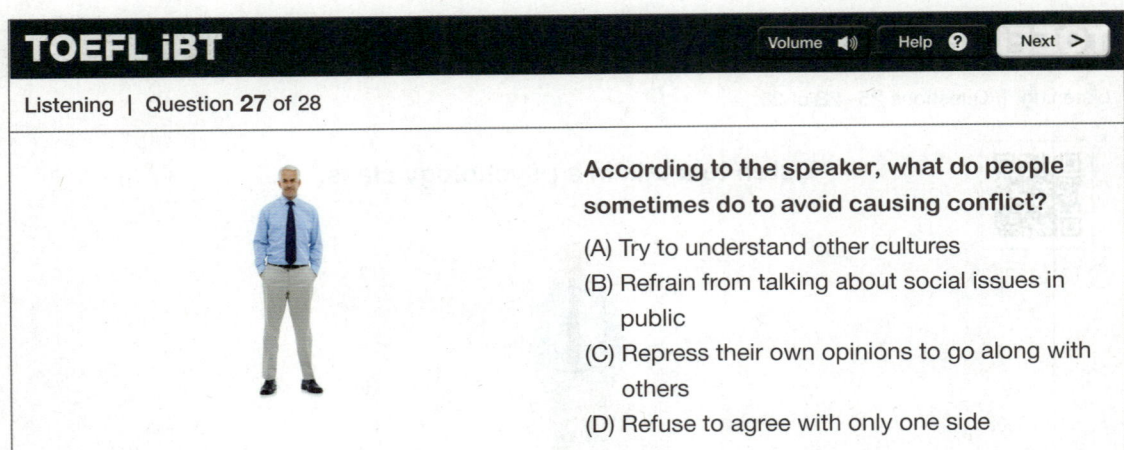

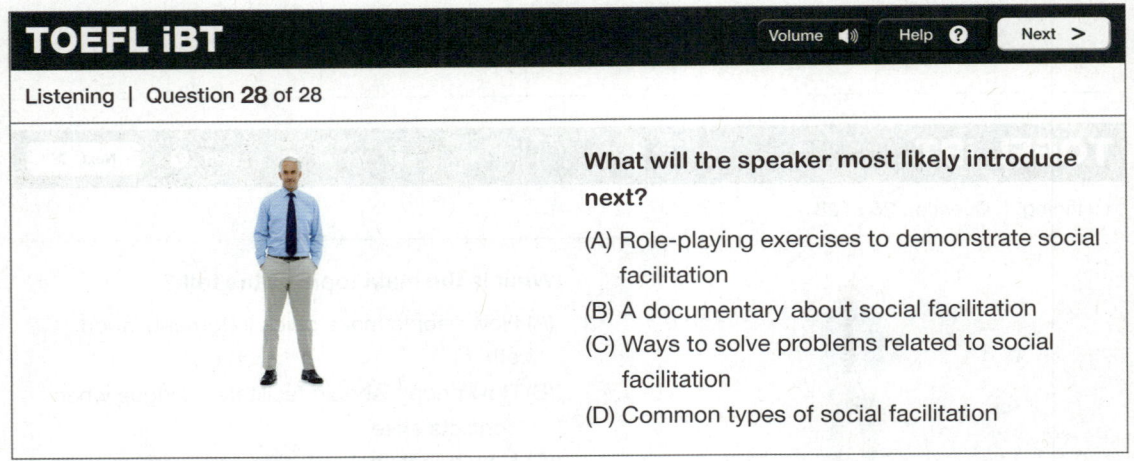

Module 2

TOEFL iBT

Listening | Question **1** of 15

T2_L2_01

Choose the best response.

(A) Yes, every night at 7.
(B) Sure, the bank stays open late.
(C) I have a paper due tomorrow.
(D) In the middle of the stage.

TOEFL iBT

Listening | Question **2** of 15

T2_L2_02

Choose the best response.

(A) It's pretty far from here, isn't it?
(B) Sure, I've been to the warehouse.
(C) Two tickets for the 10 A.M. bus, please.
(D) I prefer to take walks in the evening.

TOEFL iBT

Listening | Question **3** of 15

T2_L2_03

Choose the best response.

(A) Amy said it was a very engaging piece.
(B) The new column will be published soon.
(C) The article is about a new local tech start-up.
(D) Ms. Lee is our person for that.

Listening Module 2

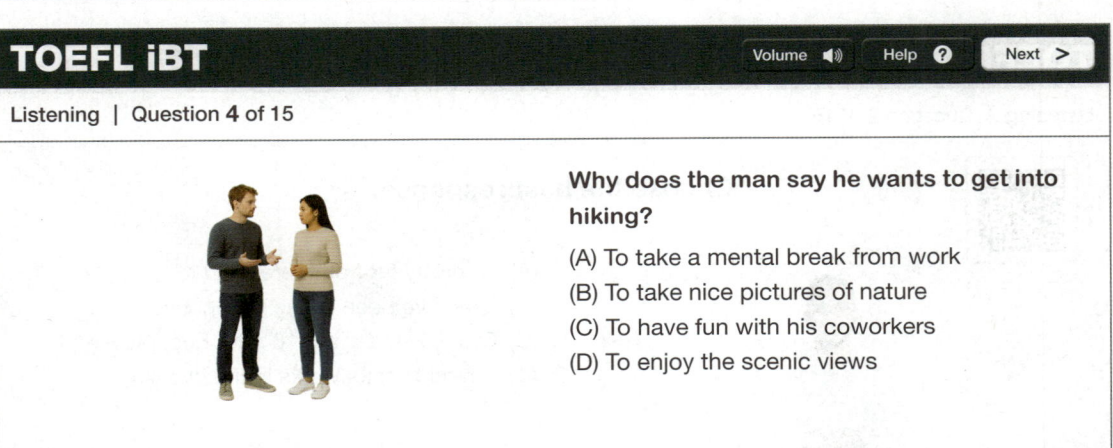

Why does the man say he wants to get into hiking?

(A) To take a mental break from work
(B) To take nice pictures of nature
(C) To have fun with his coworkers
(D) To enjoy the scenic views

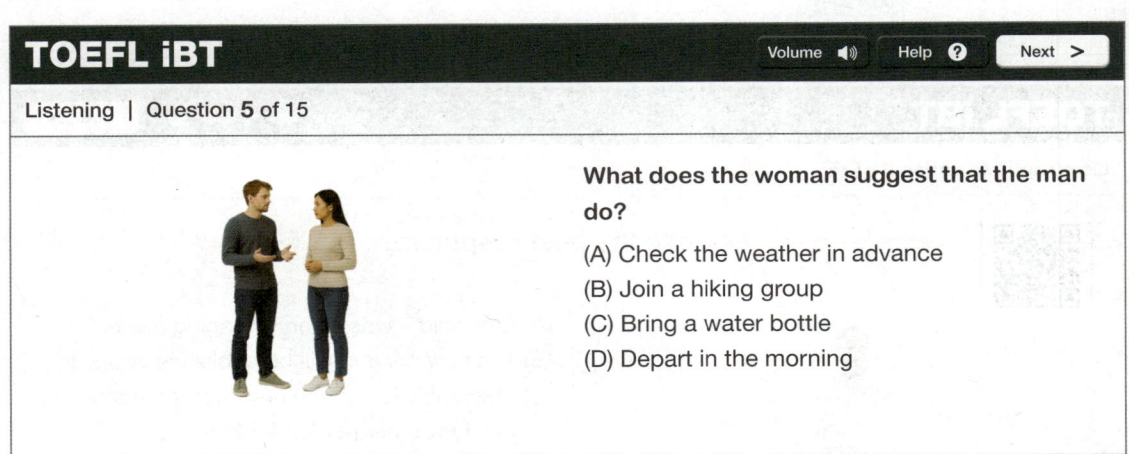

What does the woman suggest that the man do?

(A) Check the weather in advance
(B) Join a hiking group
(C) Bring a water bottle
(D) Depart in the morning

TOEFL iBT

Listening | Questions 6-7 of 15

Listen to a conversation.

T2_L2_0607

TOEFL iBT

Listening | Question 6 of 15

What does the woman imply about an album?

(A) It is topping many music charts.
(B) Online reactions to it are varied.
(C) The band produced it themselves.
(D) It should receive an award.

TOEFL iBT

Listening | Question 7 of 15

What disappointed the man about an album?

(A) It was too expensive.
(B) It did not have a clear genre.
(C) Some songs were not long enough.
(D) Its tempo was slow.

Listen to a talk in a history class.

What is the main topic of the talk?

(A) The origins of the United States Postal Service
(B) The evolution of horse-driven carriages
(C) The legacy of a mail delivery system
(D) The transition from paper to digital communication

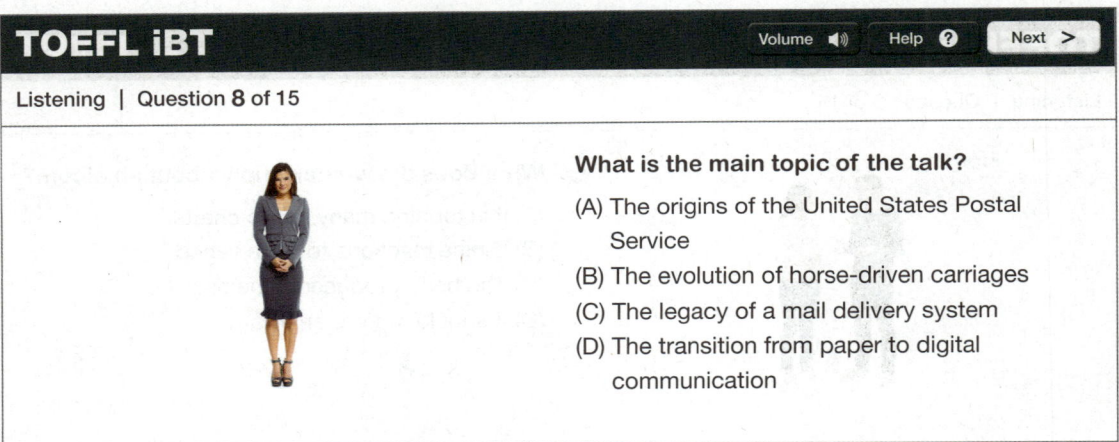

According to the talk, what aspect of the Pony Express made it well known?

(A) Its manpower
(B) Its cost
(C) Its price
(D) Its speed

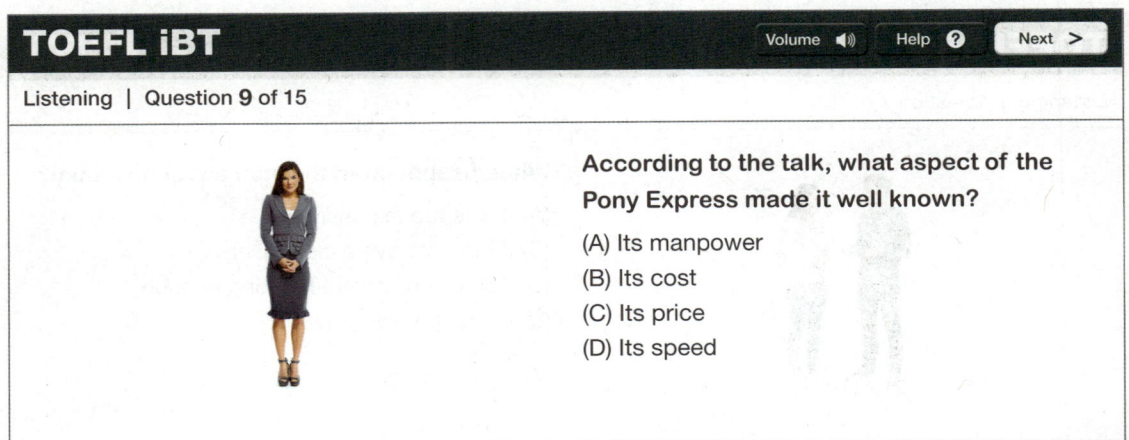

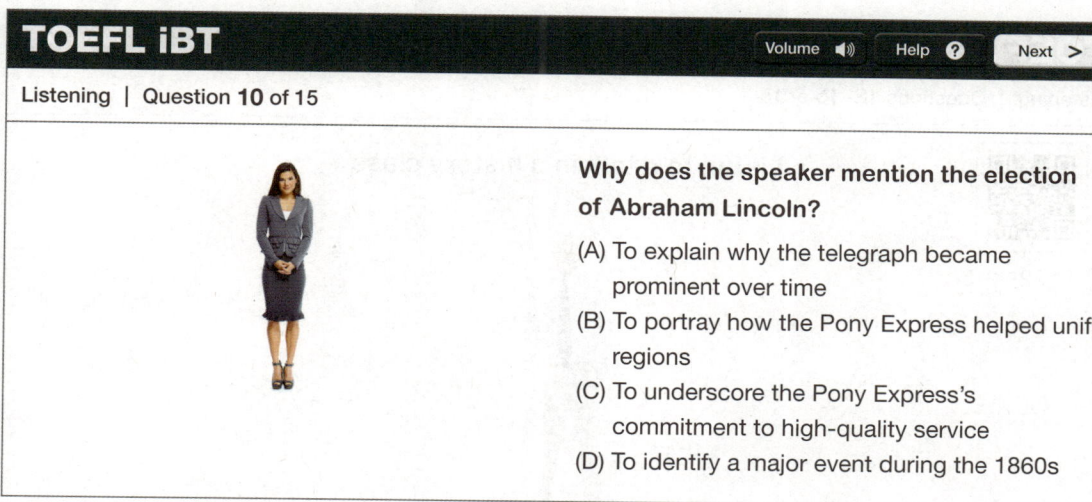

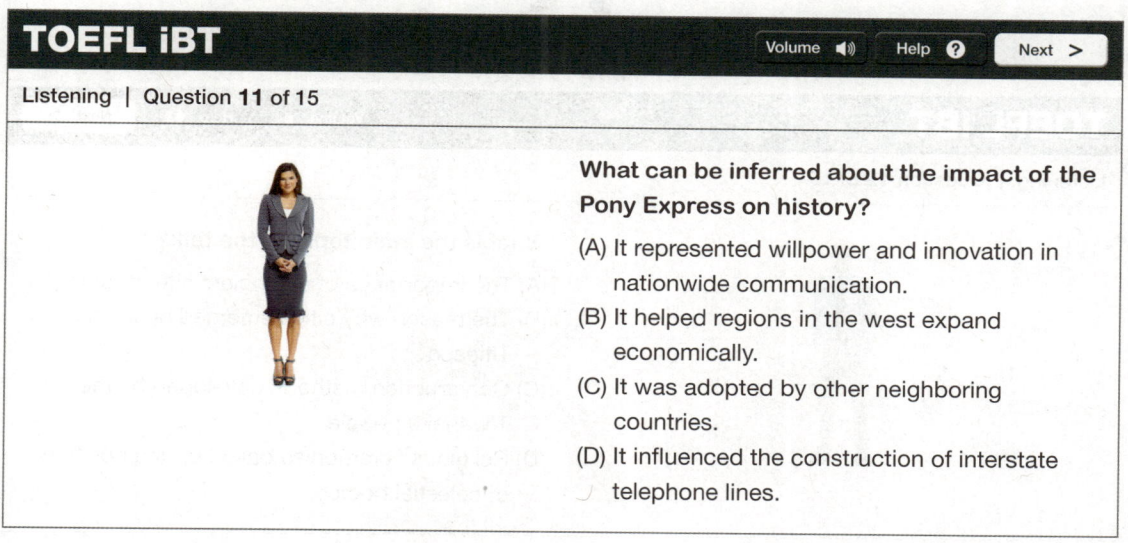

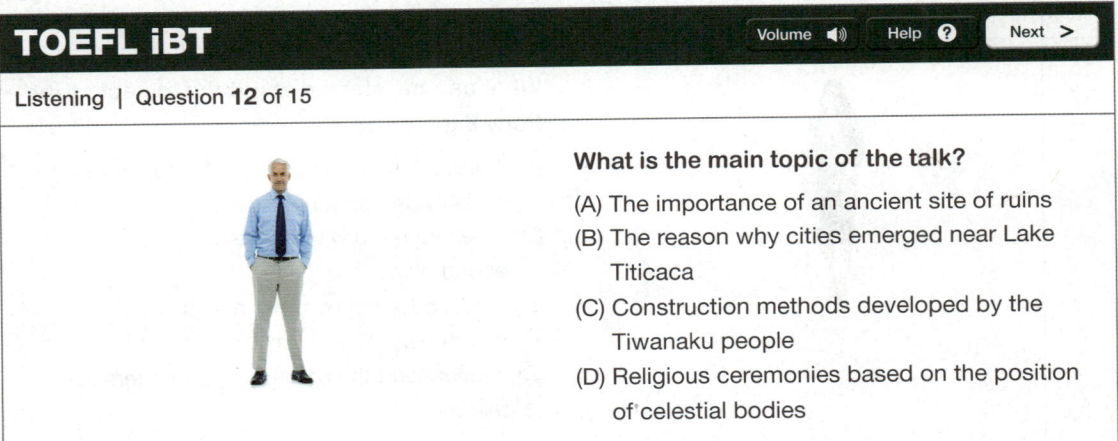

What is the main topic of the talk?

(A) The importance of an ancient site of ruins
(B) The reason why cities emerged near Lake Titicaca
(C) Construction methods developed by the Tiwanaku people
(D) Religious ceremonies based on the position of celestial bodies

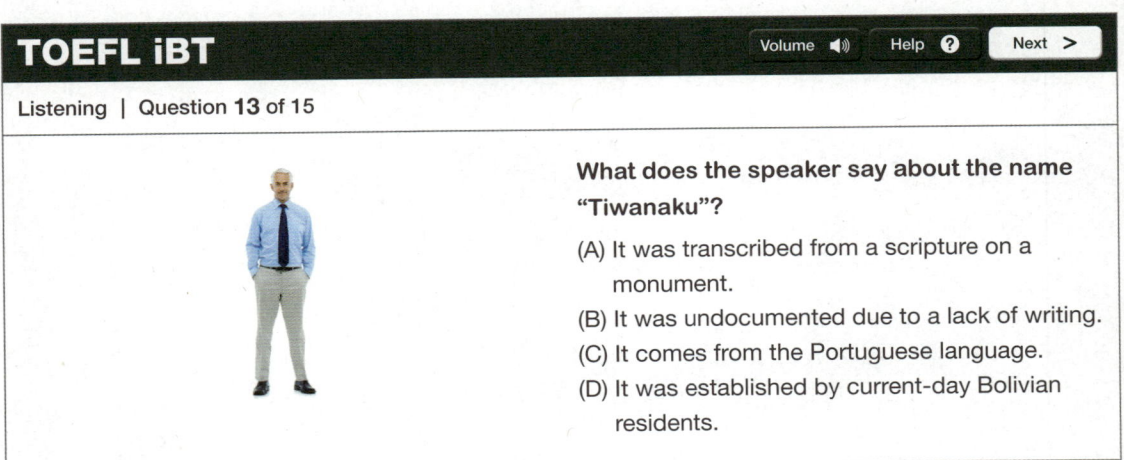

What does the speaker say about the name "Tiwanaku"?

(A) It was transcribed from a scripture on a monument.
(B) It was undocumented due to a lack of writing.
(C) It comes from the Portuguese language.
(D) It was established by current-day Bolivian residents.

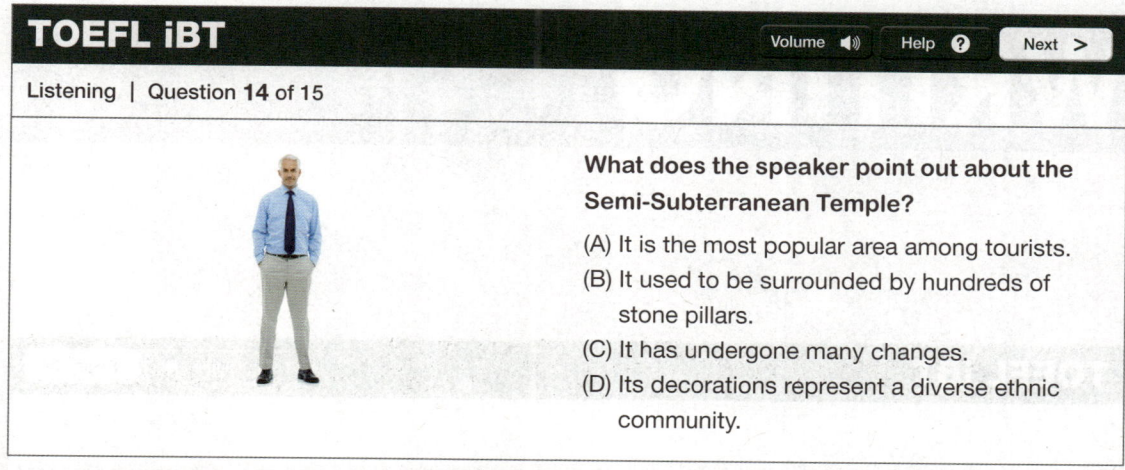

What does the speaker point out about the Semi-Subterranean Temple?

(A) It is the most popular area among tourists.
(B) It used to be surrounded by hundreds of stone pillars.
(C) It has undergone many changes.
(D) Its decorations represent a diverse ethnic community.

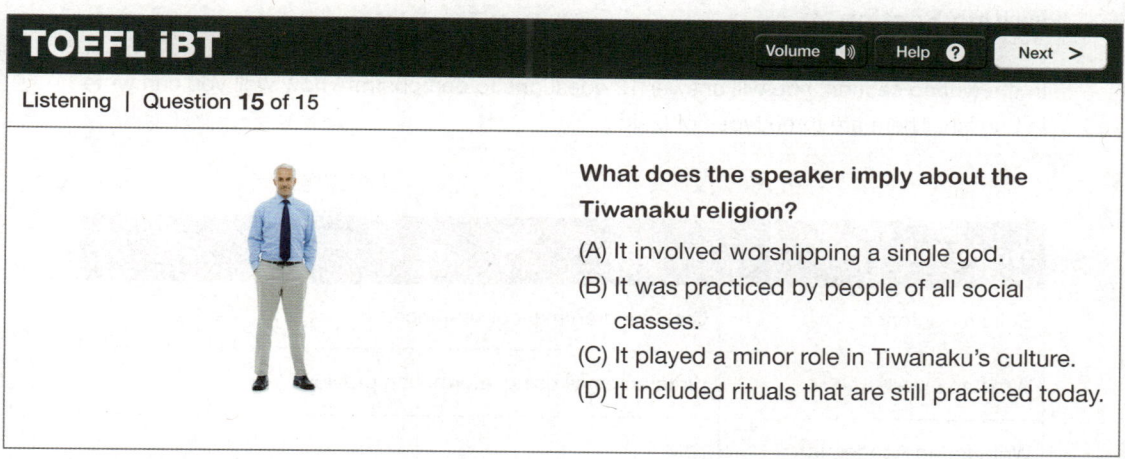

What does the speaker imply about the Tiwanaku religion?

(A) It involved worshipping a single god.
(B) It was practiced by people of all social classes.
(C) It played a minor role in Tiwanaku's culture.
(D) It included rituals that are still practiced today.

WRITING

TOEFL iBT

Writing Section

In the writing section, you will answer 12 questions to demonstrate how well you can write in English. There are three types of tasks.

Type of Task	Description
Build a Sentence	Create a grammatical sentence.
Write an Email	Write an email using information provided.
Write for an Academic Discussion	Participate in an online discussion.

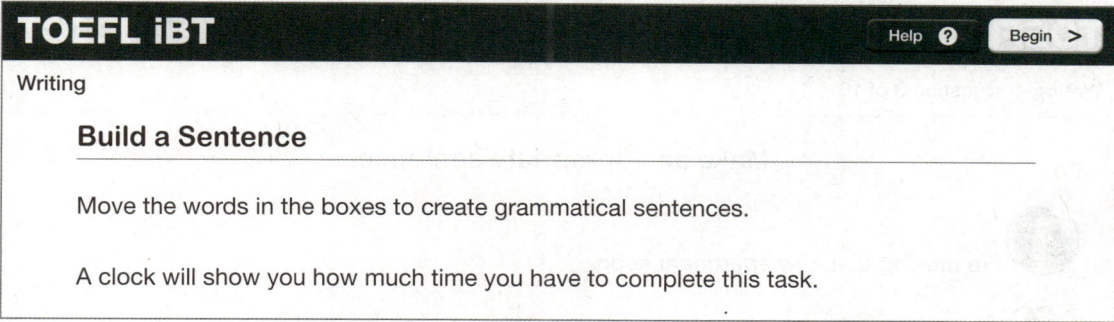

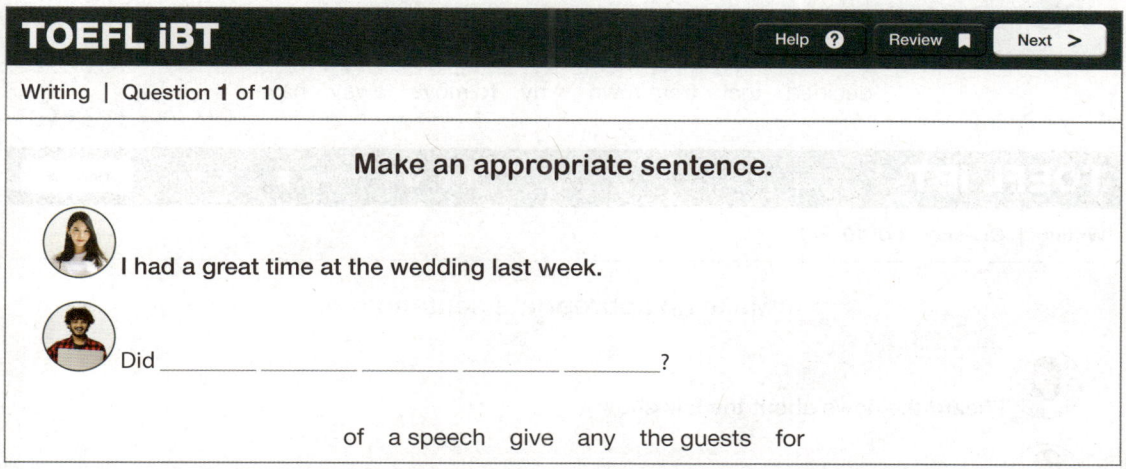

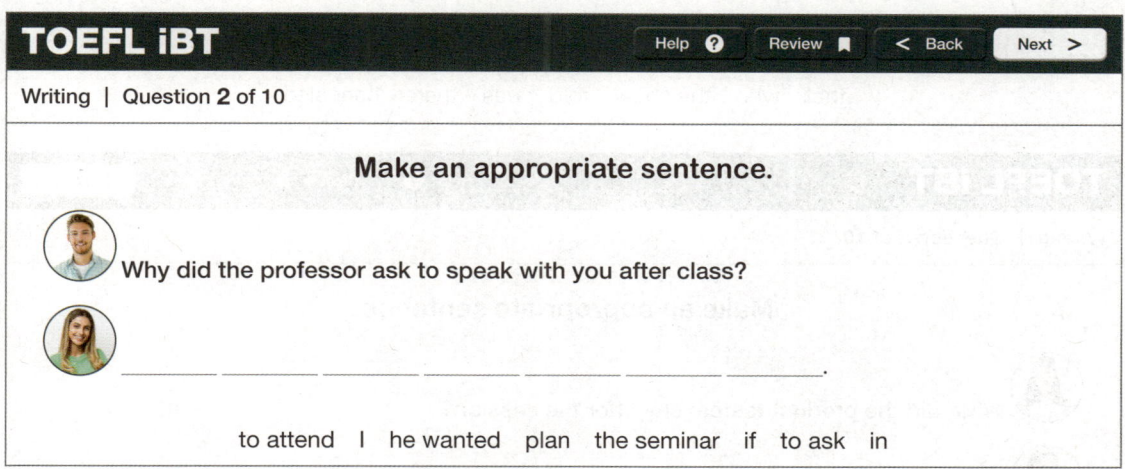

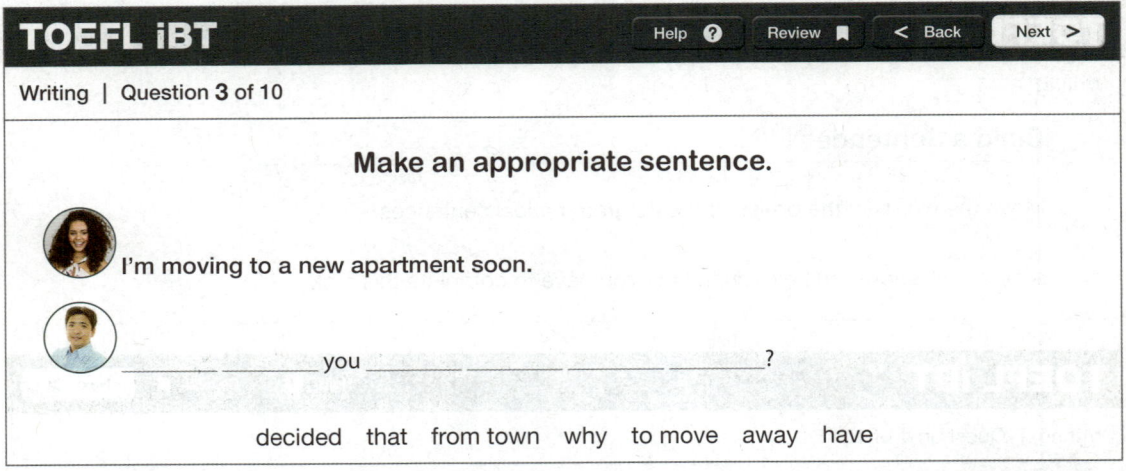

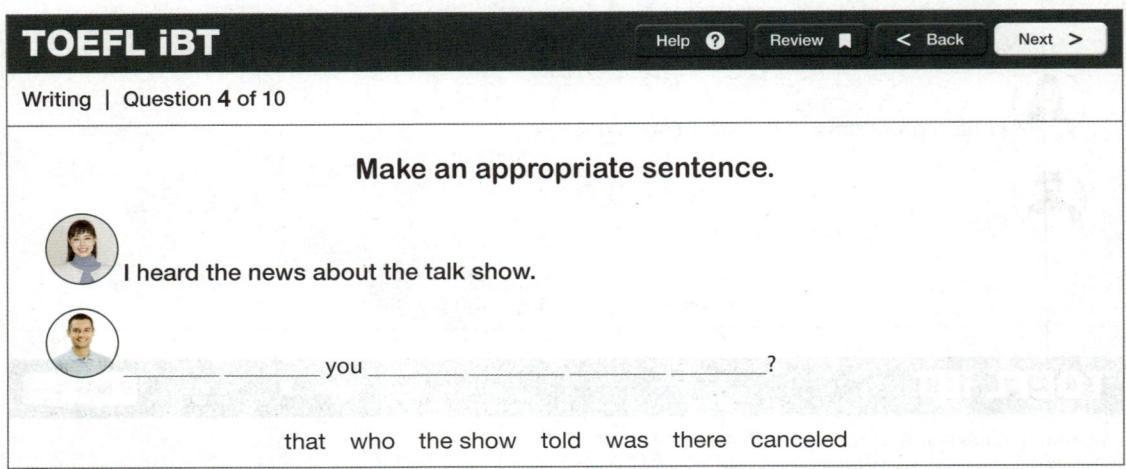

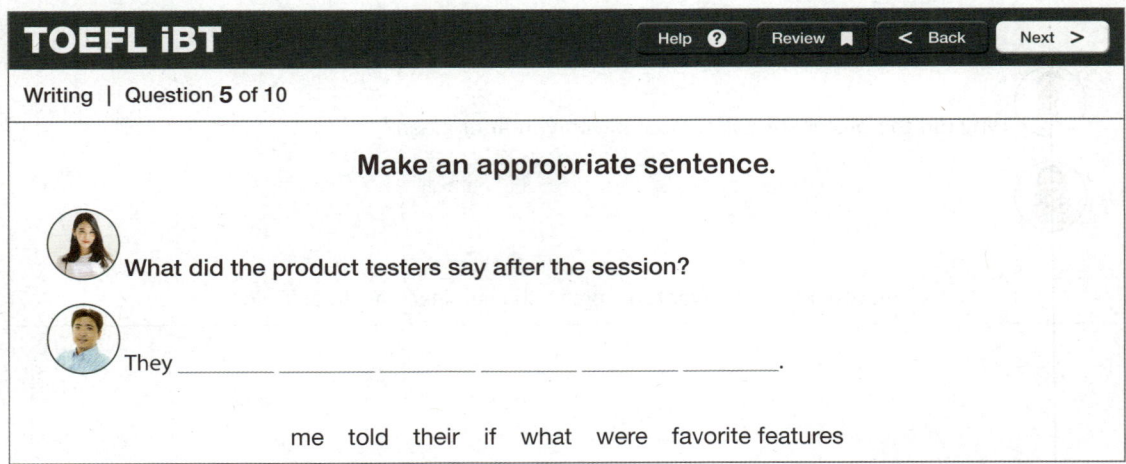

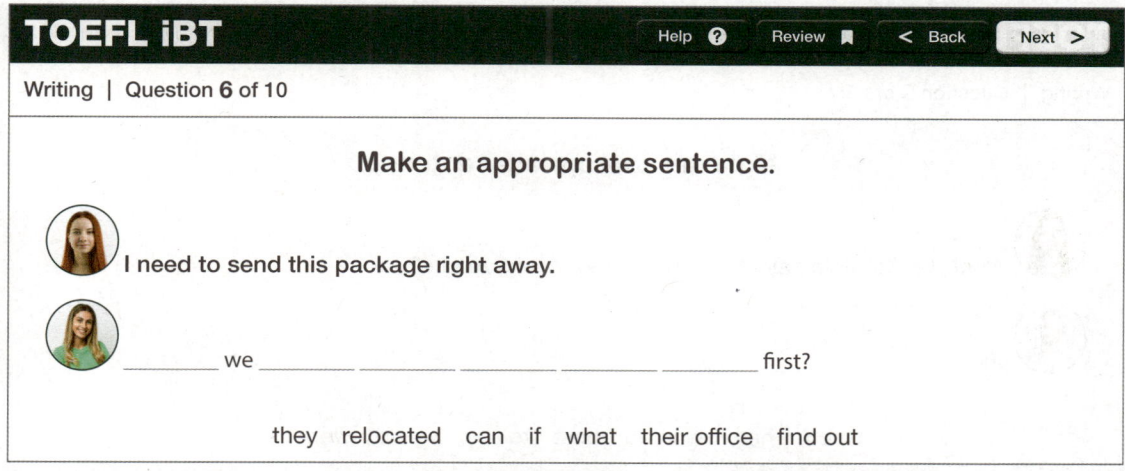

Make an appropriate sentence.

I need to send this package right away.

_____ we _____ _____ _____ _____ _____ first?

they relocated can if what their office find out

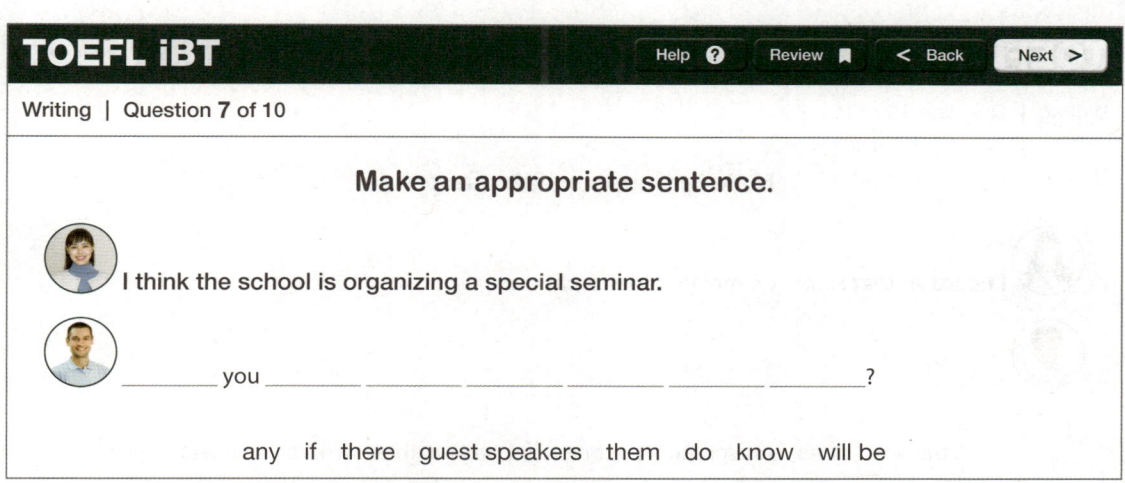

Make an appropriate sentence.

I think the school is organizing a special seminar.

_____ you _____ _____ _____ _____ _____ _____ ?

any if there guest speakers them do know will be

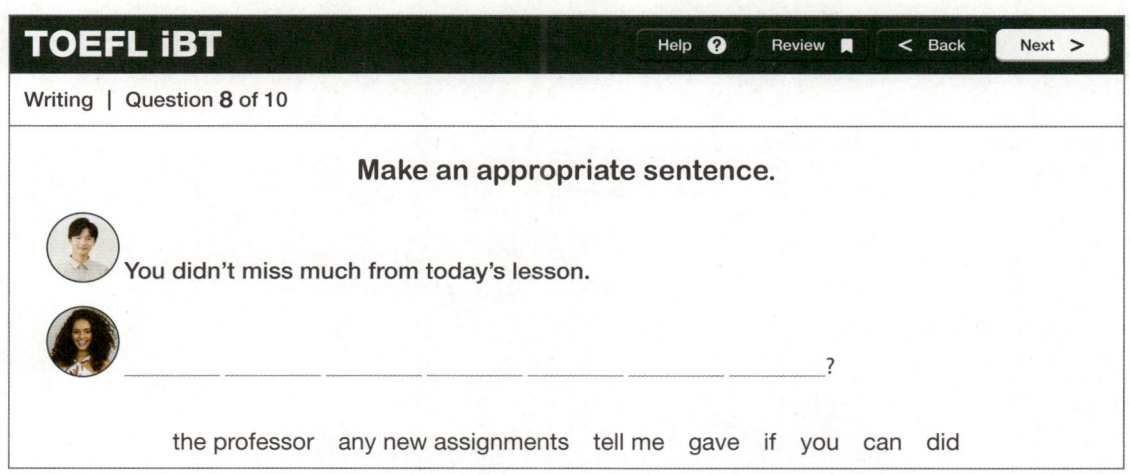

Make an appropriate sentence.

You didn't miss much from today's lesson.

_____ _____ _____ _____ _____ _____ _____ _____ ?

the professor any new assignments tell me gave if you can did

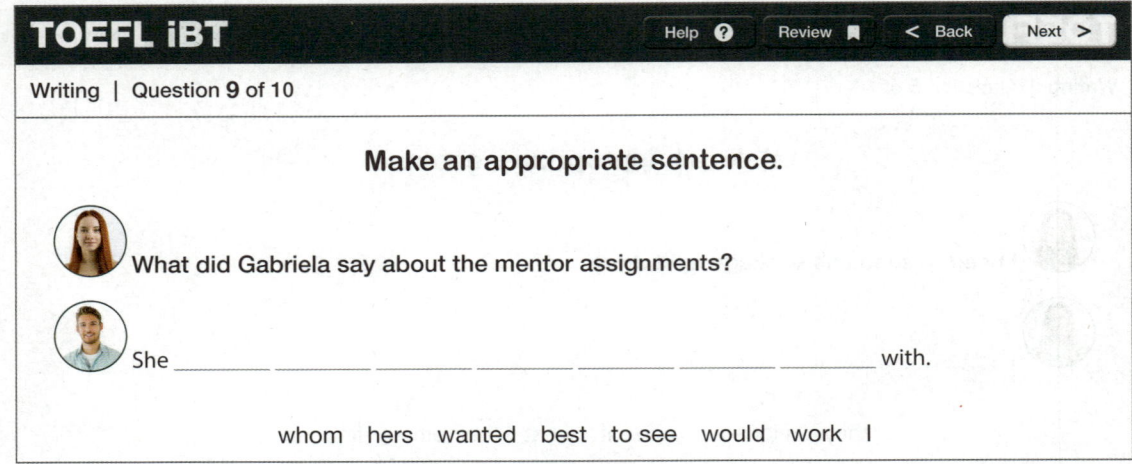

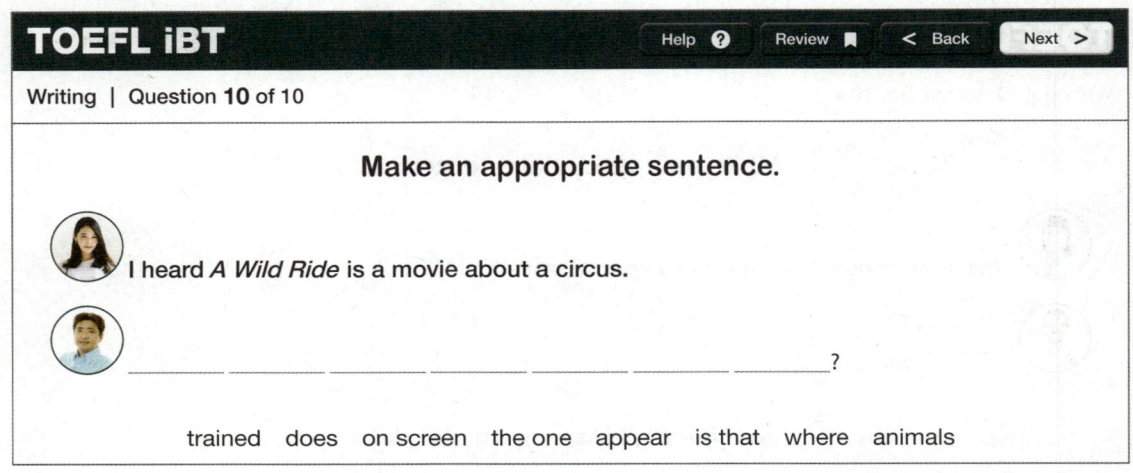

TOEFL iBT

Writing

Write an Email

You will read some information and use the information to write an email.

You will have 7 minutes to write the email.

TOEFL iBT

Writing

You recently invited your family to your house. Your next-door neighbor, Carl, has sent you a message complaining about the noise from your house. You want to apologize and reassure him that it will not happen again.

Write an email to Carl. In your email, do the following:

- Explain the reasons for the noise.
- Apologize to your neighbor.
- Describe what actions you will take.

Write as much as you can and in complete sentences.

Your Response:

To: Carl

Subject: Apology for the noise

TOEFL iBT

Writing

Write for an Academic Discussion

A professor has posted a question about a topic and students have responded with their thoughts and ideas. Make a contribution to the discussion.

You will have 10 minutes to write.

TOEFL iBT

Writing

Your professor is teaching a class on human geography. Write a post responding to the professor's question.

In your response, you should do the following:

- Express and support your opinion.
- Make a contribution to the discussion in your own words.

An effective response will contain at least 100 words.

Dr. Rodrigo

Next week, we will be discussing urbanization, which refers to the movement of people to cities and the increasing population in urban areas. Some argue that more people living in cities improves living standards, while others believe it creates a variety of problems. What is your perspective on this issue? Why?

Bella

I think more people coming to live in cities is a good thing. Cities are known to have greater opportunities for work and education. When people come to the city, they can send their children to schools with better teachers. Also, there are far more job opportunities in the city than in the country.

Jacob

I do not think more people living in cities is a good thing. Cities are densely populated, so people are often in close proximity to one another. This makes it much easier for diseases to spread quickly, increasing the risk of outbreaks and putting public health at greater risk.

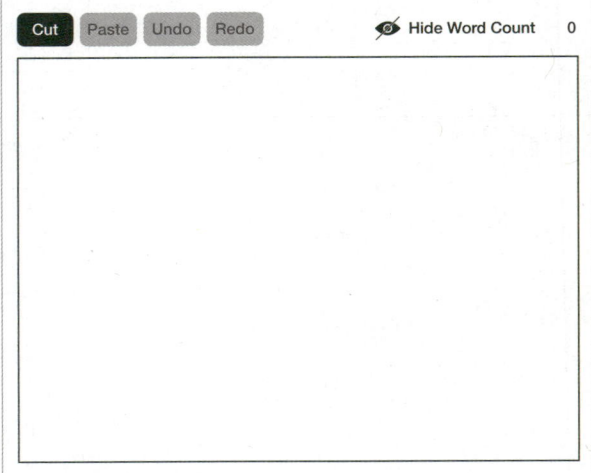

SPEAKING

Speaking Section

In the speaking section, you will answer 11 questions to demonstrate how well you can speak English. There are two types of tasks.

Type of Task	Description
Listen and Repeat	Listen and repeat what you heard.
Take an Interview	Answer questions from the interviewer.

TOEFL iBT

Speaking

Listen and Repeat

You will listen as someone speaks to you. Listen carefully and then repeat what you have heard. The clock will indicate how much time you have to speak.

No time for preparation will be provided.

TOEFL iBT

Speaking

You are being trained to assist students at the university library. Listen to your trainer and repeat what she says.

TOEFL iBT

Speaking | Question **1** of 11

T2_S_01

Listen and repeat only once.

RESPONSE TIME
00:00:08

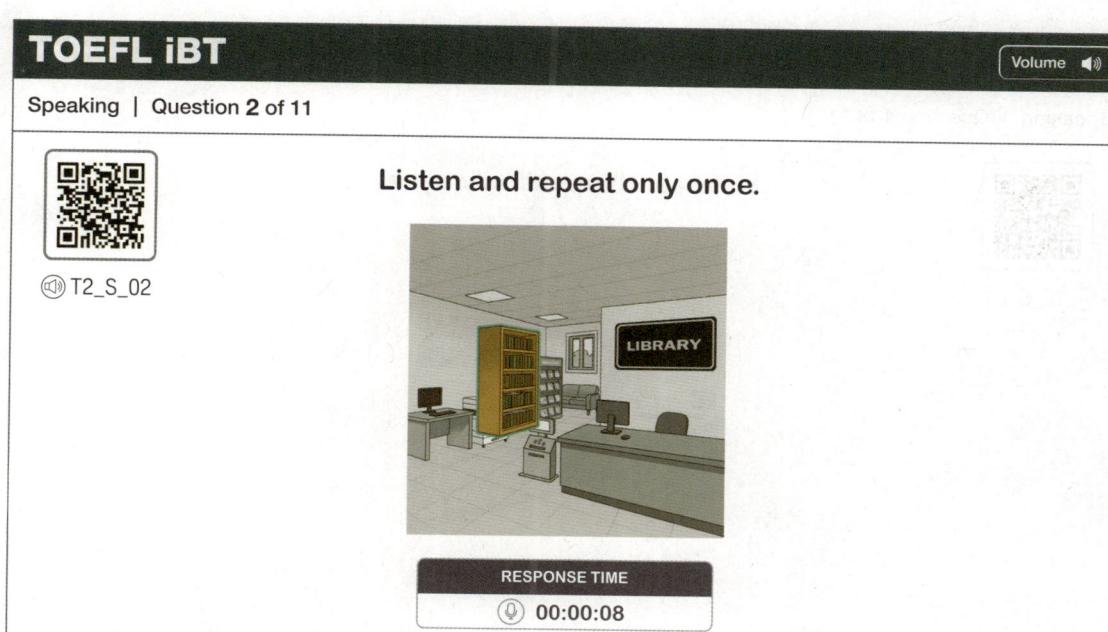

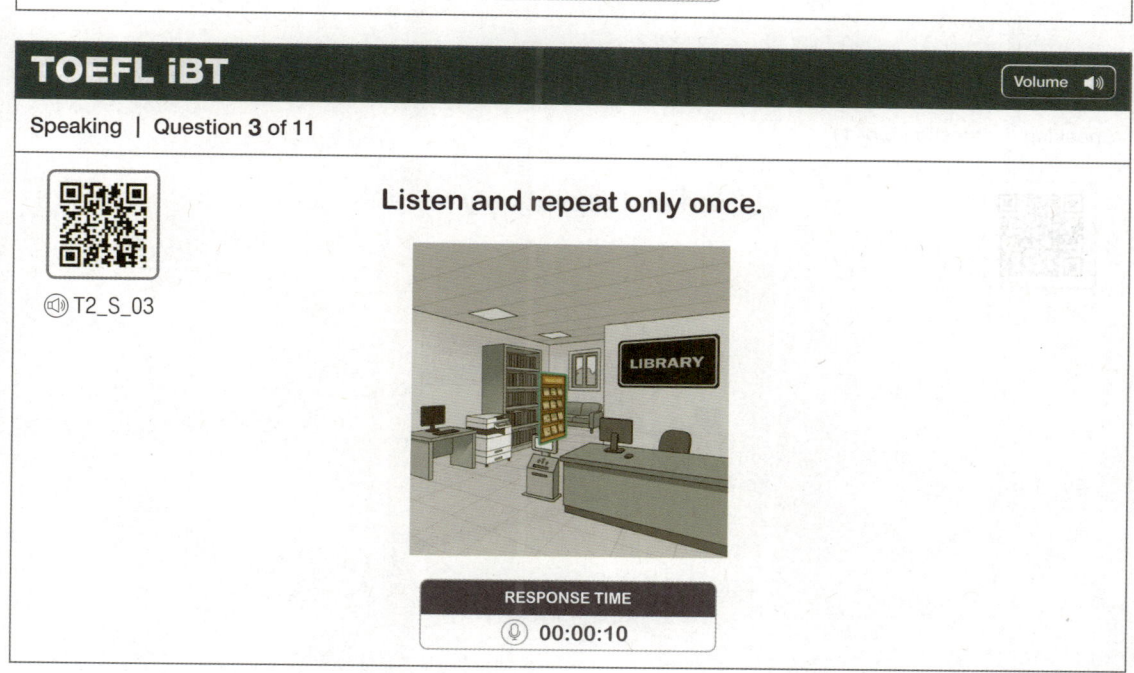

TOEFL iBT

Speaking | Question **4** of 11

T2_S_04

Listen and repeat only once.

RESPONSE TIME
00:00:10

TOEFL iBT

Speaking | Question **5** of 11

T2_S_05

Listen and repeat only once.

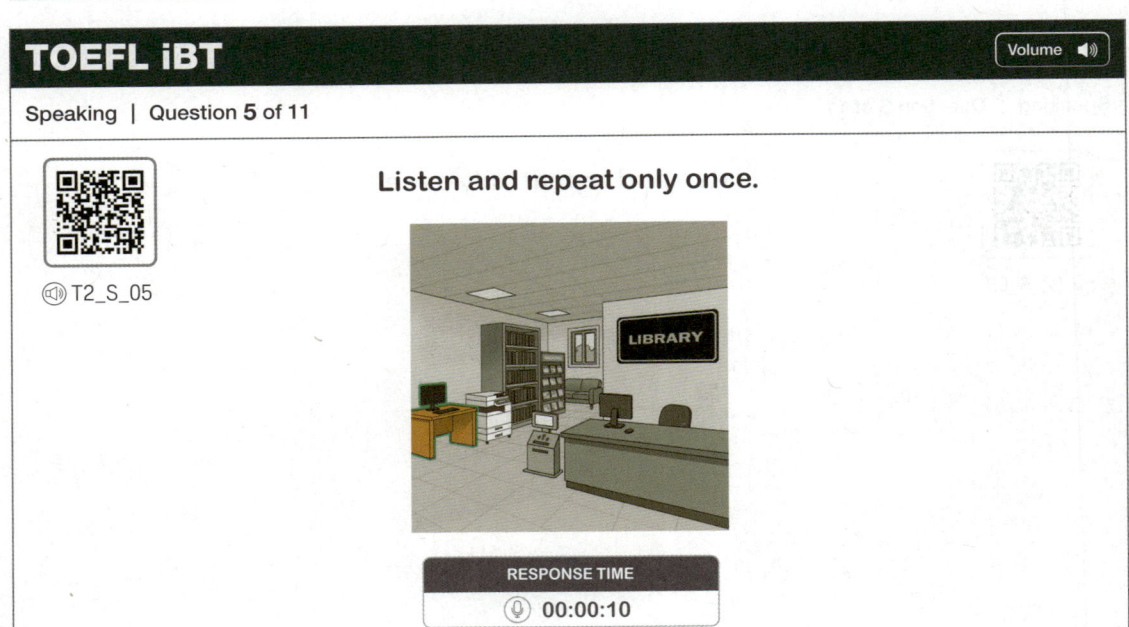

RESPONSE TIME
00:00:10

TOEFL iBT

Speaking | Question **6** of 11

T2_S_06

Listen and repeat only once.

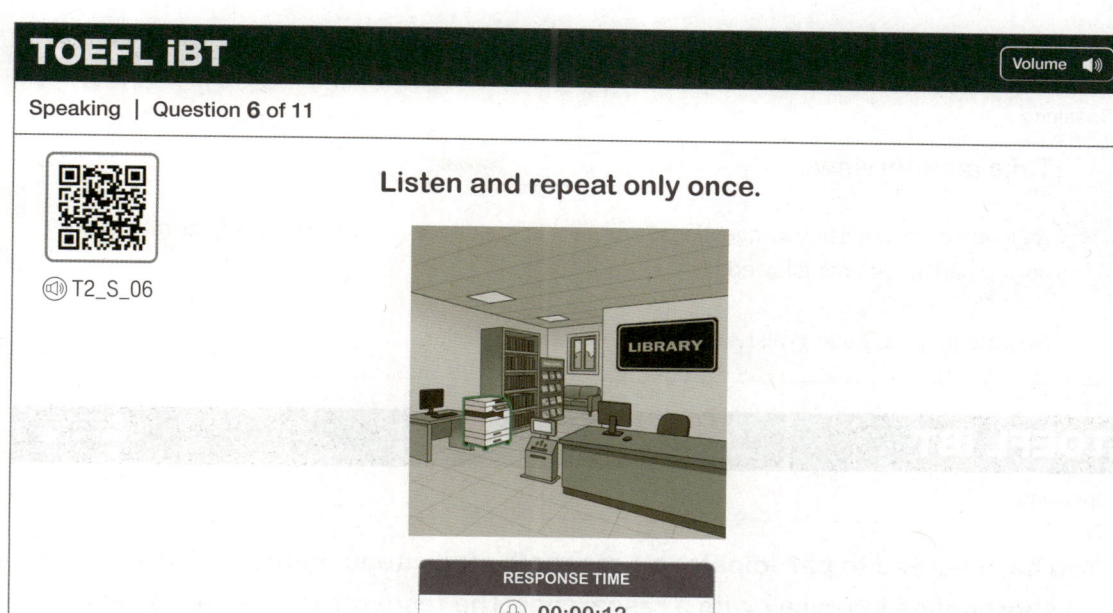

RESPONSE TIME 00:00:12

TOEFL iBT

Speaking | Question **7** of 11

T2_S_07

Listen and repeat only once.

RESPONSE TIME 00:00:12

TOEFL iBT

Speaking

Take an Interview

An interviewer will ask you questions. Answer the questions and be sure to say as much as you can in the time allowed.

No time for preparation will be provided.

TOEFL iBT

Speaking

You have agreed to participate in a research study about careers. You will have a short online interview with a researcher. The researcher will ask you some questions.

TOEFL iBT

Speaking | Question **8** of 11

T2_S_08

Please answer the interviewer's questions.

RESPONSE TIME
00:00:45

TOEFL iBT

Speaking | Question **9** of 11

T2_S_09

Please answer the interviewer's questions.

RESPONSE TIME
00:00:45

TOEFL iBT

Speaking | Question **10** of 11

🔊 T2_S_10

Please answer the interviewer's questions.

RESPONSE TIME
🎤 00:00:45

TOEFL iBT

Speaking | Question **11** of 11

🔊 T2_S_11

Please answer the interviewer's questions.

RESPONSE TIME
🎤 00:00:45

TEST 3

⚠️ 실전모의고사 유의 사항

실제 시험과 동일한 환경에서 연습하기 위해 다음 사항을 반드시 지켜 주세요.

1 Reading – Listening – Writing – Speaking 순서로 한 번에 진행
중간에 휴식 없이 네 영역을 연속으로 풀며 실제 시험 흐름에
익숙해집니다.

2 Listening은 음원을 먼저 듣기
문제를 미리 읽지 말고, 반드시 음원을 모두 들은 후에 문제를 풉니다.
실제 시험과 동일한 조건으로 문제를 푸는 것이 중요합니다.

3 Listening과 Speaking 음원은 한 번만 듣기
반복 청취는 금지하며, 한 번의 청취로 내용을 이해하고 답변하는 훈련을
합니다.

4 노트테이킹 도구 준비하기
백지와 연필을 준비해 Listening 영역에서 필요한 내용을 간단히
메모하며 문제를 풉니다.

5 시간을 재며 Writing과 Speaking 문제 풀기
각 영역의 제한 시간 내에 답안을 작성하거나 말하기 연습을 진행해 실제
시험 감각을 익힙니다.

Answers p.63

READING

TOEFL iBT

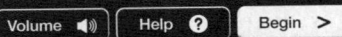

Reading Section

In the reading section, you will answer 35-48 questions to demonstrate how well you understand academic and non-academic texts in English. There are three types of tasks.

Type of Task	Description
Complete the Words	Fill in the missing letters in a paragraph.
Read in Daily Life	Answer questions about everyday reading materials.
Read an Academic Passage	Answer questions about academic passages.

Module 1

TOEFL iBT

Reading | Questions **1-10** of 33

Fill in the missing letters in the paragraph.

Recipes are instructions that guide us in making meals. They sh_ _ the various st_ _ _ of prepa_ _ _ _ _ _ like chop_ _ _ _ , mixing, a_ _ baking. Th_ _ _ step-by-step direc_ _ _ _ _ can al_ _ vary t_ suit dif_ _ _ _ _ _ preferences, such as flavor or texture. There are many types, including traditional, modern, and fusion versions. The study of cooking and culinary arts, the process by which dishes are created, can teach us about the food traditions of cultures and how flavors evolve in different regions.

TOEFL iBT

Reading | Questions **11-20** of 33

Fill in the missing letters in the paragraph.

As the demand for energy continues to grow worldwide, there is increasing interest in renewable sources of power such as sun, wind, and water power. These fo_ _ _ of ene_ _ _ are consi_ _ _ _ _ more susta_ _ _ _ _ _ than fos_ _ _ fuels bec_ _ _ _ they d_ not u_ _ up nat_ _ _ _ resources o_ pollute the atmosphere. Solar panels, for example, convert sunlight into electricity using a process known as the photovoltaic effect. Meanwhile, wind turbines capture the kinetic energy of moving air and transform it into usable power.

TOEFL iBT

Volume | Help | Review | < Back | Next >

Reading | Question **21** of 33

Read an email.

Date:	June 3
Subject:	Reserved Book Pickup

Dear Ms. Green,

This is a reminder that the book you reserved, *The History of Seafaring*, will be available for pickup on June 8 between 9:00 A.M. and 11:00 A.M. at the Harper Library front desk. Please bring your library card when you come to collect it, as items can only be released to the cardholder.

Best regards,
Laura Harper

What is the earliest time Ms. Green can pick up her book?

(A) 8:00 A.M.
(B) 9:00 A.M.
(C) 10:00 A.M.
(D) 11:00 A.M.

TOEFL iBT

Volume | Help | Review | < Back | Next >

Reading | Question **22** of 33

Read an email.

Date:	June 3
Subject:	Reserved Book Pickup

Dear Ms. Green,

This is a reminder that the book you reserved, *The History of Seafaring*, will be available for pickup on June 8 between 9:00 A.M. and 11:00 A.M. at the Harper Library front desk. Please bring your library card when you come to collect it, as items can only be released to the cardholder.

Best regards,
Laura Harper

Why must Ms. Green bring her library card?

(A) To confirm her identity
(B) To pay a fee
(C) To borrow more books
(D) To extend her reservation

Read an email.

| Date: | April 5 |
| Subject: | Staff Workshop |

Dear Ms. Valdez,

The annual professional development workshop for Johnson Office Solutions will take place on Friday, May 2, beginning promptly at 9:00 A.M. in the conference hall on Easton Avenue. All team leaders are required to attend and assist with group activities. Please ensure that your team's training reports are updated and uploaded two days prior to the event. Since the workshop is expected to last most of the day, lunch will be provided to attendees by Riverside Café.

Please review the attached employee list and confirm which of your team members will be attending the workshop. Please send a final list to Mr. Cortez. We also ask that you avoid scheduling any client calls on the morning of May 3 as team leaders will be required to attend a feedback session regarding the previous day's event.

Best regards,
Emma Johnson

Why did Ms. Johnson send the email to Ms. Valdez?

(A) To assist her with leading activities
(B) To remind her to update training reports
(C) To inform her of an upcoming event
(D) To request her input on revising procedures

Read an email.

Date: April 5
Subject: Staff Workshop

Dear Ms. Valdez,

The annual professional development workshop for Johnson Office Solutions will take place on Friday, May 2, beginning promptly at 9:00 A.M. in the conference hall on Easton Avenue. All team leaders are required to attend and assist with group activities. Please ensure that your team's training reports are updated and uploaded two days prior to the event. Since the workshop is expected to last most of the day, lunch will be provided to attendees by Riverside Café.

Please review the attached employee list and confirm which of your team members will be attending the workshop. Please send a final list to Mr. Cortez. We also ask that you avoid scheduling any client calls on the morning of May 3 as team leaders will be required to attend a feedback session regarding the previous day's event.

Best regards,
Emma Johnson

Why should Ms. Valdez contact Mr. Cortez?

(A) To request a list of supplies
(B) To suggest event activities
(C) To confirm event attendees
(D) To share a client call schedule

Read an email.

Date:	April 5
Subject:	Staff Workshop

Dear Ms. Valdez,

The annual professional development workshop for Johnson Office Solutions will take place on Friday, May 2, beginning promptly at 9:00 A.M. in the conference hall on Easton Avenue. All team leaders are required to attend and assist with group activities. Please ensure that your team's training reports are updated and uploaded two days prior to the event. Since the workshop is expected to last most of the day, lunch will be provided to attendees by Riverside Café.

Please review the attached employee list and confirm which of your team members will be attending the workshop. Please send a final list to Mr. Cortez. We also ask that you avoid scheduling any client calls on the morning of May 3 as team leaders will be required to attend a feedback session regarding the previous day's event.

Best regards,
Emma Johnson

What is indicated about the morning of May 3?

(A) The final activities of the workshop will take place.
(B) Ms. Valdez will provide her opinions of the workshop.
(C) Employees will be treated to lunch at Riverside Café.
(D) Ms. Valdez will gather feedback from company clients.

Read a text chain.

Jim Nicholson (2:00 P.M.)
Hi everyone, just a reminder—the program update is due tomorrow. Please wrap up all testing before submitting.

Sam Kim (2:05 P.M.)
Got it. I was a bit concerned about how intuitive the new version would be, but the feedback from the focus groups is really encouraging!

Eugene Bischoff (2:10 P.M.)
Glad to hear that, Sam. I'll run checks across various devices to confirm everything works seamlessly.

Craig Mori (2:15 P.M.)
If any major issues pop up, I'm available to assist. I'll be monitoring my emails closely.

Jim Nicholson (2:20 P.M.)
Thanks, Craig. Let's aim to deliver a polished and reliable update.

What is Eugene's responsibility?

(A) Finalizing all testing requirements
(B) Checking off all the testing boxes
(C) Analyzing the feedback from the focus group
(D) Testing across devices for reliability

Reading | Question **27** of 33

Read a text chain.

Jim Nicholson (2:00 P.M.)
Hi everyone, just a reminder—the program update is due tomorrow. Please wrap up all testing before submitting.

Sam Kim (2:05 P.M.)
Got it. I was a bit concerned about how intuitive the new version would be, but the feedback from the focus groups is really encouraging!

Eugene Bischoff (2:10 P.M.)
Glad to hear that, Sam. I'll run checks across various devices to confirm everything works seamlessly.

Craig Mori (2:15 P.M.)
If any major issues pop up, I'm available to assist. I'll be monitoring my emails closely.

Jim Nicholson (2:20 P.M.)
Thanks, Craig. Let's aim to deliver a polished and reliable update.

How will Craig help out?

(A) By contacting his colleagues
(B) By emailing about a reliable update
(C) By handling any emergencies
(D) By assisting the focus groups

Read a text chain.

Jim Nicholson (2:00 P.M.)
Hi everyone, just a reminder—the program update is due tomorrow. Please wrap up all testing before submitting.

Sam Kim (2:05 P.M.)
Got it. I was a bit concerned about how intuitive the new version would be, but the feedback from the focus groups is really encouraging!

Eugene Bischoff (2:10 P.M.)
Glad to hear that, Sam. I'll run checks across various devices to confirm everything works seamlessly.

Craig Mori (2:15 P.M.)
If any major issues pop up, I'm available to assist. I'll be monitoring my emails closely.

Jim Nicholson (2:20 P.M.)
Thanks, Craig. Let's aim to deliver a polished and reliable update.

What can be inferred about the updated program?

(A) It is the company's most successful product.
(B) It is easy to use.
(C) It received negative reviews.
(D) It functions on all devices.

Photosynthesis Adaptations in Desert Plants

Desert plants face extreme conditions, including intense sunlight, high temperatures, and limited water. To survive, many have developed specialized adaptations for photosynthesis—the process by which plants convert sunlight, carbon dioxide, and water into energy and oxygen.

One key adaptation is the Crassulacean Acid Metabolism (CAM) photosynthetic pathway. Unlike most plants, which open tiny pores called stomata on their leaves during the day to absorb carbon dioxide, CAM plants open them at night. This timing reduces water loss through evaporation since nighttime temperatures are cooler. The absorbed carbon dioxide is stored and then used during the day for photosynthesis.

Another strategy is the C4 photosynthetic pathway, in which desert plants have evolved a more efficient method of capturing carbon dioxide. Instead of using carbon dioxide directly in photosynthesis, they first concentrate it in special cells, allowing them to continue photosynthesizing efficiently even under intense sunlight and high temperatures. This adaptation helps desert plants thrive in hot, dry environments where other plants would quickly wilt.

These photosynthetic adaptations not only help individual species survive but also shape entire ecosystems. By maintaining vegetation cover, desert plants prevent soil erosion and support diverse forms of wildlife. Scientists continue to study these plants to understand how they manage energy and water use so efficiently. Insights from this research could contribute to developing drought-resistant crops in the future.

The word "convert" in the passage is closest in meaning to

(A) store
(B) transform
(C) absorb
(D) remove

Photosynthesis Adaptations in Desert Plants

Desert plants face extreme conditions, including intense sunlight, high temperatures, and limited water. To survive, many have developed specialized adaptations for photosynthesis—the process by which plants convert sunlight, carbon dioxide, and water into energy and oxygen.

One key adaptation is the Crassulacean Acid Metabolism (CAM) photosynthetic pathway. Unlike most plants, which open tiny pores called stomata on their leaves during the day to absorb carbon dioxide, CAM plants open them at night. This timing reduces water loss through evaporation since nighttime temperatures are cooler. The absorbed carbon dioxide is stored and then used during the day for photosynthesis.

Another strategy is the C4 photosynthetic pathway, in which desert plants have evolved a more efficient method of capturing carbon dioxide. Instead of using carbon dioxide directly in photosynthesis, they first concentrate it in special cells, allowing them to continue photosynthesizing efficiently even under intense sunlight and high temperatures. This adaptation helps desert plants thrive in hot, dry environments where other plants would quickly wilt.

These photosynthetic adaptations not only help individual species survive but also shape entire ecosystems. By maintaining vegetation cover, desert plants prevent soil erosion and support diverse forms of wildlife. Scientists continue to study these plants to understand how they manage energy and water use so efficiently. Insights from this research could contribute to developing drought-resistant crops in the future.

According to the passage, what is the main advantage of CAM photosynthesis?

(A) It increases the rate of water evaporation.
(B) It allows plants to absorb more sunlight.
(C) It reduces water loss by being active at night.
(D) It prevents plants from producing carbon dioxide.

Photosynthesis Adaptations in Desert Plants

Desert plants face extreme conditions, including intense sunlight, high temperatures, and limited water. To survive, many have developed specialized adaptations for photosynthesis—the process by which plants convert sunlight, carbon dioxide, and water into energy and oxygen.

One key adaptation is the Crassulacean Acid Metabolism (CAM) photosynthetic pathway. Unlike most plants, which open tiny pores called stomata on their leaves during the day to absorb carbon dioxide, CAM plants open them at night. This timing reduces water loss through evaporation since nighttime temperatures are cooler. The absorbed carbon dioxide is stored and then used during the day for photosynthesis.

Another strategy is the C4 photosynthetic pathway, in which desert plants have evolved a more efficient method of capturing carbon dioxide. Instead of using carbon dioxide directly in photosynthesis, they first concentrate it in special cells, allowing them to continue photosynthesizing efficiently even under intense sunlight and high temperatures. This adaptation helps desert plants thrive in hot, dry environments where other plants would quickly wilt.

These photosynthetic adaptations not only help individual species survive but also shape entire ecosystems. By maintaining vegetation cover, desert plants prevent soil erosion and support diverse forms of wildlife. Scientists continue to study these plants to understand how they manage energy and water use so efficiently. Insights from this research could contribute to developing drought-resistant crops in the future.

How does the C4 pathway differ from the CAM pathway?

(A) It depends entirely on nighttime photosynthesis.
(B) It enables plants to perform efficiently in intense sunlight.
(C) It occurs only in cool environments.
(D) It stores carbon dioxide for several days.

Photosynthesis Adaptations in Desert Plants

Desert plants face extreme conditions, including intense sunlight, high temperatures, and limited water. To survive, many have developed specialized adaptations for photosynthesis—the process by which plants convert sunlight, carbon dioxide, and water into energy and oxygen.

One key adaptation is the Crassulacean Acid Metabolism (CAM) photosynthetic pathway. Unlike most plants, which open tiny pores called stomata on their leaves during the day to absorb carbon dioxide, CAM plants open them at night. This timing reduces water loss through evaporation since nighttime temperatures are cooler. The absorbed carbon dioxide is stored and then used during the day for photosynthesis.

Another strategy is the C4 photosynthetic pathway, in which desert plants have evolved a more efficient method of capturing carbon dioxide. Instead of using carbon dioxide directly in photosynthesis, they first concentrate it in special cells, allowing them to continue photosynthesizing efficiently even under intense sunlight and high temperatures. This adaptation helps desert plants thrive in hot, dry environments where other plants would quickly wilt.

These photosynthetic adaptations not only help individual species survive but also shape entire ecosystems. By maintaining vegetation cover, desert plants prevent soil erosion and support diverse forms of wildlife. Scientists continue to study these plants to understand how they manage energy and water use so efficiently. Insights from this research could contribute to developing drought-resistant crops in the future.

What is the relationship between paragraphs 2 and 3?

(A) Paragraph 2 introduces a type of system, and paragraph 3 describes another.
(B) Paragraph 2 states an argument, and paragraph 3 refutes it.
(C) Paragraph 2 explains a problem, and paragraph 3 offers a solution.
(D) Paragraph 2 presents a theory, and paragraph 3 provides supporting evidence.

Photosynthesis Adaptations in Desert Plants

Desert plants face extreme conditions, including intense sunlight, high temperatures, and limited water. To survive, many have developed specialized adaptations for photosynthesis—the process by which plants convert sunlight, carbon dioxide, and water into energy and oxygen.

One key adaptation is the Crassulacean Acid Metabolism (CAM) photosynthetic pathway. Unlike most plants, which open tiny pores called stomata on their leaves during the day to absorb carbon dioxide, CAM plants open them at night. This timing reduces water loss through evaporation since nighttime temperatures are cooler. The absorbed carbon dioxide is stored and then used during the day for photosynthesis.

Another strategy is the C4 photosynthetic pathway, in which desert plants have evolved a more efficient method of capturing carbon dioxide. Instead of using carbon dioxide directly in photosynthesis, they first concentrate it in special cells, allowing them to continue photosynthesizing efficiently even under intense sunlight and high temperatures. This adaptation helps desert plants thrive in hot, dry environments where other plants would quickly wilt.

These photosynthetic adaptations not only help individual species survive but also shape entire ecosystems. By maintaining vegetation cover, desert plants prevent soil erosion and support diverse forms of wildlife. Scientists continue to study these plants to understand how they manage energy and water use so efficiently. Insights from this research could contribute to developing drought-resistant crops in the future.

Why does the author mention developing drought-resistant crops in the last paragraph?

(A) To illustrate how desert plants can benefit humans
(B) To compare the nutritional value of desert plants and crops
(C) To emphasize the dangers of climate change
(D) To explain the chemical structure of desert plants

Module 2

TOEFL iBT

Reading | Questions **1-10** of 15

Fill in the missing letters in the paragraph.

Penguins are flightless birds that thrive in groups called colonies. They commu_ _ _ _ _ _ using voc _ _ calls, phy_ _ _ _ _ gestures, a_ _ touch. These bi_ _ _ are kn_ _ _ for th_ _ _ strong soc_ _ _ bonds and of_ _ _ help ea_ _ other in times of danger. They can remember the locations of feeding grounds and safe nesting areas, which helps them survive in harsh climates. These resilient animals play a crucial role in their ecosystems, controlling fish populations, cycling nutrients, and supporting marine biodiversity.

TOEFL iBT

Reading | Question **11** of 15

The History of Written Scripts

The invention of writing transformed human civilization by allowing knowledge to be stored and transmitted across generations. Early scripts included pictographs, which represented objects with simple images. Over time, systems evolved into symbols representing sounds and ideas, laying the **foundation** for alphabets and logographic scripts. Writing played a crucial role in administration, trade, and the preservation of cultural identity.

Linguistic research shows that writing systems have been shaped by geography, available materials, and societal needs. For example, cuneiform was inscribed on clay tablets, while Egyptian hieroglyphs were carved into stone and painted on papyrus. Each script reflected not only linguistic features but also the resources available to the societies that created them.

Today, scholars study the development of scripts to understand how communication shaped human progress. They examine how alphabets spread through cultural contact, how scripts adapted to new languages, and how literacy changed social structures. Understanding the evolution of writing helps explain the growth of education, the rise of bureaucracies, and the transmission of ideas across continents.

The word "foundation" in the passage is closest in meaning to

(A) limit
(B) establishment
(C) basis
(D) translation

The History of Written Scripts

The invention of writing transformed human civilization by allowing knowledge to be stored and transmitted across generations. Early scripts included pictographs, which represented objects with simple images. Over time, systems evolved into symbols representing sounds and ideas, laying the foundation for alphabets and logographic scripts. Writing played a crucial role in administration, trade, and the preservation of cultural identity.

Linguistic research shows that writing systems have been shaped by geography, available materials, and societal needs. For example, cuneiform was inscribed on clay tablets, while Egyptian hieroglyphs were carved into stone and painted on papyrus. Each script reflected not only linguistic features but also the resources available to the societies that created them.

Today, scholars study the development of scripts to understand how communication shaped human progress. They examine how alphabets spread through cultural contact, how scripts adapted to new languages, and how literacy changed social structures. Understanding the evolution of writing helps explain the growth of education, the rise of bureaucracies, and the transmission of ideas across continents.

Early writing systems contributed to all of the following EXCEPT

(A) cultural preservation
(B) administrative purposes
(C) trade activities
(D) religious events

The History of Written Scripts

The invention of writing transformed human civilization by allowing knowledge to be stored and transmitted across generations. Early scripts included pictographs, which represented objects with simple images. Over time, systems evolved into symbols representing sounds and ideas, laying the foundation for alphabets and logographic scripts. Writing played a crucial role in administration, trade, and the preservation of cultural identity.

Linguistic research shows that writing systems have been shaped by geography, available materials, and societal needs. For example, cuneiform was inscribed on clay tablets, while Egyptian hieroglyphs were carved into stone and painted on papyrus. Each script reflected not only linguistic features but also the resources available to the societies that created them.

Today, scholars study the development of scripts to understand how communication shaped human progress. They examine how alphabets spread through cultural contact, how scripts adapted to new languages, and how literacy changed social structures. Understanding the evolution of writing helps explain the growth of education, the rise of bureaucracies, and the transmission of ideas across continents.

According to paragraph 2, what influenced the form of early writing systems?

(A) Seasonal weather
(B) Political leadership
(C) Local materials
(D) The spread of agriculture

The History of Written Scripts

The invention of writing transformed human civilization by allowing knowledge to be stored and transmitted across generations. Early scripts included pictographs, which represented objects with simple images. Over time, systems evolved into symbols representing sounds and ideas, laying the foundation for alphabets and logographic scripts. Writing played a crucial role in administration, trade, and the preservation of cultural identity.

Linguistic research shows that writing systems have been shaped by geography, available materials, and societal needs. For example, cuneiform was inscribed on clay tablets, while Egyptian hieroglyphs were carved into stone and painted on papyrus. Each script reflected not only linguistic features but also the resources available to the societies that created them.

Today, scholars study the development of scripts to understand how communication shaped human progress. They examine how alphabets spread through cultural contact, how scripts adapted to new languages, and how literacy changed social structures. Understanding the evolution of writing helps explain the growth of education, the rise of bureaucracies, and the transmission of ideas across continents.

What is the relationship between paragraphs 2 and 3?

(A) Paragraph 3 contradicts the historical examples in paragraph 2.
(B) Paragraph 3 elaborates on the cultural impact of scripts mentioned in paragraph 2.
(C) Paragraph 3 dismisses the importance of geography introduced in paragraph 2.
(D) Paragraph 3 focuses only on modern alphabets, while paragraph 2 describes ancient scripts.

The History of Written Scripts

The invention of writing transformed human civilization by allowing knowledge to be stored and transmitted across generations. Early scripts included pictographs, which represented objects with simple images. Over time, systems evolved into symbols representing sounds and ideas, laying the foundation for alphabets and logographic scripts. Writing played a crucial role in administration, trade, and the preservation of cultural identity.

Linguistic research shows that writing systems have been shaped by geography, available materials, and societal needs. For example, cuneiform was inscribed on clay tablets, while Egyptian hieroglyphs were carved into stone and painted on papyrus. Each script reflected not only linguistic features but also the resources available to the societies that created them.

Today, scholars study the development of scripts to understand how communication shaped human progress. They examine how alphabets spread through cultural contact, how scripts adapted to new languages, and how literacy changed social structures. Understanding the evolution of writing helps explain the growth of education, the rise of bureaucracies, and the transmission of ideas across continents.

What are scholars currently exploring?

(A) The link between alphabets and religion
(B) The adaptation of scripts to new languages
(C) The role of trade in replacing old systems
(D) The influence of climate on literacy rates

LISTENING

TOEFL iBT

Volume Begin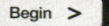

Listening Section

In the listening section, you will answer 35 to 45 questions to demonstrate how well you understand spoken English. There are three types of tasks.

Type of Task	Description
Listen and Choose a Response	Select the best response to the question or statement.
Conversations	Answer questions about short conversations.
Announcements and Academic Talks	Answer questions about announcements and academic talks.

You WILL NOT be able to return to previous questions.

Module 1

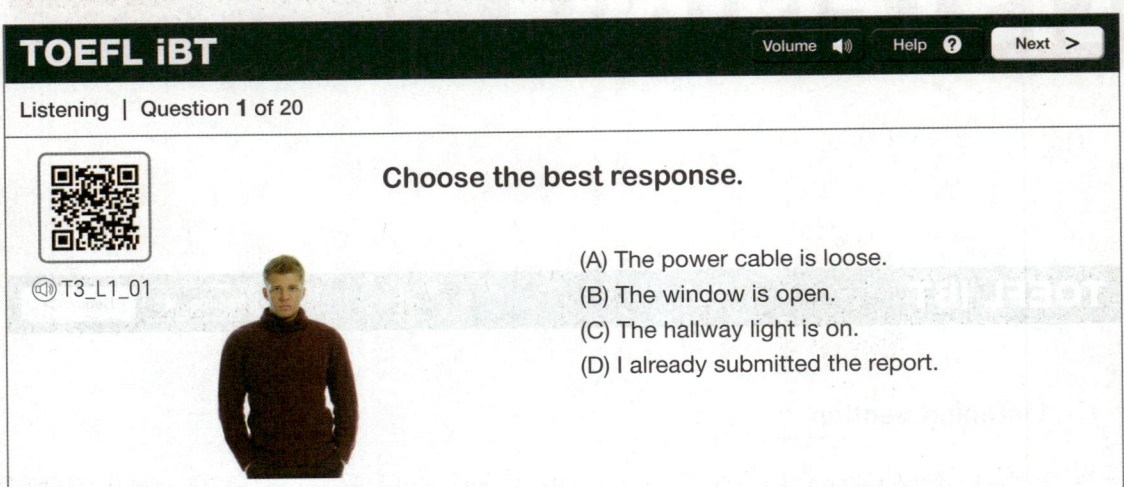

Listening | Question 1 of 20

T3_L1_01

Choose the best response.

(A) The power cable is loose.
(B) The window is open.
(C) The hallway light is on.
(D) I already submitted the report.

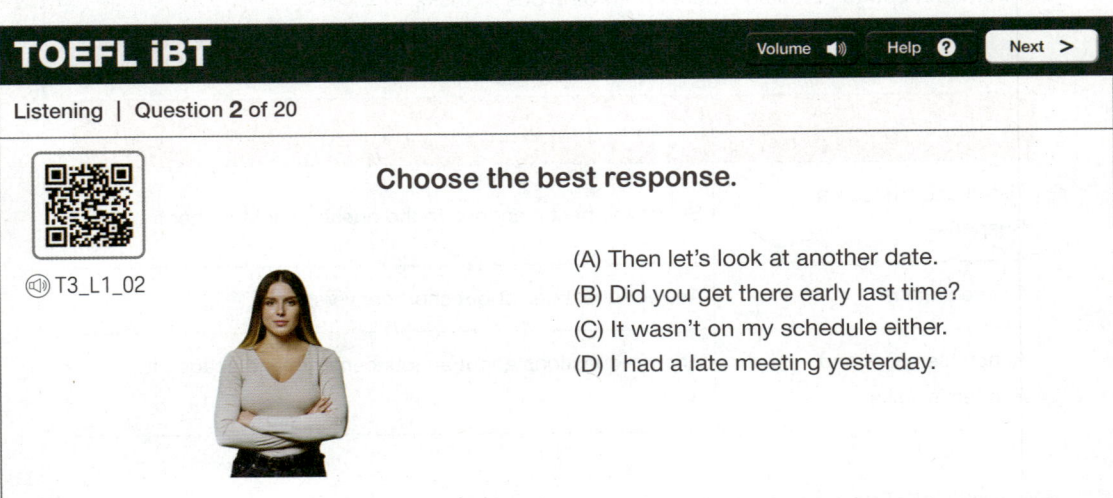

Listening | Question 2 of 20

T3_L1_02

Choose the best response.

(A) Then let's look at another date.
(B) Did you get there early last time?
(C) It wasn't on my schedule either.
(D) I had a late meeting yesterday.

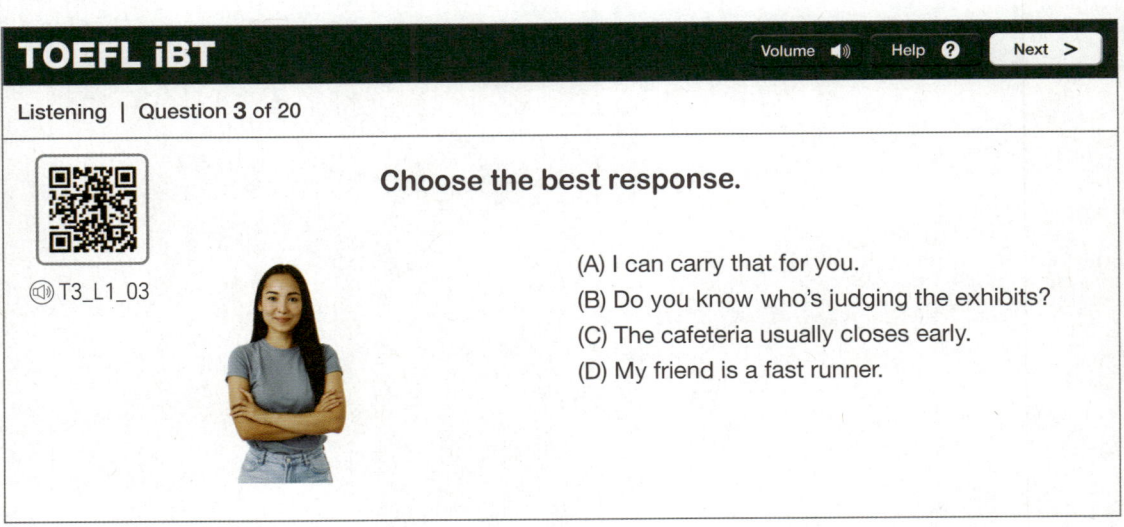

Listening | Question 3 of 20

T3_L1_03

Choose the best response.

(A) I can carry that for you.
(B) Do you know who's judging the exhibits?
(C) The cafeteria usually closes early.
(D) My friend is a fast runner.

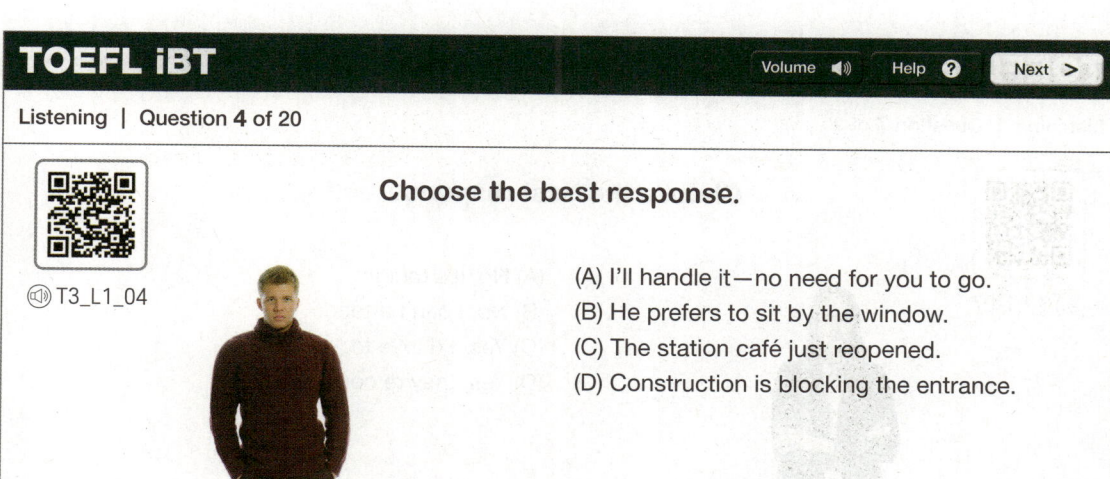

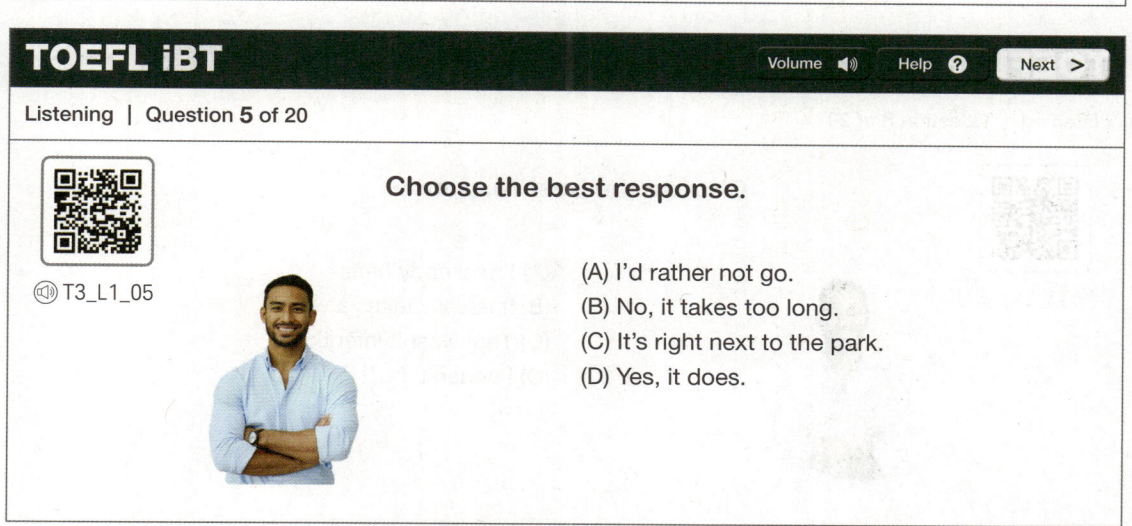

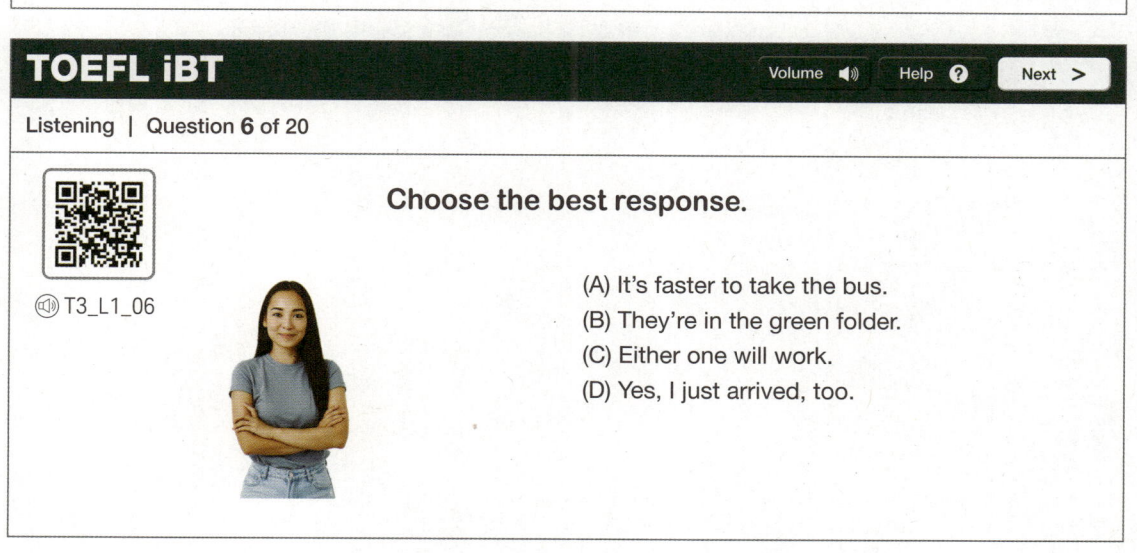

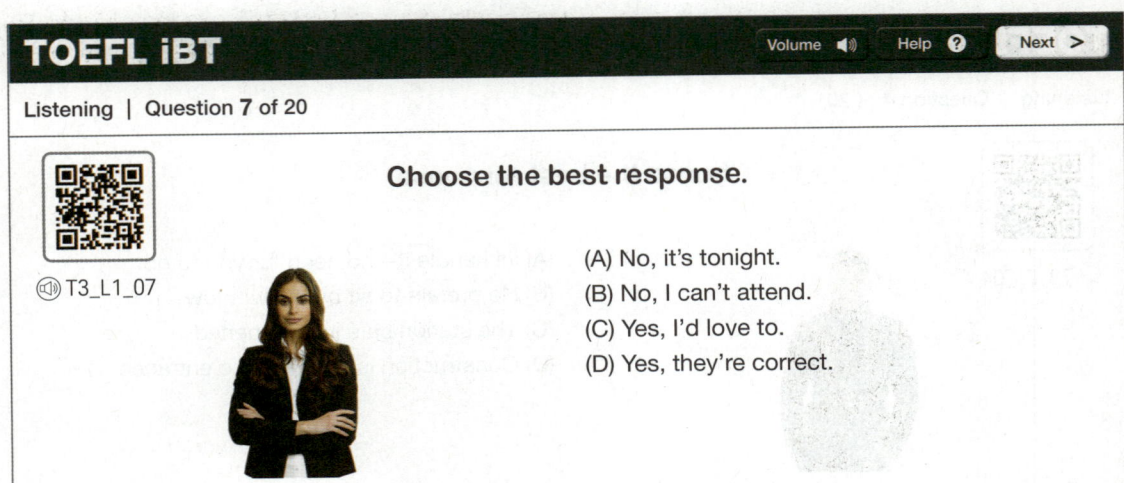

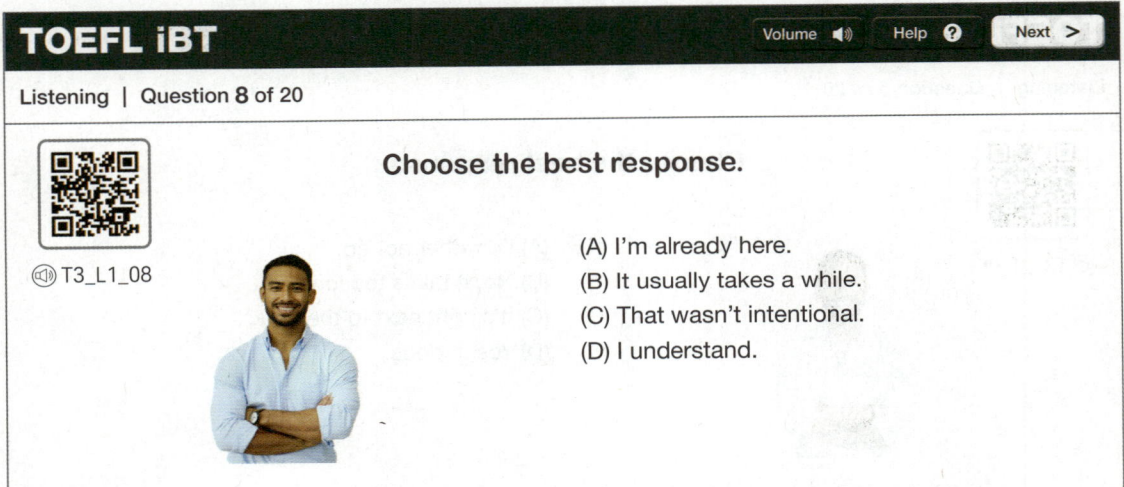

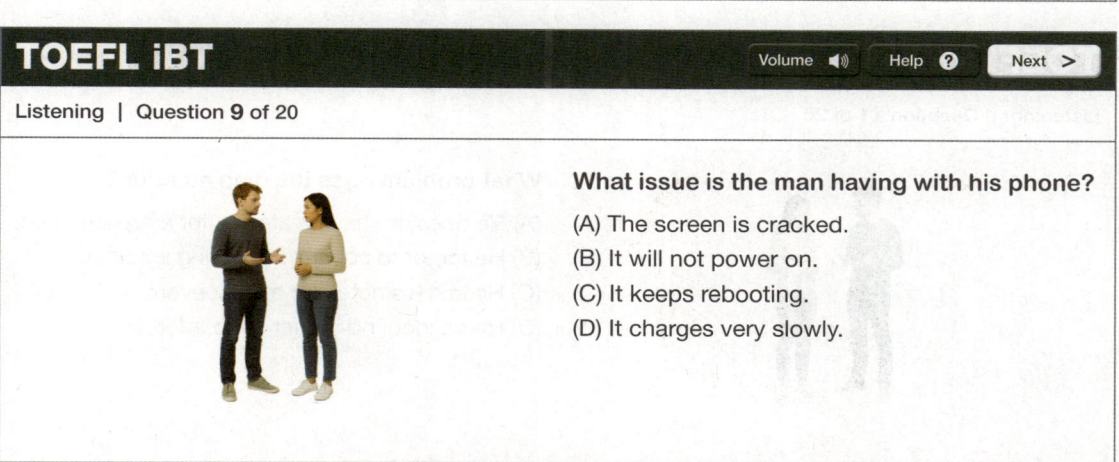

What issue is the man having with his phone?

(A) The screen is cracked.
(B) It will not power on.
(C) It keeps rebooting.
(D) It charges very slowly.

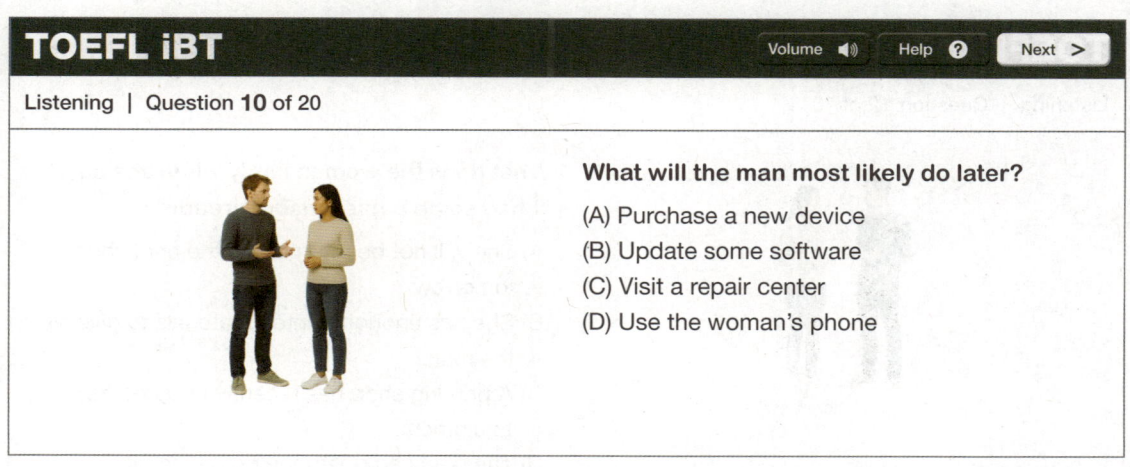

What will the man most likely do later?

(A) Purchase a new device
(B) Update some software
(C) Visit a repair center
(D) Use the woman's phone

What problem does the man mention?

(A) He does not have materials for a presentation.
(B) He forgot to confirm a meeting location.
(C) He lost his notes for a work event.
(D) He cannot find a print shop address.

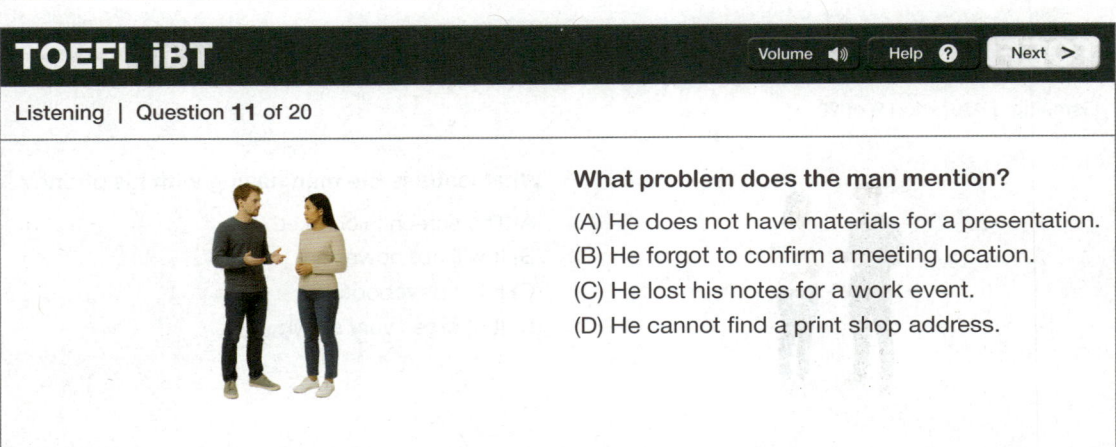

What does the woman imply when she says, "I had some copies made already"?

(A) She will not be returning to the print shop tomorrow.
(B) She has enough printed materials to give to the man.
(C) A printing shop has recently updated its equipment.
(D) The man can postpone preparing his presentation.

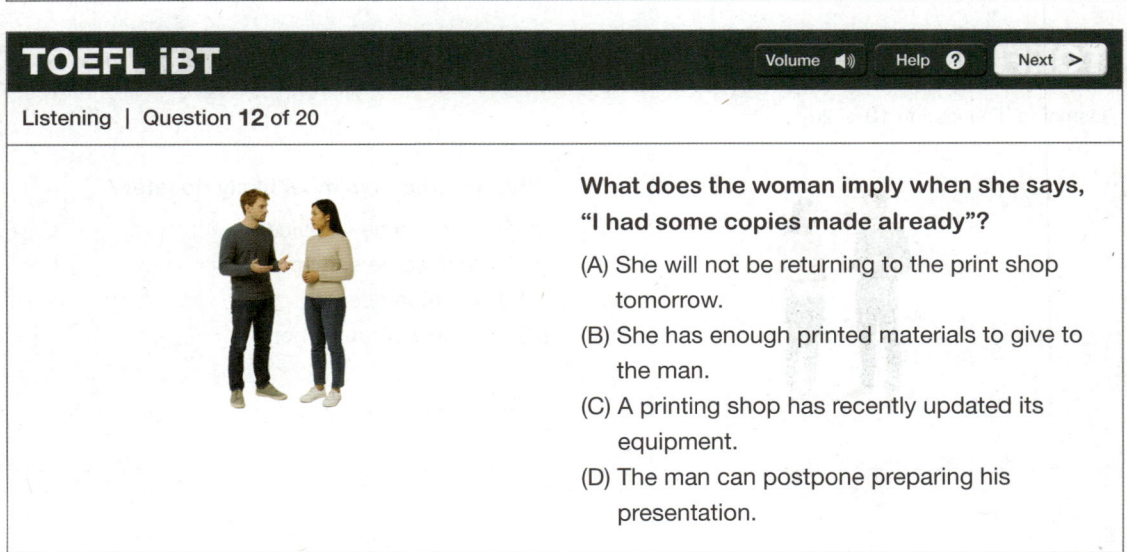

TOEFL iBT

Listening | Questions 13-14 of 20

Listen to an announcement at a university club meeting.

🔊 T3_L1_1314

TOEFL iBT

Listening | Question 13 of 20

Why does the speaker mention city life?

(A) It is the theme of an exhibition.
(B) It will be discussed by a special guest.
(C) It is the topic of today's lecture.
(D) Some club members are new to the city.

TOEFL iBT

Listening | Question 14 of 20

What does the speaker encourage participants to do?

(A) Submit work by a deadline
(B) Review last year's photos
(C) Apply for a job opening
(D) Sign up for a special course

TOEFL iBT

Listening | Questions 15-16 of 20

T3_L1_1516

Listen to an announcement at a university event.

TOEFL iBT

Listening | Question 15 of 20

What is the main topic of the announcement?

(A) A donation drive
(B) A student orientation
(C) An upcoming charity auction
(D) A new university event

TOEFL iBT

Listening | Question 16 of 20

What does the speaker hope the listeners will do?

(A) Volunteer at the event
(B) Donate online
(C) Support international students
(D) Attend the event

Listen to a talk in an astronomy class.

T3_L1_1720

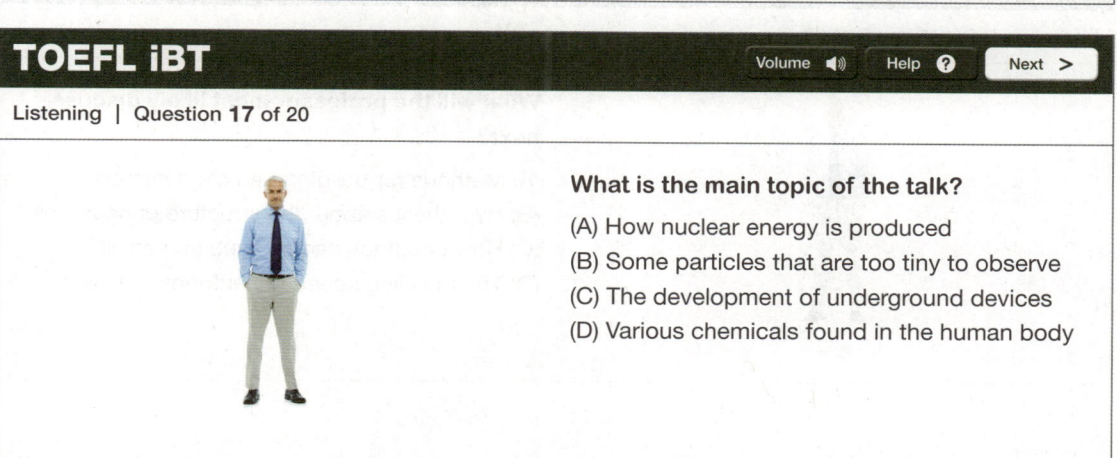

What is the main topic of the talk?

(A) How nuclear energy is produced
(B) Some particles that are too tiny to observe
(C) The development of underground devices
(D) Various chemicals found in the human body

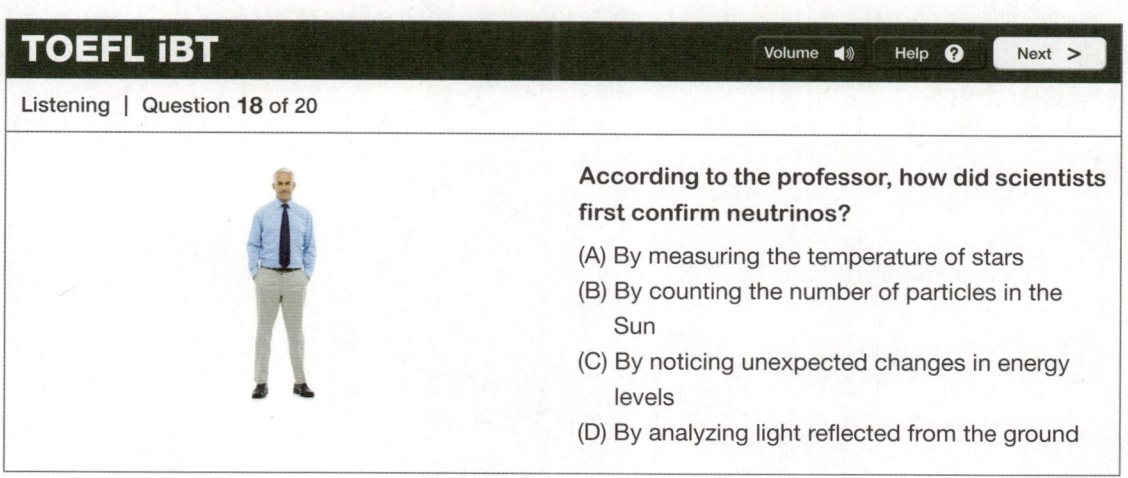

According to the professor, how did scientists first confirm neutrinos?

(A) By measuring the temperature of stars
(B) By counting the number of particles in the Sun
(C) By noticing unexpected changes in energy levels
(D) By analyzing light reflected from the ground

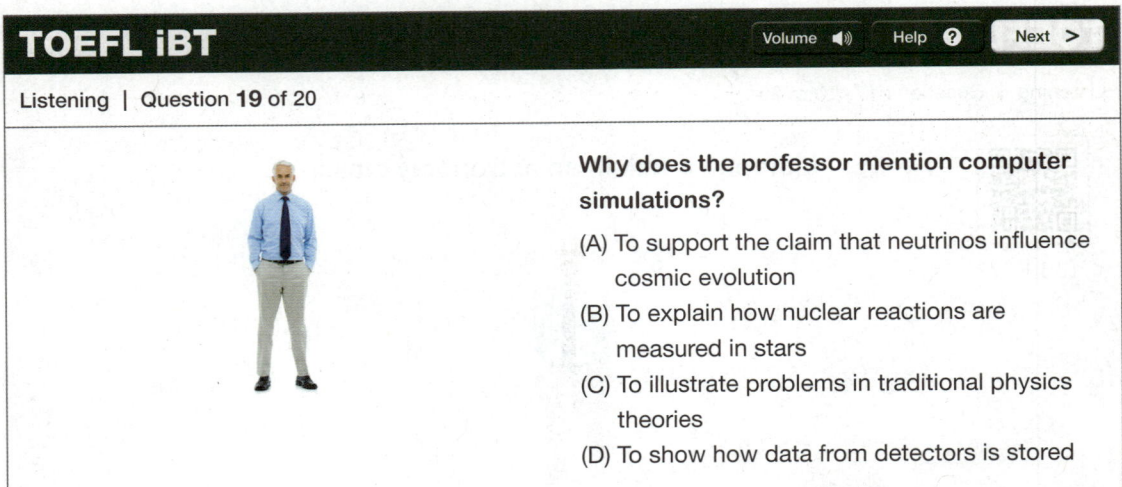

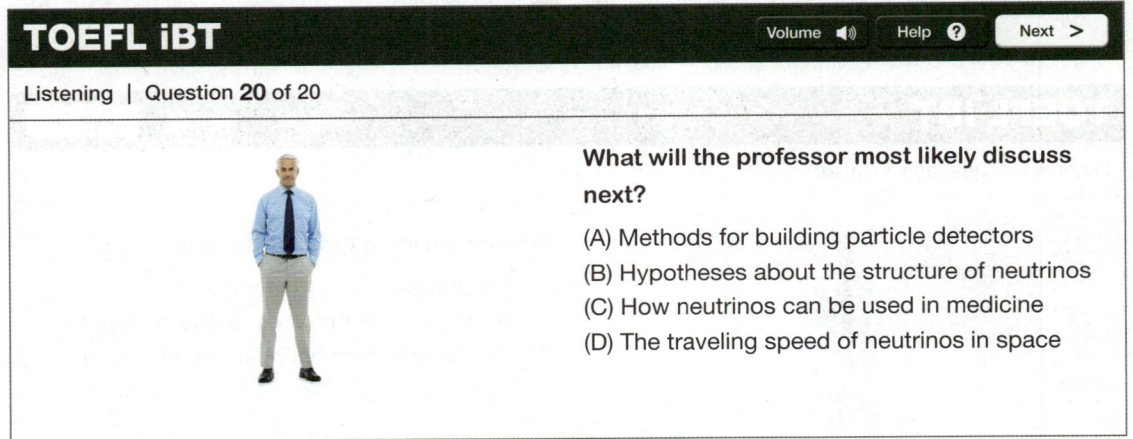

Module 2

TOEFL iBT

Listening | Question **1** of 15

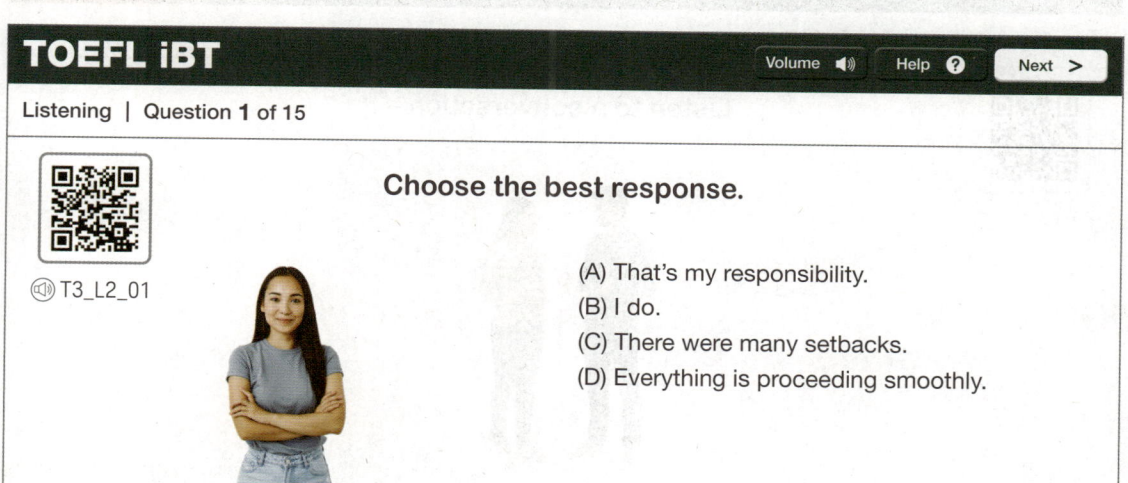

🔊 T3_L2_01

Choose the best response.

(A) That's my responsibility.
(B) I do.
(C) There were many setbacks.
(D) Everything is proceeding smoothly.

TOEFL iBT

Listening | Question **2** of 15

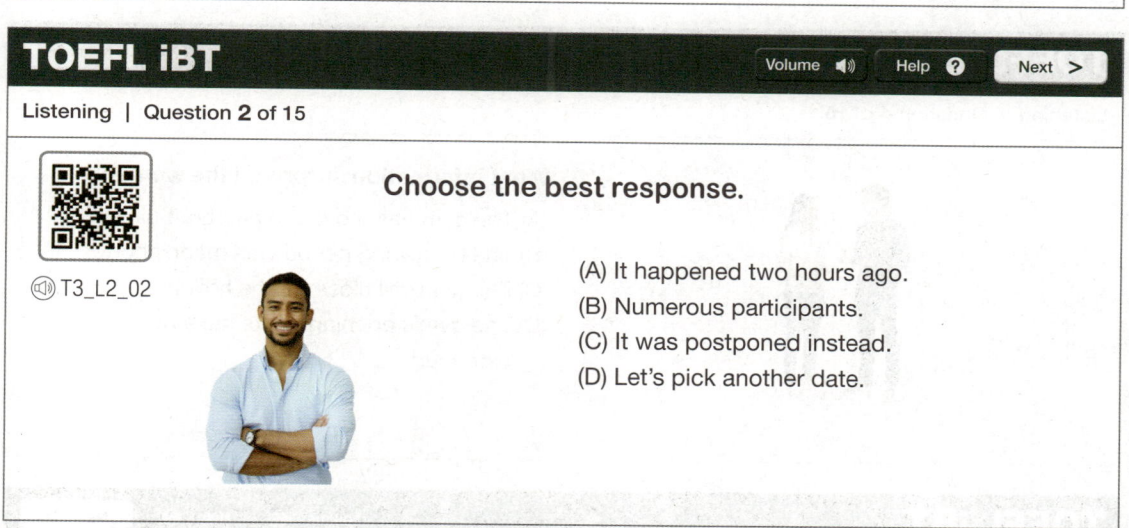

🔊 T3_L2_02

Choose the best response.

(A) It happened two hours ago.
(B) Numerous participants.
(C) It was postponed instead.
(D) Let's pick another date.

TOEFL iBT

Listening | Question **3** of 15

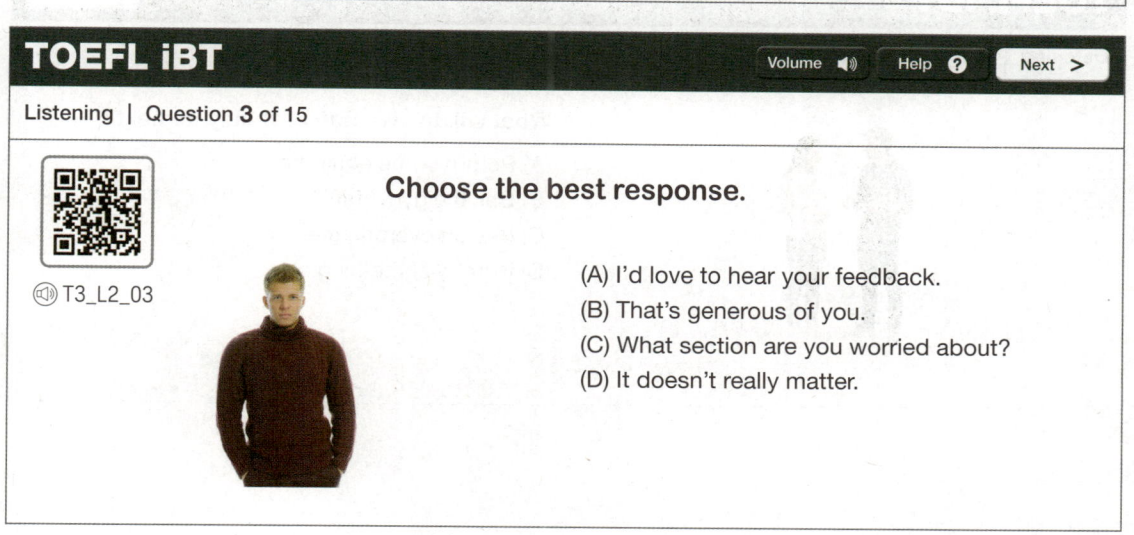

🔊 T3_L2_03

Choose the best response.

(A) I'd love to hear your feedback.
(B) That's generous of you.
(C) What section are you worried about?
(D) It doesn't really matter.

Listening | Questions 4-5 of 15

Listen to a conversation.

T3_L2_0405

Listening | Question 4 of 15

What information surprised the woman?

(A) The gym has moved to another building.
(B) The borrowing period was made shorter.
(C) The gym will close for the holidays.
(D) The gym's opening hours have been extended.

Listening | Question 5 of 15

What will the woman probably do next?

(A) Return some equipment
(B) Call the gym staff
(C) Pay an overdue fee
(D) Borrow something else

TOEFL iBT

Listening | Questions 6-7 of 15

Listen to a conversation.

T3_L2_0607

TOEFL iBT

Listening | Question 6 of 15

What event are the speakers discussing?

(A) A food festival
(B) A craft fair
(C) A book fair
(D) An art exhibit

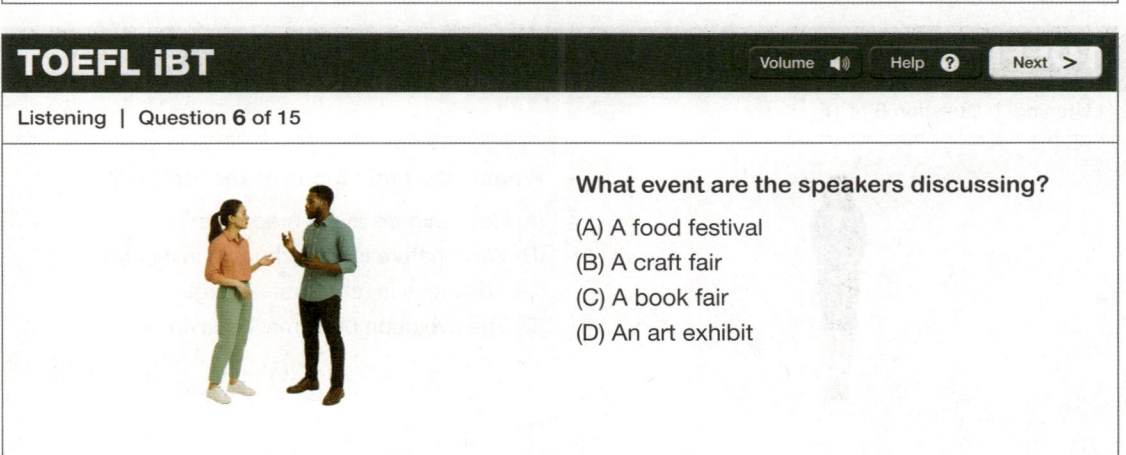

TOEFL iBT

Listening | Question 7 of 15

What does the man plan to bring to the event?

(A) A book
(B) A laptop
(C) A camera
(D) A timetable

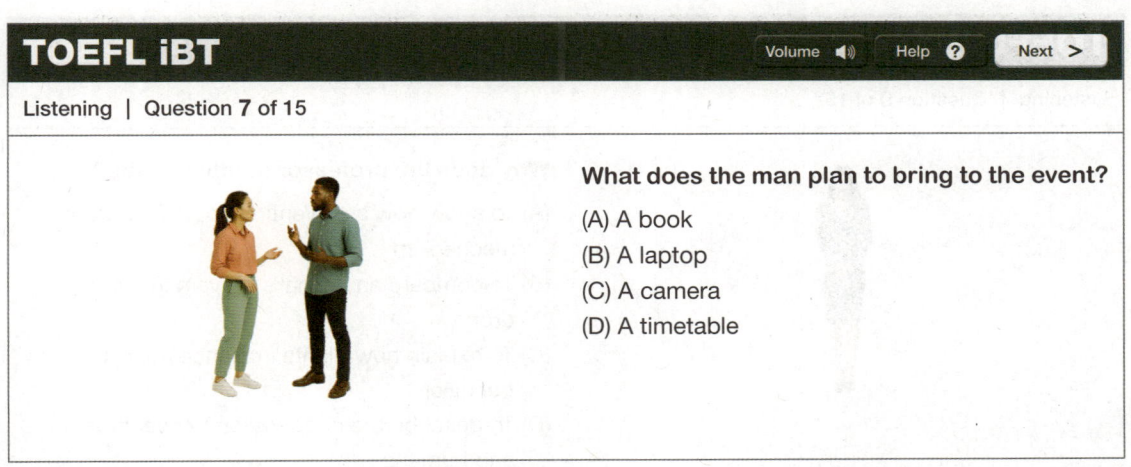

Listen to a lecture in a design class.

T3_L2_0811

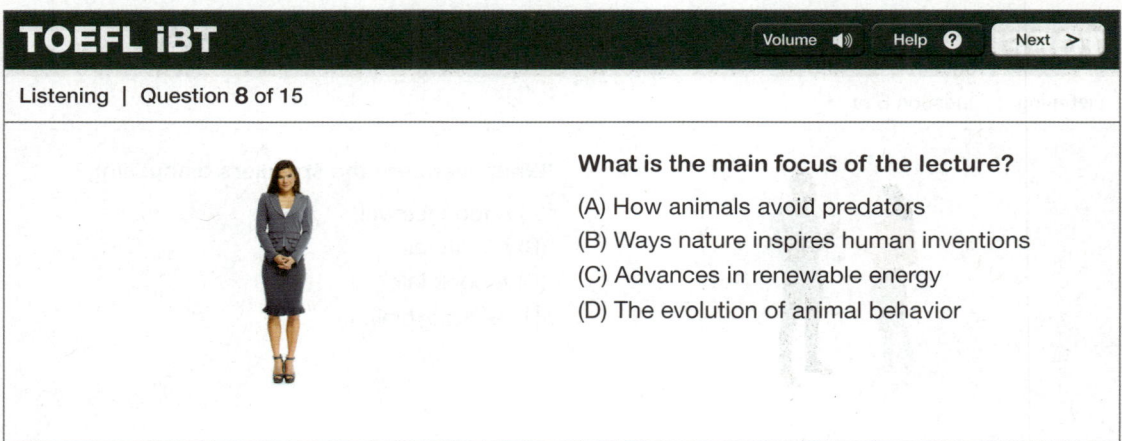

What is the main focus of the lecture?

(A) How animals avoid predators
(B) Ways nature inspires human inventions
(C) Advances in renewable energy
(D) The evolution of animal behavior

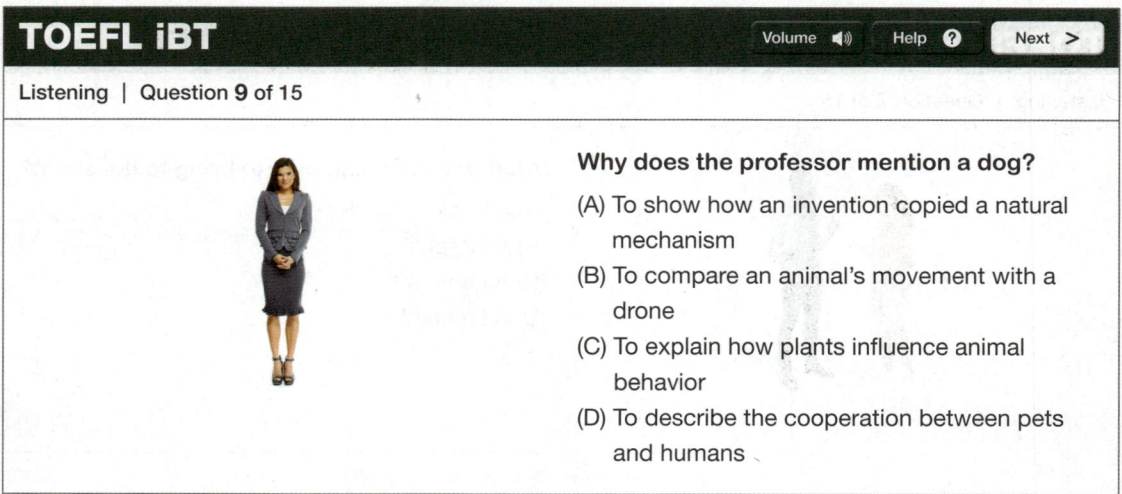

Why does the professor mention a dog?

(A) To show how an invention copied a natural mechanism
(B) To compare an animal's movement with a drone
(C) To explain how plants influence animal behavior
(D) To describe the cooperation between pets and humans

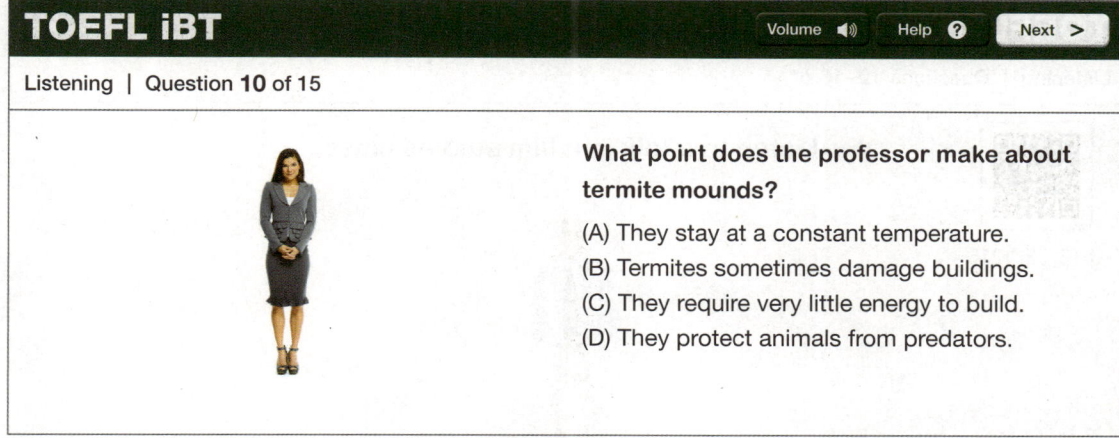

What point does the professor make about termite mounds?

(A) They stay at a constant temperature.
(B) Termites sometimes damage buildings.
(C) They require very little energy to build.
(D) They protect animals from predators.

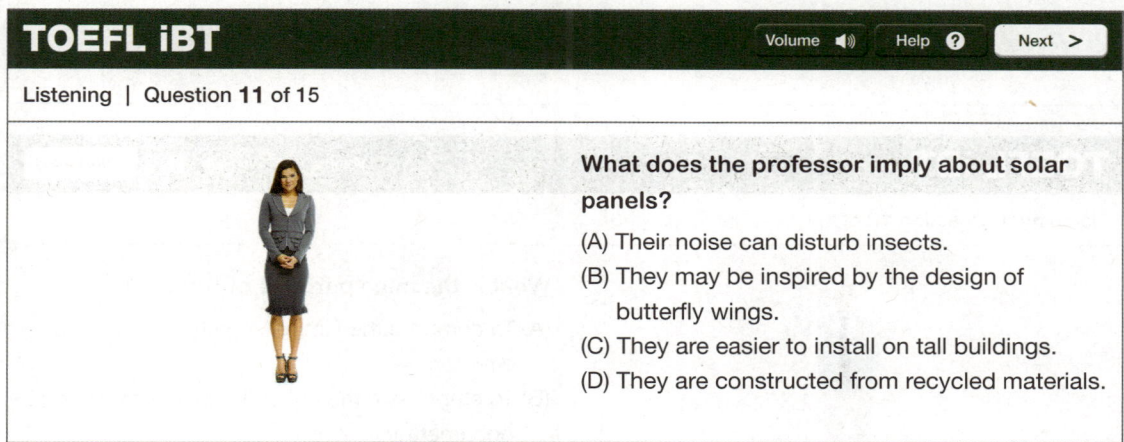

What does the professor imply about solar panels?

(A) Their noise can disturb insects.
(B) They may be inspired by the design of butterfly wings.
(C) They are easier to install on tall buildings.
(D) They are constructed from recycled materials.

Listen to a talk in a film studies class.

T3_L2_1215

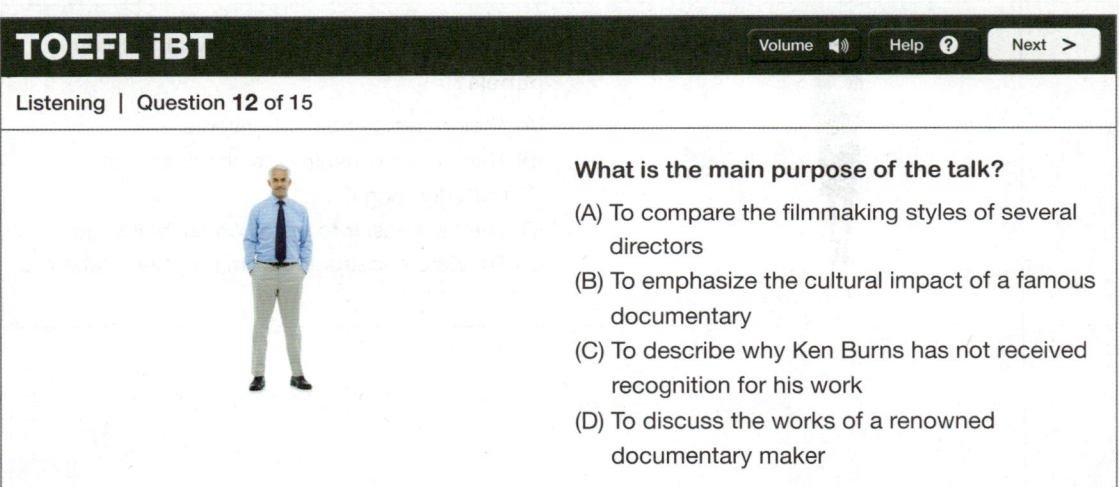

What is the main purpose of the talk?

(A) To compare the filmmaking styles of several directors
(B) To emphasize the cultural impact of a famous documentary
(C) To describe why Ken Burns has not received recognition for his work
(D) To discuss the works of a renowned documentary maker

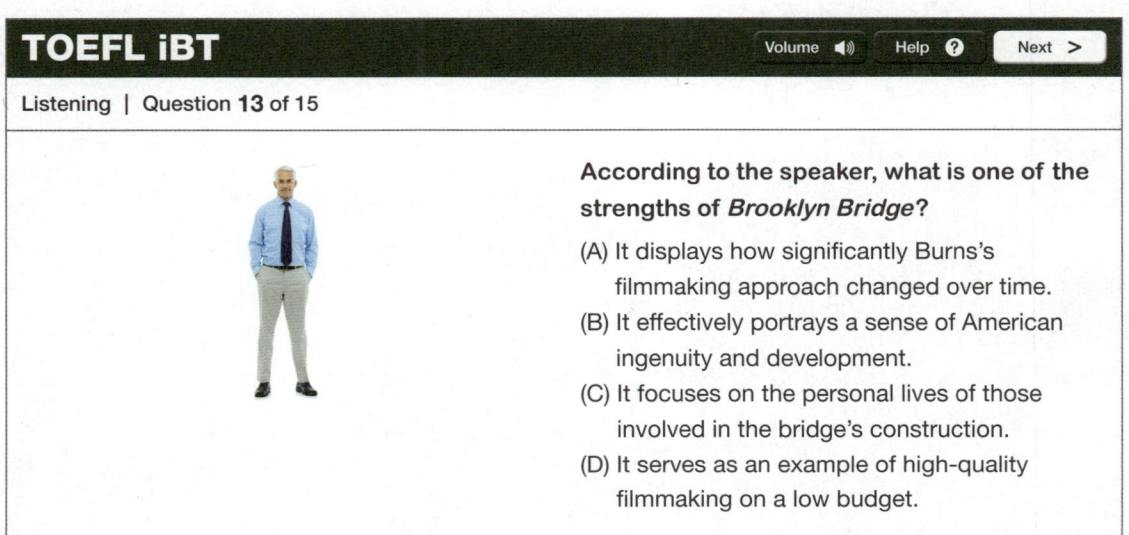

According to the speaker, what is one of the strengths of *Brooklyn Bridge*?

(A) It displays how significantly Burns's filmmaking approach changed over time.
(B) It effectively portrays a sense of American ingenuity and development.
(C) It focuses on the personal lives of those involved in the bridge's construction.
(D) It serves as an example of high-quality filmmaking on a low budget.

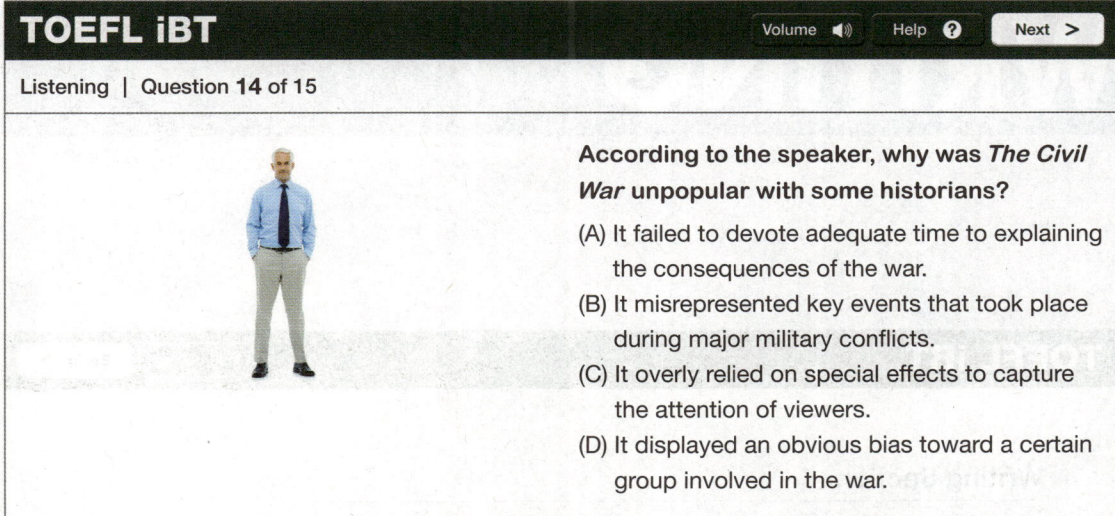

According to the speaker, why was *The Civil War* unpopular with some historians?

(A) It failed to devote adequate time to explaining the consequences of the war.
(B) It misrepresented key events that took place during major military conflicts.
(C) It overly relied on special effects to capture the attention of viewers.
(D) It displayed an obvious bias toward a certain group involved in the war.

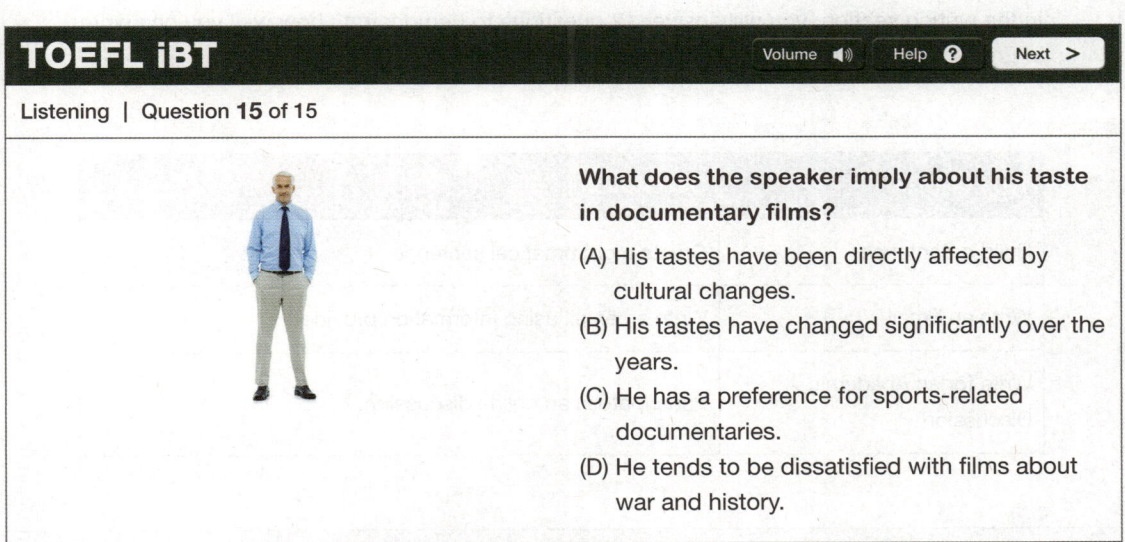

What does the speaker imply about his taste in documentary films?

(A) His tastes have been directly affected by cultural changes.
(B) His tastes have changed significantly over the years.
(C) He has a preference for sports-related documentaries.
(D) He tends to be dissatisfied with films about war and history.

WRITING

TOEFL iBT

Volume 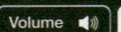 Begin

Writing Section

In the writing section, you will answer 12 questions to demonstrate how well you can write in English. There are three types of tasks.

Type of Task	Description
Build a Sentence	Create a grammatical sentence.
Write an Email	Write an email using information provided.
Write for an Academic Discussion	Participate in an online discussion.

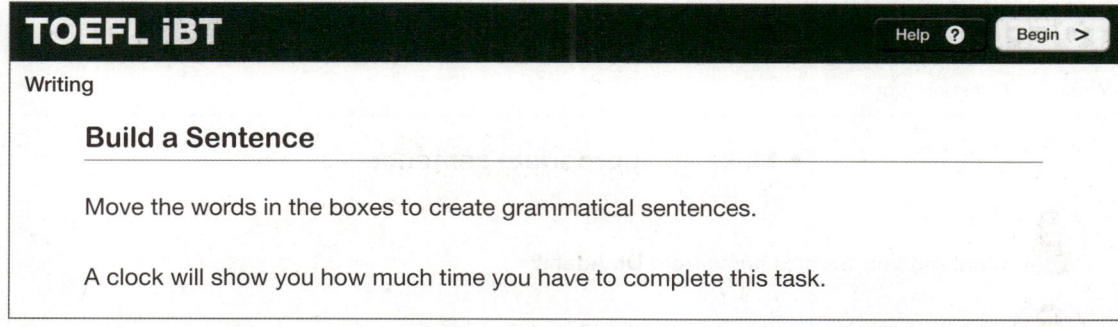

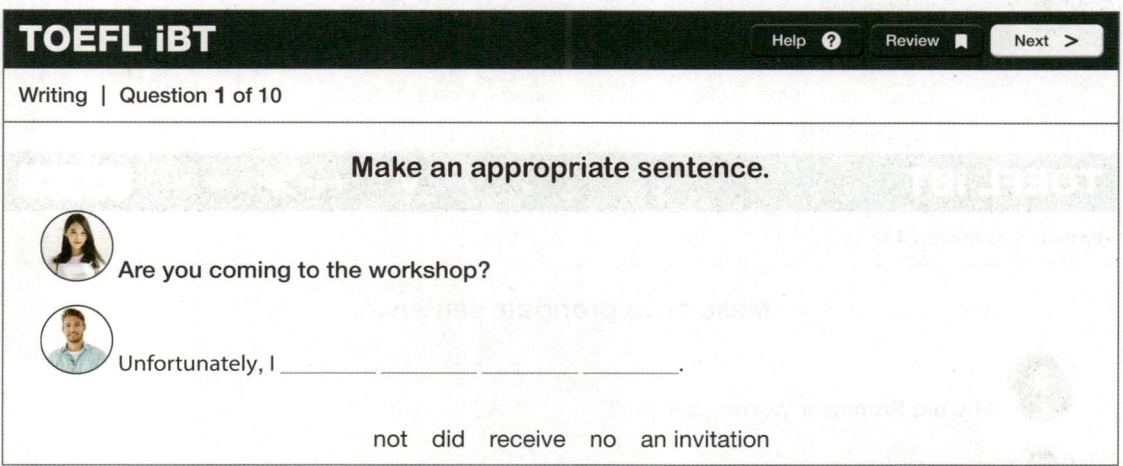

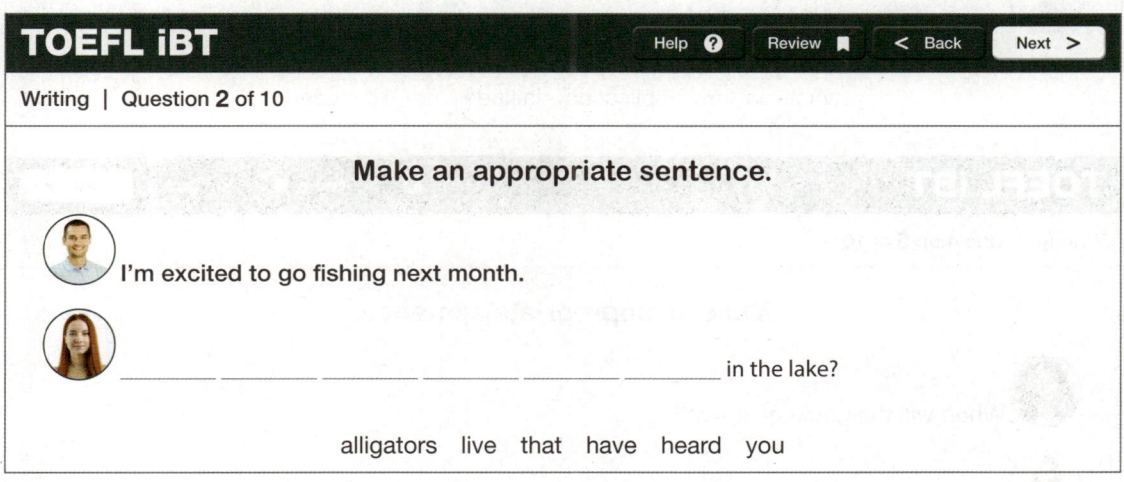

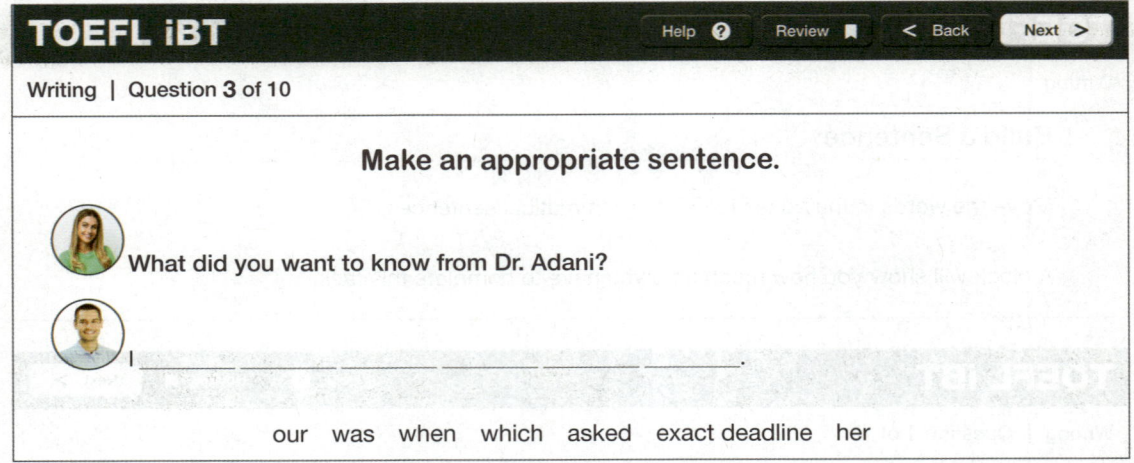

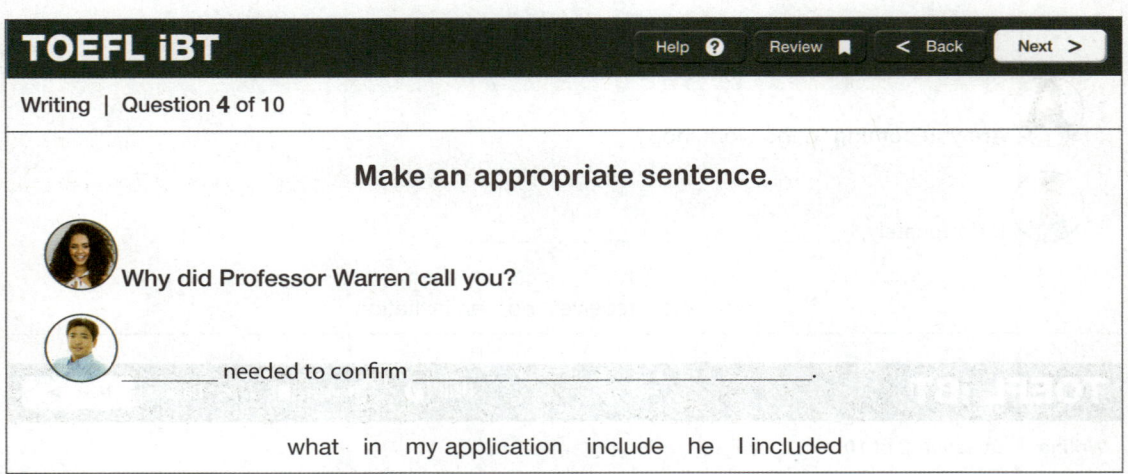

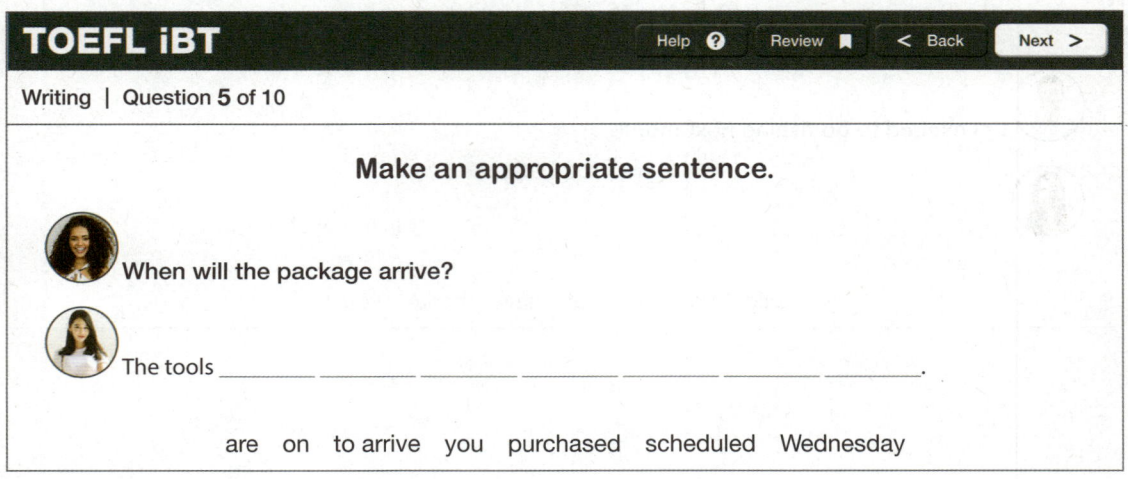

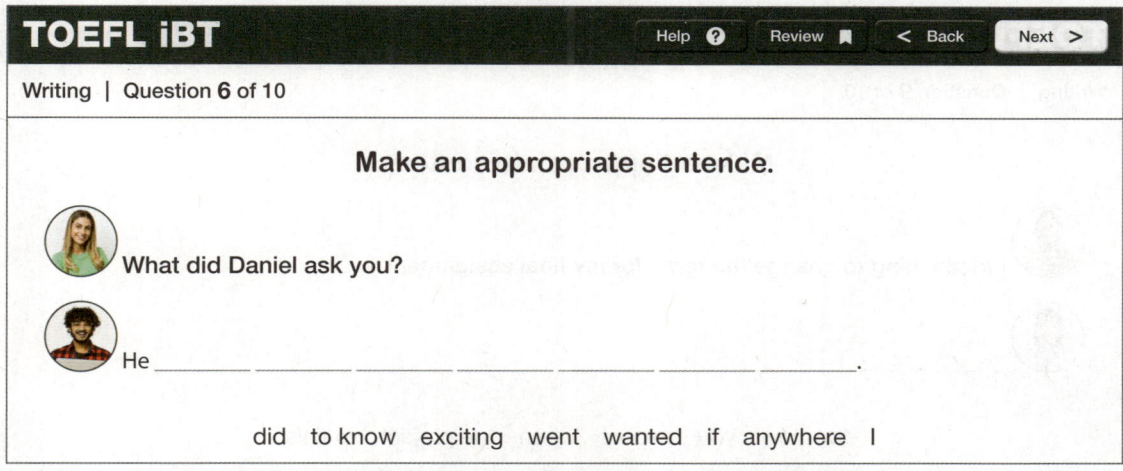

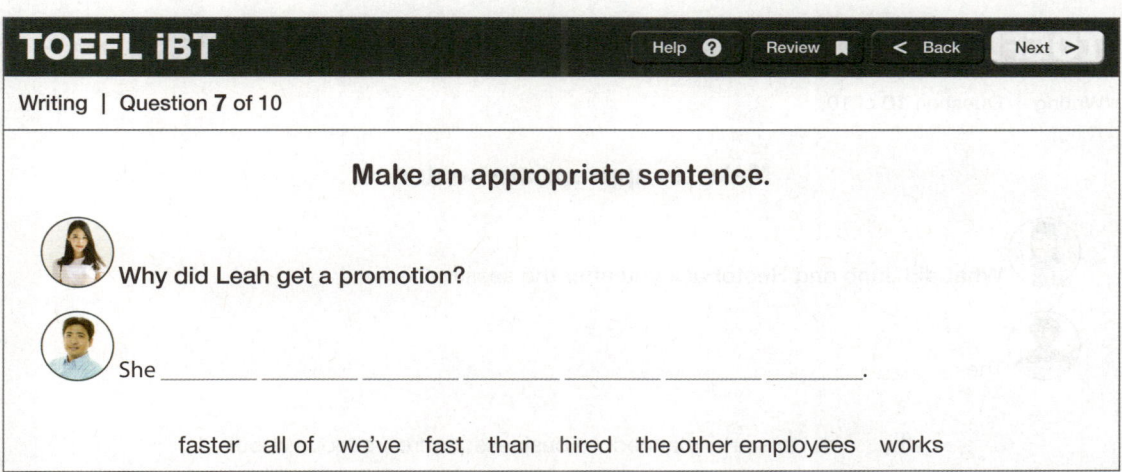

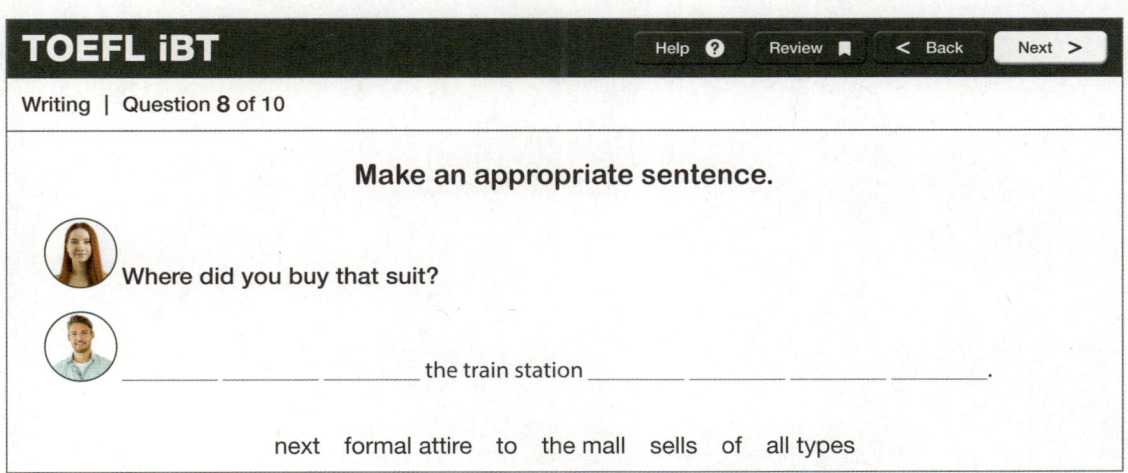

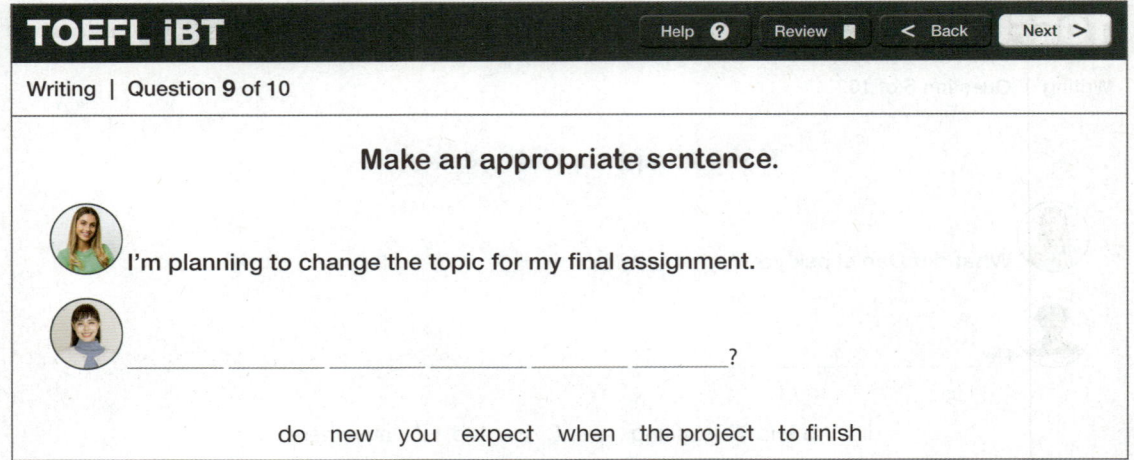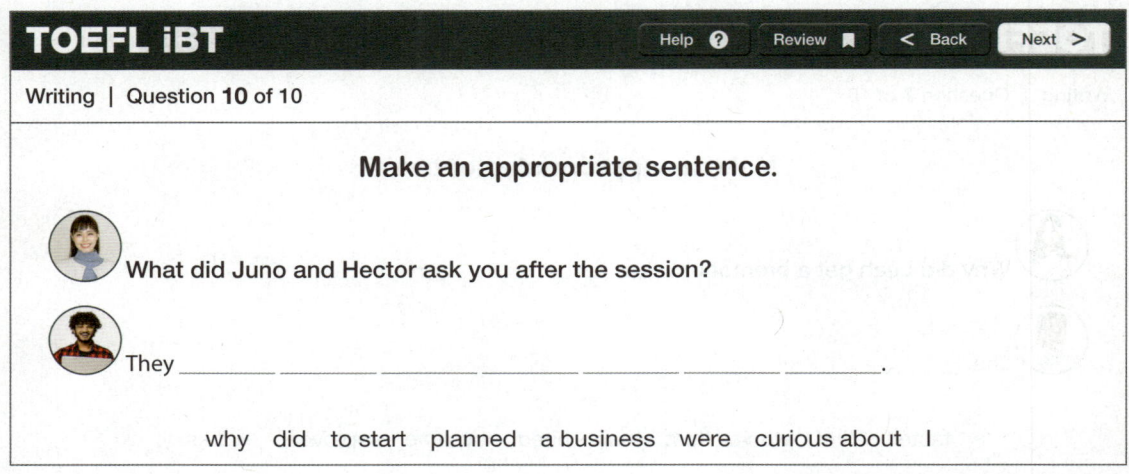

TOEFL iBT

Writing

Write an Email

You will read some information and use the information to write an email.

You will have 7 minutes to write the email.

TOEFL iBT

Writing

You have recently joined a new gym. You need to contact the owner, Mr. Nadal, to cancel your membership because of a health issue. You hope to return once your health improves.

Write an email to Mr. Nadal. In your email, do the following:

- Mention what membership you have.
- Explain why you need to cancel your membership.
- Describe what you would like to happen next.

Write as much as you can and in complete sentences.

Your Response:

To: Mr. Nadal

Subject: Gym membership cancellation

TOEFL iBT

Writing

Write for an Academic Discussion

A professor has posted a question about a topic and students have responded with their thoughts and ideas. Make a contribution to the discussion.

You will have 10 minutes to write.

TOEFL iBT

Writing

Your professor is teaching a class on sociology. Write a post responding to the professor's question.

In your response, you should do the following:

- Express and support your opinion.
- Make a contribution to the discussion in your own words.

An effective response will contain at least 100 words.

Dr. Johns

As we have discussed in class, life expectancy has risen across the world over the past few centuries and is expected to continue climbing in the future. Some believe that improvements in sanitation were the key factor, while others think that medical advancements were more influential. Which viewpoint do you agree with, and why?

Jane

I think improvements in sanitation have played a key role in why people are living longer. Before, people threw their waste on the streets, and many became sick from unpurified water. We now live in much more sanitary conditions with a sewer system and easy access to clean water.

Sam

I believe advancements in medicine are the biggest reason for the increased life expectancy. We are now able to treat illnesses that would have been fatal before. What might have been a pandemic in the past can now be prevented with a simple vaccine, contributing to longer lifespans.

SPEAKING

TOEFL iBT Volume 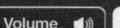 Begin >

Speaking Section

In the speaking section, you will answer 11 questions to demonstrate how well you can speak English. There are two types of tasks.

Type of Task	Description
Listen and Repeat	Listen and repeat what you heard.
Take an Interview	Answer questions from the interviewer.

TOEFL iBT

Speaking

Listen and Repeat

You will listen as someone speaks to you. Listen carefully and then repeat what you have heard. The clock will indicate how much time you have to speak.

No time for preparation will be provided.

TOEFL iBT

Speaking

You are being trained to welcome visitors to the park. Listen to your trainer and repeat what he says. Repeat only once.

TOEFL iBT

Speaking | Question **1** of 11

T3_S_01

Listen and repeat only once.

RESPONSE TIME
00:00:08

TOEFL iBT

Speaking | Question **2** of 11

T3_S_02

Listen and repeat only once.

RESPONSE TIME 00:00:08

TOEFL iBT

Speaking | Question **3** of 11

T3_S_03

Listen and repeat only once.

RESPONSE TIME 00:00:10

TOEFL iBT

Speaking | Question **6** of 11

T3_S_06

Listen and repeat only once.

RESPONSE TIME 00:00:12

TOEFL iBT

Speaking | Question **7** of 11

T3_S_07

Listen and repeat only once.

RESPONSE TIME 00:00:12

TOEFL iBT

Speaking

Take an Interview

An interviewer will ask you questions. Answer the questions and be sure to say as much as you can in the time allowed.

No time for preparation will be provided.

TOEFL iBT

Speaking

You have agreed to participate in a research study about commuting habits. You will have a short online interview with a researcher. The researcher will ask you some questions.

TOEFL iBT

Speaking | Question **8** of 11

T3_S_08

Please answer the interviewer's questions.

RESPONSE TIME
00:00:45

TOEFL iBT

Speaking | Question **9** of 11

T3_S_09

Please answer the interviewer's questions.

RESPONSE TIME
00:00:45

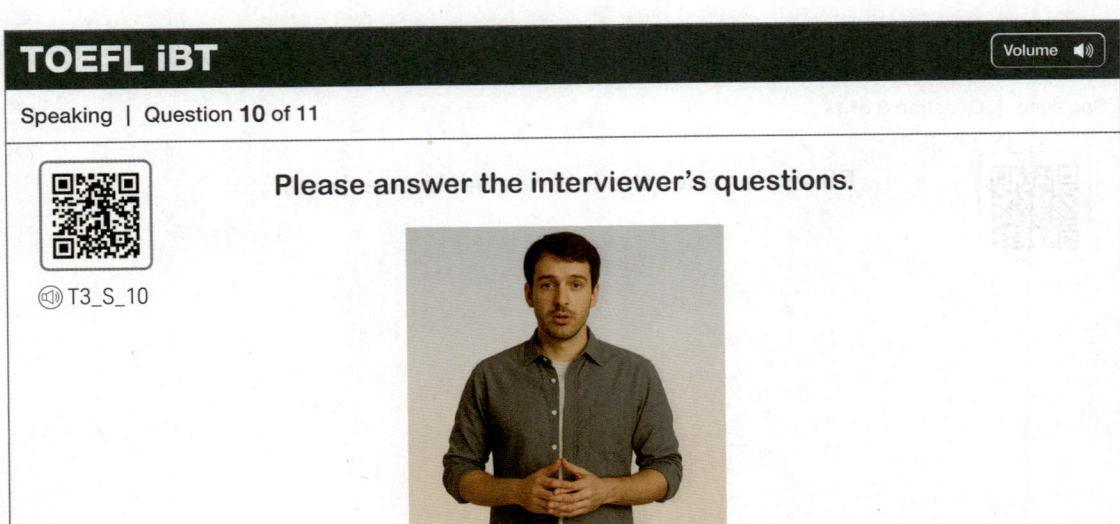

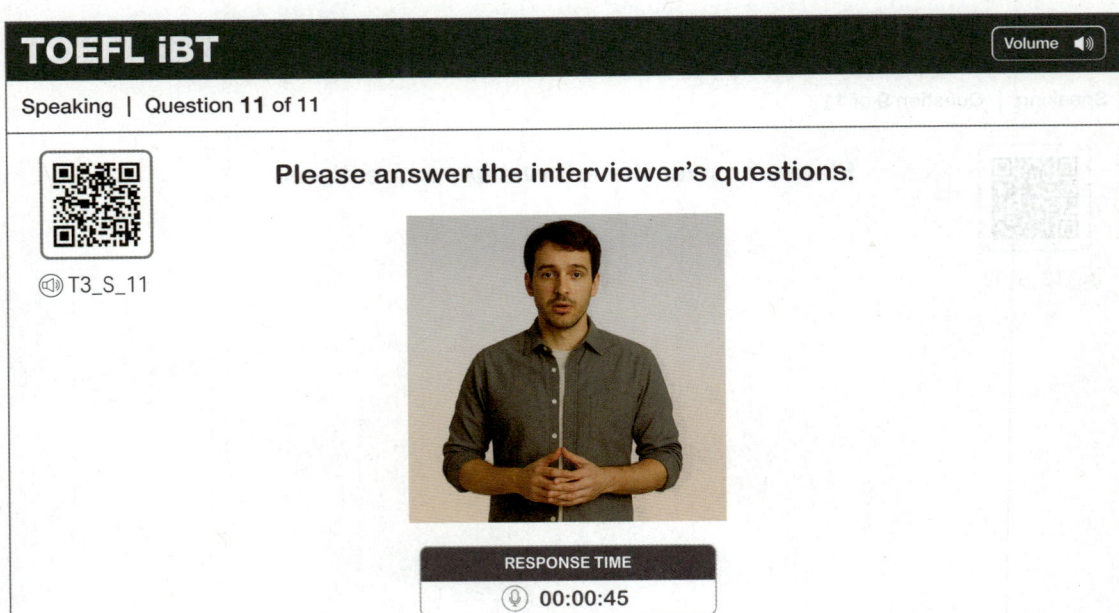

MEMO

*toefl 실전모의고사 온라인 강의

2026 NEW

시원스쿨 토플 전문강사
박주영 선생님

ETS 토플 공식 파트너 시원스쿨랩의
최신 개정 강의로 빠르게 목표 달성!

2026 개정
토플에 대한 기준을
제공

영역별 핵심 전략
+실전 문제 연습으로
개정 시험 완벽 대비

실제 시험 화면과
동일한 실전 모의고사
풀 세트 제공

*toefl. × 시원스쿨 LAB

2026 Updated!
개정 시험 ETS 토플 제공 컨텐츠로 최단기 목표 달성!

ETS 토플 제공 컨텐츠 학습 + **2026 개정 내용 완벽 반영** + **이론-실전까지 한 번에**

ETS 토플 공식 파트너 시원스쿨랩이 쏜다!

토플 패키지
3만원 할인권
쿠폰번호 : SIWONTOEFL1

토플 단과
1만원 할인권
쿠폰번호 : SIWONTOEFL2

유효기간 : 발급일로부터 7일간
할인내용 : 토플 패키지 3만원 할인
사용방법 : 시원스쿨랩 사이트 ▶ 내강의실 ▶ 내쿠폰함
▶ 쿠폰번호 등록 후, 결제 시 사용

유효기간 : 발급일로부터 7일간
할인내용 : 토플 단과 1만원 할인
사용방법 : 시원스쿨랩 사이트 ▶ 내강의실 ▶ 내쿠폰함
▶ 쿠폰번호 등록 후, 결제 시 사용

toefl × SIWONSCHOOL

ETS 토플 공식 파트너

TOEFL
실전모의고사

Answers

시원스쿨 LAB

TOEFL 실전모의고사

Answers

시원스쿨 LAB

Reading Module 1

TEST 1

정답

Complete the Words
1-10   dies, ms, ey, ity, tions, nect, ross, tries, own, ical

Read in Daily Life
11-12   (A), (B)
13-15   (B), (A), (C)

Read an Academic Passage
16-20   (A), (A), (B), (C), (B)

해석/어휘

Complete the Words
1-10   다음 문단에서 빠진 글자를 채우시오.

> 음악은 인간 문화의 보편적인 요소로서, 감정과 사회적 관계 둘 모두에 영향을 미친다. 멜로디와 리듬이 확산되면서, 여러 세대에 걸쳐 창의성에 영감을 불어넣고, 전통을 보존하며, 공동체들을 연결해 준다. 어떤 국가들은 고전적인 작품들이나 민속 유산으로 알려져 있는 반면, 다른 국가들은 문화적 독자성과 일상 생활을 재형성하는 현대적인 장르들을 수용한다. 그 장르가 무엇이든, 음악은 전 세계의 여러 문화에 걸쳐 표현과 이해에 있어 여전히 필수적이다.

어휘 및 표현

universal 보편적인   element 요소, 원소   influence ~에 영향을 미치다   social connection 사회적 관계   spread 확산되다   inspire ~에 영감을 불어넣다   creativity 창의성   preserve ~을 보존하다   tradition 전통   connect ~을 연결하다   community 공동체, 집단   generation 세대   be known for ~로 알려져 있다   composition 작곡(된 작품)   folk heritage 민속 유산   embrace ~을 수용하다   reshape ~을 재형성하다   identity 독자성, 정체(성)   no matter A A가 무엇이든   remain 여전히 ~한 상태이다   vital 필수적인   expression 표현(력)

Read in Daily Life
11-12   이메일을 읽으시오.

> 제목: 부족한 저장 공간
>
> 헤이즐 씨께,
>
> 귀하의 계정에 저장 공간이 부족해지고 있다는 사실을 알려 드립니다. 5월 5일까지 아무런 조치도 취해지지 않을 경우, 일부 메시지 전송 기능들이 제대로 작동하지 않을 수 있습니다. 오래된 파일들을 삭제해 저장 공간을 늘릴 수 있습니다. 이 문제에 대한 귀하의 관심에 감사드립니다.

안녕히 계십시오.
잭 키팅

11 이메일의 주된 목적은?
(A) 알림 메시지를 제공하는 것
(B) 새로운 서비스를 제안하는 것
(C) 계정을 인증해 주는 것
(D) 기술적인 문제를 알리는 것

12 이메일에서 메시지 전송 기능과 관련해 언급하는 것은?
(A) 몇몇 업데이트를 거칠 것이다.
(B) 이용 불가능한 상태가 될 수 있다.
(C) 서비스 구독을 필요로 한다.
(D) 사용자 지정이 가능하다.

어휘 및 표현

storage 저장, 보관 **notify A that ~** A에게 ~라고 알리다 **account** 계정 **run low** 부족해지다, 다 떨어지다 **action** 조치, 움직임 **feature** 기능, 특징 **work** (기계 등이) 작동하다 **properly** 제대로, 적절히 **increase** ~을 늘리다, ~을 증가시키다 **delete** ~을 삭제하다 **attention** 관심, 주목, 주의 **matter** 문제, 사안(=issue) **notification** 알림 (메시지) **verify** ~을 인증하다, ~을 확인하다 **undergo** ~을 거치다, ~을 겪다 **unavailable** 이용 불가능한 **subscription** (서비스 등의) 가입, 구독 **customizable** 사용자 지정이 가능한, 주문 제작할 수 있는

13-15 이메일을 읽으시오.

제목: 화재 안전 점검

우리 건물의 다음 번 화재 안전 점검이 6월 21일 오전 10시부터 오후 4시까지 예정되어 있습니다. 이 점검은 공인 화재 안전 전문가들에 의해 실시될 것입니다.

이 시간대에, 스프링클러와 연기 감지기, 화재 경보기, 소화기, 그리고 비상구가 테스트될 것입니다. 구내에 계실 경우, 큰 경보음이 들리고 복도 또는 계단실에서 일시적인 제약을 겪으실 수 있습니다. 주거용 세대 및 사무실 공간은 점검관들에 의해 곧바로 출입이 차단될 것입니다.

명심하시기 바랍니다: 화재 안전 점검은 건물 안전 규정을 충족하기 위해 주기적으로 실시됩니다. 연기 감지기에 대한 조작 또는 소화기 제거 같은, 소방 장비의 의도적 손상 또는 절도는 엄격히 금지되며, 형사 범죄에 해당할 수 있습니다.

질문이 있으시거나 도움이 필요하신 경우, 건물 관리소에 연락 주시기 바랍니다. 점검 결과는 며칠 내로 지역 게시판에 게시되고 모든 분께 이메일로 발송될 것입니다. 안전한 생활 및 근무 환경을 유지하도록 도움이 되는 데 있어 여러분의 협조에 감사드립니다.

13 이 이메일은 ~에게 보내지는 것일 가능성이 크다.
(A) 지역 소방서 근무자들
(B) 주민과 사무실 입주자들
(C) 해당 건물을 지은 회사

(D) 아파트를 임대하는 데 관심이 있는 사람들

14 건물 내 소방 장비과 관련해 유추할 수 있는 것은?
(A) 법으로 보호된다.
(B) 몇몇 새로운 업그레이드를 필요로 할 수 있다.
(C) 건물 관리자들에 의해 점검된다.
(D) 여러 연기 감지기가 최근 오작동했다.

15 이 이메일의 수신인은 ~을 통보받을 것이다.
(A) 6월 21일 점검 일정상의 변동 사항
(B) 시에서 제공하는 새로운 화재 안전 가이드라인
(C) 6월 21일 점검의 결과
(D) 건물 유지 관리에 대한 요금

어휘 및 표현
inspection 점검 carry out ~을 실시하다(=conduct) certified 공인된, 자격증이 있는 professional 전문가 detector 감지기 extinguisher 소화기 emergency exit 비상구 on site 구내에 있는, 현장에 있는 temporary 일시적인 restriction 제약 stairwell 계단실 residential 주거의 unit (아파트, 상가 등의) 세대, 점포 access ~에 출입하다 inspector 점검관 regularly 주기적으로, 규칙적으로 meet (조건 등) ~을 충족하다 code 규정, 법규 willful 의도적인 damage 손상, 피해 theft 절도 equipment 장비 tamper with ~을 조작하다 remove ~을 제거하다 strictly 엄격히 prohibit ~을 금지하다 constitute ~에 해당하다, ~을 구성하다 criminal offense 형사 범죄 findings 결과 post ~을 게시하다 cooperation 협조 maintain ~을 유지하다 local 지역의, 현지의 resident 주민 tenant 입주자 lease ~을 임대하다 property 건물, 부동산 malfunction 오작동하다 recently 최근 be notified of ~을 통보받다 result 결과 maintenance 유지 관리

Read an Academic Passage
16-20 해조류의 역할

해조류는 해양 생태계와 인간 사회에 모두 필수적인 혜택을 제공해 주면서, 먹을 것과 산소, 그리고 필수 영양분의 공급원으로서 역할을 한다. 육지 식물과 달리, 해조류는 진정한 뿌리와 잎이 부족하다. 대신 바닷물로부터 직접적으로 무기물과 이산화탄소를 흡수한다. 이러한 능력은 다른 식물들이 생존하지 못하는 환경에서 성장할 수 있게 해 준다. 해안 침식을 줄여 주고, 산소를 만들어 내며, 많은 해양 먹이 그물의 기반을 형성함으로써, 해조류는 해양 생태계의 건강에 있어 아주 중요하다.

한 가지 대단히 흥미로운 해조류 집단은 켈프인데, 이들은 수 마일에 걸쳐 이어지는 거대 해저 숲을 형성할 수 있다. 이 우뚝 솟은 구조물은 물고기와 무척추동물, 그리고 심지어 해달 같은 해양 포유류들에게도 쉼터를 만들어 줄 수 있다. 그 보답으로, 많은 이 종들이 생태계로 다시 유기물을 제공해, 켈프 숲의 생명력을 증진시킨다. 이 역동적인 협력 관계는 생물 다양성을 지탱해 줄 뿐만 아니라 강력한 파도와 폭풍에 대해 해안 지대를 보호해 주는 데에도 도움이 된다.

해조류의 모든 측면이 긍정적인 것은 아니다. 일부 침입 해조류 종은 공격적으로 확산되면서, 토종 식물을 밀어내고 지역 생태계를 바꿔 놓는다. 예를 들어, 콜레르파 탁시폴리아의 유입은 지중해의 여러 지역에서 해안 서식지를 붕괴시켜 왔다. 해조류의 다양한 역할을 연구함으로써, 연구가들은 그 유해한 영향을 더 잘 관리함과 동시에 식량과 의학, 바이오 연료, 그리고 기후 관련 해결책을 위한 잠재성도 활용할 수 있다.

16 지문 내용에 따르면, 해조류는 ~의 측면에 있어 유익하다.
(A) 해안 지역에서 필수 영양분을 생성하는 것
(B) 바닷물로부터 산소를 흡수하는 것
(C) 해양 먹이 그물 내에서 1차 소비자로서 역할을 하는 것
(D) 밀집한 뿌리를 이용해 해안을 보호하는 것

17 지문의 단어 "crucial"에 가장 가까운 의미는?
(A) 필요한
(B) 활동적인, 적극적인
(C) 신선한
(D) 견고한, 튼튼한

18 다음 중 지문에서 해조류의 역할로써 언급되지 않은 것은?
(A) 산소 생산에 기여하는 일
(B) 뿌리를 통해 영양분을 바다로 옮기는 일
(C) 물고기와 해양 포유류에게 쉼터를 제공하는 일
(D) 해안 지역의 퇴화를 방지하는 일

19 켈프와 관련해 유추할 수 있는 것은?
(A) 대부분 햇빛이 잘 드는 환경에서 자란다.
(B) 그 숲이 때때로 해수면보다 더 높이 솟아 오를 수 있다.
(C) 다른 생물체들을 위험한 환경으로부터 보호해 준다.
(D) 폭풍우가 바다 상공에서 형성되는 것을 막아 준다.

20 해조류의 다양한 역할과 관련해 유추할 수 있는 것은?
(A) 이 다양성이 해조류를 지중해 일부 지역에서 위협 요소로 만든다.
(B) 이 다양성이 미래에 여러 실용적인 용도를 초래할 수 있다.
(C) 이 다양성이 전 세계 국가들의 관리 및 협조를 필요로 한다.
(D) 이 다양성이 다른 해양 식물 유형들의 진화와 관련되어 있다.

어휘 및 표현
vital 필수적인(=essential) benefit 혜택, 이점 ecosystem 생태계 serve as ~의 역할을 하다(=act as) nutrient 영양분 lack ~이 부족하다 absorb ~을 흡수하다 mineral 무기물 ability 능력 reduce ~을 줄이다, ~을 감소시키다 erosion 침식 form ~을 형성하다 base 기반 crucial 아주 중요한 vast 거대한, 방대한 stretch 이어지다, 뻗어 있다 towering 우뚝 솟은 shelter 쉼터, 대피소 invertebrate 무척추동물 mammal 포유류 sea otter 해달 in return 결과적으로 species (동식물의) 종 contribute ~을 제공하다 organic matter 유기물 reinforce ~을 증진하다, ~을 강화하다 dynamic 역동적인 biodiversity 생물 다양성 buffer ~을 보호하다, ~을 완화하다 aspect 측면, 양상 positive 긍정적인 spread 확산되다 aggressively 공격적으로 crowd out ~을 밀어내다, ~을 몰아내다 alter ~을 바꾸다 introduction 유입, 도입 disrupt ~을 붕괴시키다 habitat 서식지 the Mediterranean 지중해 harmful 유해한 impact 영향 utilize ~을 활용하다 potential 잠재성 solution 해결책 beneficial 유익한 in terms of ~의 측면에 있어, ~와 관련해 primary consumer 1차 소비자 dense 밀집한 transfer ~을 옮기다 deterioration 퇴화, 악화 sea level 해수면 safeguard ~을 보호하다 organism 생물체 threat 위협 (요소) result in ~을 초래하다 practical 실용적인 be related to ~와 관련되다 evolution 진화, 발전

Reading Module 2

TEST 1

정답

Complete the Words
1-10   nd, ieve, ch, ments, st, es, lity, as, own, fe

Read an Academic Passage
11-15   (C), (B), (C), (D), (B)

해석/어휘

Complete the Words
1-10   다음 문단에서 빠진 글자를 채우시오.

> 잠수함에 의해 포착된 동영상에 이상한 생물들이 바다의 가장 깊은 곳에 번성하고 있는 것으로 나타났다. 사람들은 그렇게 극한의 환경이 그저 척박한 지대라고 생각하는 경향이 있다. 실제로는, 생명체가 그곳에 풍부하다는 사실이 연구를 통해 명확하게 드러났다. 과학자들은 다른 어떤 심해 서식지보다 열수 분출공 근처에서 더 많은 종을 기록했다. 이 생태계들은 독특한 먹이 사슬을 지속하고 있으며, 생명체의 기원에 관한 단서를 드러낸다.

어휘 및 표현
footage 동영상 capture ~을 포착하다, ~을 담아내다 submarine 잠수함 thrive 번성하다 tend to do ~하는 경향이 있다 extreme 극한의, 극심한 barren 척박한 abundant 풍부한 species (동식물의) 종 hydrothermal vent 열수 분출공 habitat 서식지 ecosystem 생태계 sustain ~을 지속하다, ~을 지탱하다 unique 독특한, 특별한 reveal ~을 드러내다 clue 단서 origin 기원, 유래

Read an Academic Passage
11-15   생물학적 정화

> 환경 과학은 인간 사회가 어떻게 오염을 관리하고 그에 대응하는지 탐구한다. 산업 지역 및 도시 지역은 흔히 오염된 토양 및 물 문제로 힘겨워한다. 역사적으로, 정화 노력은 화학 약품 처리 또는 굴착 작업에 의존했는데, 이는 비용도 많이 들고 파괴적일 수 있다. 이 방법들이 오염원을 제거해 주기는 했지만, 종종 생태계를 손상시켰으며, 재오염을 방지하는 데 지속적인 유지 관리가 필요했다.
>
> 최근 몇 년 사이에, 생물학적 정화가 하나의 대안으로 떠올랐다. 생물학적 정화는 박테리아나 균류, 또는 식물 같이, 살아 있는 생물체를 이용해 오염원을 분해하거나 흡수하는 과정이다. 생물학적 정화는 오염된 곳을 회복시키는 동안 생태학적 기능을 보존하고, 토양 건강을 지탱해 주며, 심지어 야생 동물의 귀환을 촉진할 수 있다. 자연적 수단을 이용함으로써, 이 접근법은 전통적인 방법보다 덜 파괴적인 방식으로 환경을 회복시킬 수 있다.
>
> 경제적, 기술적 요인들이 생물학적 정화의 채택에 영향을 미친다. 관찰 도구 및 미생물 유전자 변형 분야의 발전이 정화 프로젝트의 효율성을 향상시켜, 많은 산업 부지에 대해 비용 효율이 높은 해결책이 되어 왔다. 정부 및 민간

회사들은 환경 규제 및 공동체의 기대치를 충족시킬 수 있는 잠재성을 인식해, 생물학적 정화 분야에 점점 더 많이 투자하고 있다.

하지만, 생물학적 정화에 제약이 없는 것은 아니다. 화학적 방법보다 느릴 수 있으며, 모든 유형의 오염원에 대해 효과적이지 못할 수 있다. 정화 작업에 이용되는 일부 생물체는 의도치 않은 생태학적 영향을 방지하기 위해 신중한 관리를 필요로 할 수 있다. 이러한 고려 사항들에도 불구하고, 생물학적 정화는 환경 복원에 대한 유망하고 지속 가능한 접근법에 해당하며, 과학이 인간에 의해 초래된 문제를 해결하는 데 자연적 과정을 어떻게 이용할 수 있는지 보여 준다.

11 지문에서 생물학적 정화와 관련해 시사하는 것은?
(A) 전통적인 방법보다 더 빠른 속도로 오염원을 없애 준다.
(B) 관찰 도구 및 미생물 유전자 변형 기술에 대한 필요성을 최소화해 준다.
(C) 오염된 땅을 회복시키면서 생태학적 기능을 보전하는 데 도움을 준다.
(D) 재오염을 방지하기 위해 화학적 처리 방식을 이용한다.

12 지문에서 생물학적 정화의 이점으로 언급하는 것은?
(A) 더 높은 균류 성장률
(B) 동물 개체군의 회복
(C) 낮아진 물 낭비 수준
(D) 토양 속 중요 박테리아의 보호

13 지문 마지막에 있는 단어 "harness"에 가장 가까운 의미는?
(A) 부착하다
(B) 해결하다
(C) 활용하다
(D) 차지하다

14 글쓴이가 정부와 민간 회사를 언급한 이유는?
(A) 생물학적 정화를 가장 많이 이용하는 단체를 강조하기 위해
(B) 글을 읽는 사람들에게 두 독립체가 보인 모범을 따르도록 권하기 위해
(C) 환경 규제가 매우 중요하다는 사실을 나타내기 위해
(D) 생물학적 정화의 상당한 잠재성을 강조하기 위해

15 3 문단과 4 문단의 관계는?
(A) 4 문단이 3 문단에 제기된 의문에 대한 답을 제공해 준다.
(B) 4 문단이 3 문단에 제시된 장점에 대한 몇몇 단점을 소개한다.
(C) 4 문단이 3 문단에 소개된 다양한 기술을 설명해 준다.
(D) 4 문단이 3 문단에 언급된 문제에 대한 해결책을 이야기한다.

어휘 및 표현

bioremediation 생물학적 정화 **explore** ~을 탐구하다 **pollution** 오염 **struggle with** ~로 힘겨워하다 **contaminate** ~을 오염시키다 **rely on** ~에 의존하다 **chemical treatment** 화학 약품 처리 **excavation** 굴착, 발굴 **disruptive** 파괴적인, 지장을 주는 **remove** ~을 없애다 **pollutant** 오염원 **ecosystem** 생태계 **constant** 지속적인 **maintenance** 유지 관리 **recontamination** 재오염 **emerge** 떠오르다, 나타나다

organism 생물체 fungi 균류 break down ~을 분해하다 absorb ~을 흡수하다 restore ~을 회복시키다, ~을 복원하다(=rehabilitate) preserve ~을 보존하다 ecological 생태학적인 means 수단 approach 접근법 traditional 전통적인 method 방법 factor 요인, 요소 influence ~에 영향을 미치다 adoption 채택 advance 발전, 진보 monitoring 관찰, 감시 engineer ~의 유전자를 조작하다 microorganism 미생물 improve ~을 향상시키다 efficiency 효율성 cost-effective 비용 효율이 좋은 solution 해결책 invest in ~에 투자하다 recognize ~을 인식하다 potential 잠재성 regulation 규제, 규정 expectation 기대(치) limitation 제약, 한계 prevent ~을 방지하다 unintended 의도치 않은 impact 영향 consideration 고려 (사항) represent ~에 해당하다 promising 유망한 sustainable 지속 가능한 demonstrate ~을 보여 주다 harness ~을 이용하다 address (문제 등) ~을 해결하다 human-caused 인간에 의해 초래된 rate 속도, 비율, 등급, 요금 minimize ~을 최소화하다 wastage 낭비 highlight ~을 강조하다(=underscore) follow the example 모범을 따르다 entity 독립체 considerable 상당한 pose (문제 등) ~을 제기하다 drawback 단점, 결점 advantage 장점 present ~을 제시하다 introduce ~을 소개하다

TEST 1
Listening Module 1

정답

Listen and Choose a Response

1-12   (B), (C), (A), (B), (D), (D), (C), (C), (C), (B), (D), (C)

Listen to a Conversation

13-14   (C), (B)
15-16   (C), (D)
17-18   (B), (D)

Listen to an Announcement

19-20   (C), (B)
21-22   (D), (C)
23-24   (A), (C)
25-26   (B), (D)

Listen to an Academic Talk

27-30   (D), (B), (C), (B)

스크립트/해석/어휘

Listen and Choose a Response

1-12   가장 적절한 응답을 고르시오.

1   How did the experiment turn out?
   실험은 어떻게 되었어?

(A) 실험실이 꽤 작긴 하지만, 아주 깨끗해.
(B) 내가 생각한 것보다 더 순조롭게 진행되었어.
(C) 아마 이번엔 다른 방법을 시도해 볼 수 있을 거야.
(D) 고마워. 우리는 그것에 대해 정말 열심히 노력했어.

2   How long will it continue to rain tonight?
   오늘밤에 얼마나 오래 계속 비가 내릴까?

(A) 바깥 기온이 약 75도야.
(B) 아냐, 그렇지 않을 거야.
(C) 적어도 두 시간은 오는 게 분명해.
(D) 날씨가 허락한다면.

3   Did you check the store inventory?
   매장 재고를 확인해 보셨어요?

(A) 네, 출근한 직후에요.

(B) 아뇨, 그분들은 아직 체크인하시지 않았어요.
(C) 저는 저 티셔츠가 마음에 들어요.
(D) 제가 그게 작동하는지 확인했습니다.

4 Mr. Hudson has decided to lead the interviews.
허드슨 씨가 면접을 진행하기로 결정하셨어요.

(A) 질문들이 꽤 어려웠어요.
(B) 저, 저는 그날 그곳에 없을 겁니다.
(C) 아뇨, 저는 지원서를 전혀 받지 못했어요.
(D) 공연이 막 시작하려는 참입니다.

5 How about a quick coffee break?
간단히 커피 한 잔 하면서 쉬는 게 어때요?

(A) 그건 인턴 직원 전용입니다.
(B) 제가 5달러를 지불한 것 같아요.
(C) 그 위치를 기억하세요?
(D) 제가 지금 회의가 있습니다.

6 We'd appreciate it if you posted your photos later.
사진들을 나중에 게시해 주신다면 감사하겠습니다.

(A) 그 행사가 순조롭게 진행되었다는 얘기를 들었어요.
(B) 저도 아까 그 게시물을 봤어요.
(C) 제가 아는 사진 작가에게 연락해 보겠습니다.
(D) 그러면 좋겠지만, 제가 아무것도 찍지 않았습니다.

7 Isn't the musical play showing tomorrow?
그 뮤지컬 공연이 내일 상연하지 않아?

(A) 응, 훌륭했어.
(B) 내가 선약이 있어.
(C) 지역 문화 센터 웹사이트를 확인해 보자.
(D) 대본이 아주 잘 쓰여졌어.

8 Would you like a paperback or a hardcover copy?
종이 표지 책으로 하시겠어요, 아니면 양장본으로 하시겠어요?

(A) 아뇨, 그게 저에겐 그렇게 어렵지 않았어요.
(B) 플라스틱 버전들이 있는 것 같아요.
(C) 무엇이든 즉시 이용할 수 있는 것으로요.
(D) 저는 가방이 없어요.

9 Do you mind closing the door?
문 좀 닫아 줄래?

(A) 난 그걸 이미 살펴 봤어.

(B) 응, 아주 가까이 있어.
(C) 물론이지.
(D) 그곳은 이미 문을 닫았어.

10 Please email me the details for tomorrow's event.
내일 행사의 상세 정보를 내게 이메일로 보내 줘.

(A) 3층 사무실 라운지야.
(B) 비키가 그 일을 책임지고 있어.
(C) 새로운 대리인이야.
(D) 메이슨이 개회사를 했어.

11 Do you know what kind of car Nick drives?
닉이 어떤 종류의 자동차를 운전하는지 아니?

(A) 우리가 택시를 한번 불러 볼 수 있을 거야.
(B) 그래, 그녀가 그걸 가져왔어.
(C) 나는 운전 면허증이 없어.
(D) 그는 매일 버스를 타고 다녀.

12 Can you mail out this package?
이 소포 좀 우편으로 보내 주시겠어요?

(A) 그건 무료 배송 서비스를 포함합니다.
(B) 그 유통 센터는 1번가에 있어요.
(C) 제가 점심 식사 후에 처리하겠습니다.
(D) 제가 비용 환급 요청서를 제출할 겁니다.

어휘 및 표현

experiment 실험 turn out (진행, 결과 등) 되어 가다 lab 실험실 go smooth 순조롭게 진행되다 method 방법 continue to do 계속 ~하다 I doubt it 그렇지 않을 거야 at least 적어도, 최소한 permit 허락하다 inventory 재고 (목록) make sure (that) ~인지 확인하다, 반드시 ~하도록 하다 application 지원(서), 신청(서) be about to do 막 ~하려는 참이다 how about ~? ~는 어때요? post ~을 게시하다, 게시(물) contact ~에게 연락하다 prior commitment 선약 script 대본 paperback 종이 표지 책 hardcover copy 양장본 available 이용 가능한, 구입 가능한 immediately 즉시 review ~을 살펴 보다 details 상세 정보 in charge of ~을 책임지고 있는 opening remarks 개회사 pick A up A를 가져오다, A를 차로 태우러 가다 include ~을 포함하다 free 무료의 shipping 배송 distribution 유통, 배부 take care of ~을 처리하다 submit ~을 제출하다 reimbursement 비용 환급 request 요청(서)

Listen to a Conversation
13-14 대화를 들으시오.

> W: I noticed the Halloween decorations on the porch are still up. Weren't you planning to take them down?
> 현관에 할로윈 장식물이 여전히 서 있는 게 보였어. 치우려고 계획하지 않았어?

> M: I'm hosting a seminar this Friday, so I've been busy preparing. I'll do it over the weekend.
> 내가 이번 주 금요일에 세미나를 주최하기 때문에, 준비하느라 바빴어. 그건 주말 동안 할 거야.
>
> W: Well, I heard there's going to be a bad storm this Saturday. It's probably a good idea to get it done before then.
> 저기, 이번 주 토요일에 거센 폭풍우가 있을 거라고 하던데. 아마 그 전에 해 놓는 게 좋은 생각일 거야.
>
> M: Alright. I don't remember what the passcode for the outdoor storage shed is, though. I guess I'll have to call our landlord, Marie, since she's the one who made it.
> 알겠어. 그런데, 실외 보관 창고 비밀번호가 뭔지 기억이 나지 않아. 집주인인 마리 씨에게 전화해 봐야 할 것 같은데, 그분이 그걸 만드신 분이거든.

13 여자가 남자에게 주말 전에 일을 완료하도록 권하는 이유는?
(A) 세미나가 연기되었다.
(B) 시에서 새로운 규정을 만들었다.
(C) 토요일에 날씨가 좋지 않을 것이다.
(D) 두 사람이 토요일에 다른 지역으로 간다.

14 남자가 집주인과 관련해 말하는 것은?
(A) 집주인이 곧 건물을 방문할 예정이다.
(B) 집주인이 출입 코드를 설정했다.
(C) 집주인이 실외 용품을 주문했다.
(D) 집주인이 업체를 설립했다.

어휘 및 표현
notice (보거나 듣고) ~임을 알아차리다 decoration 장식(물) take down ~을 치우다 host ~을 주최하다 be busy -ing ~하느라 바쁘다 shed 창고, 헛간 landlord 집주인 postpone ~을 연기하다 regulation 규정, 규제 property 건물, 부동산 set up ~을 설정하다, ~을 설치하다 access 출입, 접근 place an order for ~을 주문하다 supplies 용품, 물품 establish ~을 설립하다

15-16 대화를 들으시오.

> M: I want to buy my mom a nice gift for Mother's Day. She likes candles, but I'm not sure which kind to get her.
> 어머니날에 엄마에게 멋진 선물을 사 드리고 싶어. 엄마가 양초를 좋아하시는데, 어떤 종류로 사 드려야 할지 잘 모르겠어.
>
> W: How about getting her an orange-scented one? She mentioned she likes citrus.
> 오렌지향이 나는 걸 사 드리는 건 어때? 감귤류를 좋아하신다고 하셨거든.
>
> M: Oh, good thinking. Do you have any brand recommendations?
> 오, 좋은 생각이야. 추천하는 브랜드라도 있어?
>
> W: Hmm… I believe Flame & Bath is really popular nowadays. You should look them up.
> 흠… 플레임 앤 배스가 요즘 정말 인기 있는 것 같아. 정보를 한번 찾아 봐.

M: OK. Thanks so much!
알겠어. 정말 고마워!

15 남자가 찾고 있는 것은?
(A) 꽃다발
(B) 탁상용 등
(C) 양초
(D) 핸드백

16 여자가 권하는 향은?
(A) 복숭아
(B) 코튼
(C) 레몬
(D) 오렌지

어휘 및 표현
A-scented A 향이 나는 citrus 감귤류 look up ~에 관한 정보를 찾아 보다

17-18 대화를 들으시오.

M: Did you see the new course they added for history majors this semester? It's called "The Global History of Immigration".
이번 학기에 역사 전공생들을 위해 추가한 새로운 강의 확인해 봤어? "세계 이민의 역사"라고 부르던데.

W: I heard about it but decided not to sign up. Did you get in?
그에 관한 얘기는 들었는데, 난 신청하지 않기로 결정했어. 넌 했어?

M: Yes, and the professor just sent out the syllabus. The readings look intriguing and seem to have a lot of diversity.
응. 그리고 담당 교수님께서 막 강의 계획서를 보내 주셨어. 읽기 자료가 아주 흥미로워 보이고 많은 다양성이 있는 것 같아.

W: That sounds fun! Maybe I should take that class the next time it gets offered.
재미있겠다! 아마 다음 번에 제공될 때 나도 그 수업을 들어야 할 것 같아.

17 남자가 언급하는 수업 종류는?
(A) 문학
(B) 역사학
(C) 철학
(D) 정치학

18 남자가 읽기 자료와 관련해 말하는 것은?
(A) 자극적이다.
(B) 고급 수준이다.

(C) 난해하다.
(D) 다양하다.

어휘 및 표현

add ~을 추가하다 semester 학기 immigration 이민, 이주 decide (not) to do ~하기로(하지 않기로) 결정하다 sign up 신청하다, 등록하다 syllabus 강의 계획서 intriguing 아주 흥미로운 diversity 다양성 stimulating 자극하는 advanced 고급의, 상급의 dense (글이) 난해한

Listen to an Announcement

19-20 대학교 동아리 모임에서 공지 사항을 들으시오.

> Welcome, everyone. Today, we're going to be talking about the professional development event for this semester. This time, we'll be hosting a panel discussion with experts from the engineering industry. Students of all majors are welcome. We'd like you all to recommend at least one potential guest speaker.
>
> 환영합니다, 여러분. 오늘, 우리는 이번 학기 전문 능력 개발 행사에 관해 이야기해 볼 예정입니다. 이번에, 우리가 엔지니어링 업계의 전문가들과 함께 하는 패널 토론회를 주최할 것입니다. 모든 전공 분야의 학생들을 환영합니다. 여러분 모두 최소 한 분의 잠재적인 초청 연사를 추천해 주셨으면 합니다.

19 공지의 주제는?
(A) 장기 자랑
(B) 지도 교수
(C) 특별 패널 행사
(D) 회원 모집 과정

20 학생들이 하도록 권장되는 것은?
(A) 연설문을 만드는 일
(B) 제안 사항을 제출하는 일
(C) 각자의 부모님을 초대하는 일
(D) 동아리 회비를 내는 일

어휘 및 표현

professional development 전문 능력 개발 semester 학기 host ~을 주최하다 expert 전문가 industry 업계, 산업 major 전공 (분야) at least 최소한, 적어도 potential 잠재적인 recruitment 모집 submit ~을 제출하다 suggestion 제안, 의견

21-22 대학교 동아리 모임에서 공지 사항을 들으시오.

> Welcome, everyone. I have some exciting news: our club will be holding a hiking trip next weekend! It'll be happening on Saturday at 9 A.M. We've decided on Mission Peak, which is great for beginners. If you'd like to come, please write your name on the sign-up sheet that's being passed around.

> 환영합니다, 여러분. 흥미로운 소식이 좀 있는데, 우리 동아리가 다음 주말에 하이킹 여행을 개최할 예정입니다! 이 여행은 토요일 오전 9시에 진행됩니다. 미션 피크에서 하기로 결정했는데, 이곳이 초보자들에게 아주 좋습니다. 오시고 싶으시면, 지금 돌리고 있는 신청 용지에 이름을 적어 주시기 바랍니다.

21 공지의 주제는?
(A) 인적 교류 행사
(B) 교육 워크숍
(C) 스포츠 토너먼트
(D) 야외 활동

22 학생들이 하도록 권장되는 것은?
(A) 조를 구성하는 일
(B) 양식을 가져가는 일
(C) 여행을 신청하는 일
(D) 초보자용 교육 영상 시청하는 일

어휘 및 표현

hold ~을 개최하다 decide on ~을 결정하다 sign-up 신청, 등록 pass around (여럿이 볼 수 있게) ~을 돌리다 networking 인적 교류 training 교육, 훈련 form 양식, 서식 sign up for ~을 신청하다, ~에 등록하다 tutorial (교육용) 영상, 설명서

23-24 대학교 행사에서 공지 사항을 들으시오.

> Good afternoon, everyone. We are excited to announce that the university's annual career fair will be happening next Wednesday from 10 A.M. to 5 P.M. at Gateway Plaza. Make sure to stop by and pick up a free canvas bag, too!
>
> 안녕하세요, 여러분. 우리 대학교의 연례 취업 박람회가 다음 수요일 오전 10시부터 오후 5시까지 게이트웨이 플라자에서 진행될 예정이라는 사실을 알려 드리게 되어 기쁩니다. 꼭 들러 보시고 무료 캔버스 가방도 받아가시기 바랍니다!

23 공지의 주제는?
(A) 다가오는 취업 박람회
(B) 신입생 오리엔테이션
(C) 강연 시리즈
(D) 공개 연설 대회

24 화자가 청자들이 하기를 바라는 것은?
(A) 몇몇 고용주들과 이야기하는 일
(B) 부스 한 곳을 방문하는 일
(C) 선물을 받는 일
(D) 티켓을 구입하는 일

어휘 및 표현

annual 연례적인, 해마다의 career fair 취업 박람회 make sure to do 꼭 ~하세요 stop by (잠깐) 들르다 pick up ~을 가져가다, ~을 가져오다 free 무료의 upcoming 다가오는, 곧 있을 public speaking 공개 연설, 대중 연설 employer 고용주

25-26 대학교 행사에서 공지 사항을 들으시오.

> Attention, everyone. I'm delighted to announce that the university's autumn music festival will be held next Friday from 7 P.M. to 11 P.M. in Aldridge Park. There will be live performances, food trucks, and merchandise giveaways. We hope you come and join the fun!
>
> 여러분께 알립니다. 우리 대학교의 가을 음악 축제가 다음 주 금요일 오후 7시부터 오후 11시까지 앨드리지 파크에서 개최될 것임을 알려 드리게 되어 기쁩니다. 라이브 공연과 푸드 트럭, 그리고 상품 증정 행사가 있을 것입니다. 오셔서 함께 즐기시기 바랍니다!

25 공지의 주제는?
(A) 기념일 축하 행사
(B) 계절 음악 축제
(C) 지역 퍼레이드
(D) 신작 영화 상영회

26 화자가 청자들이 하기를 바라는 것은?
(A) 한 가지 공연에 참가하는 일
(B) 경품 추첨 행사에 참가하는 일
(C) 친구들을 데리고 오는 일
(D) 축제에 참석하는 일

어휘 및 표현

hold ~을 개최하다 performance 공연, 연주(회) merchandise 상품 giveaway 증정(식) anniversary (해마다 돌아오는) 기념일 celebration 축하 행사, 기념 행사 screening 상영(회) participate in ~에 참가하다 raffle 경품 추첨 행사

Listen to an Academic Talk

27-30 역사학 수업에서의 강연을 들으시오.

> The Code of Hammurabi, created around 1750 BCE by King Hammurabi of Babylon, is one of the earliest and most influential written law codes in history. It was a monumental achievement that established a clear set of rules to govern daily life and reinforced the king's authority over his expanding empire.
>
> The Code outlined hundreds of laws addressing commerce, property, family relations, and criminal justice, many of which followed the principle of proportional punishment,

often described as "an eye for an eye." Central to the Code was the idea that justice should be guided by publicly available laws rather than by arbitrary decisions, a concept that would echo throughout later civilizations.

Although originally intended to bring order and unity to Hammurabi's realm, its influence spread well beyond Mesopotamia, shaping later traditions such as Mosaic Law in the Hebrew Bible. Over time, it has come to symbolize the beginnings of codified law and the enduring human search for fairness and order in society. Next, let's examine some of the key laws and consider where we see them today.

함무라비 법전은 바빌론의 함무라비 왕에 의해 기원전 1750년 무렵에 만들어진 것으로서, 역사상 가장 초기에 쓰여지고 가장 영향력 있는 성문 법전들 중 하나입니다. 이는 일상 생활을 통제하는 일련의 명확한 규칙을 확립하고 확장되는 제국에 대한 왕의 권위를 강화해 준 기념비적인 업적이었습니다.

함무라비 법전은 상업과 부동산, 친족 관계, 그리고 형사 사법을 다루는 수백 가지 법률의 윤곽을 그렸으며, 그 중 많은 것이 흔히 "눈에는 눈"으로 묘사되는, 비례 원칙 처벌의 원리를 따랐습니다. 이 법전의 중심을 이룬 아이디어는 정의가 자의적인 결정에 의한 것이 아니라 공적으로 이용 가능한 법률을 따라야 한다는 점이었으며, 이는 이후의 여러 문명 사회 전반에 걸쳐 반향을 일으키게 된 개념이었습니다.

원래 함무라비 왕국에 질서와 통합을 가져오기 위한 것이었지만, 그 영향력은 메소포타미아를 훨씬 더 뛰어넘어 확산되면서, 히브리어 성경에 나오는 모세의 율법 같은 이후의 전통을 형성했습니다. 시간이 흐르면서, 함무라비 법전은 성문화된 법률의 시초 및 사회 속의 공정성과 질서에 대한 인간의 끊임없는 추구를 상징하게 되었습니다. 다음으로, 몇몇 주요 법률의 일부를 살펴 보고 오늘날 어디에서 이 법률들이 보이는지 생각해 보겠습니다.

27 강연의 주제는?
(A) 바빌로니아 문화의 기원
(B) 제국 통치의 어려움
(C) 바빌론의 함무라비 왕이 이룬 업적
(D) 일련의 법률이 지닌 의의

28 화자의 말에 따르면, 함무라비 법전의 주요 개념은?
(A) 법률이 민간인에 의해 쓰여져야 한다.
(B) 사람들이 공정하게 판결받아야 한다.
(C) 발전된 사회에 복잡한 법률이 있다.
(D) 모든 행동에 결과가 따를 것이다.

29 화자가 모세의 율법을 언급하는 이유는?
(A) 다른 유사한 기념비적인 것의 예를 들기 위해
(B) 메소포타미아의 주요 정책을 설명하기 위해
(C) 함무라비 법전의 지속적인 영향력을 강조하기 위해
(D) 함무라비 법전에 대한 또 다른 용어를 확인하기 위해

30 화자가 다음에 논의할 것은?
(A) 공정하고 질서 있는 사회의 정의

(B) 현대에 잔존하는 함무라비 법전
(C) 바빌로니아 문헌을 해독하는 한 가지 방법
(D) 형사 사법 제도의 발전

어휘 및 표현

Code of Hammurabi 함무라비 법전 **influential** 영향력 있는 **monumental** 기념비적인 **achievement** 업적, 성취 **establish** ~을 확립하다 **govern** ~을 통치하다, ~을 다스리다(=rule) **reinforce** ~을 강화하다 **authority** 권위 **expanding** 확장되는 **empire** 제국 **outline** ~의 윤곽을 그리다, ~의 개요를 설명하다 **address** ~을 다루다 **property** 부동산, 건물 **criminal justice** 형사 사법 **principle** 원리, 원칙 **proportional punishment** 비례 원칙 처벌 **describe** ~을 묘사하다, ~을 설명하다 **publicly** 공적으로 **available** 이용 가능한 **arbitrary** 자의적인 **echo** 반향을 일으키다 **civilization** 문명 (사회) **intended to do** ~하기 위한, ~하려는 의도인 **order** 질서 **unity** 통합 **realm** 왕국, 영역 **spread** 확산되다 **shape** ~을 형성하다 **tradition** 전통 **Mosaic Law** 모세의 율법 **Hebrew Bible** 히브리어 성경 **come to do** ~하게 되다 **symbolize** ~을 상징하다 **codified** 성문화된 **enduring** 끊임없는 **origin** 기원, 유래 **significance** 의의, 중요성 **civilian** 민간인 **judge** ~을 판결하다 **advanced** 발전된 **complex** 복잡한 **consequence** 결과 **monument** 기념비(적인 것) **policy** 정책 **emphasize** ~을 강조하다 **impact** 영향(력) **identify** ~을 확인하다 **term** 용어 **definition** (말 등의) 정의 **remnant** 잔존(하는 것), 나머지 **method** 방법 **decode** ~을 해독하다 **text** 문헌, 문서

TEST 1
Listening Module 2

정답

Listen and Choose a Response
1-3 (C), (D), (C)

Listen to a Conversation
4-5 (B), (B)
6-7 (A), (D)

Listen to an Academic Talk
8-11 (C), (D), (D), (A)
12-15 (B), (C), (D), (A)

스크립트/해석/어휘

Listen and Choose a Response

1-3 가장 적절한 응답을 고르시오.

1 Did you use my notebook?
내 노트북 썼어?
(A) 일주일에 한두 번.
(B) 난 펜을 갖고 있지 않아.
(C) 몇 분 동안만.
(D) 출판사야.

2 Do you prefer studying alone or in a group?
넌 혼자 공부하는 게 더 좋아, 아니면 그룹으로 하는 게 더 좋아?
(A) 그녀가 함께 할 수 있을지 내 친구가 물어 보고 있어.
(B) 그 그룹 프로젝트는 잘 진행됐어.
(C) 스터디룸 예약은 무료야.
(D) 혼자일 때 덜 시끄러워.

3 Do you approve of the manager's decision?
부장님의 결정에 찬성하세요?
(A) 아뇨, 그게 전보다 더 좋습니다.
(B) 영수증을 제출하시는 것도 잊지 마세요.
(C) 저는 완전히 동의하는 건 아니에요.
(D) 그 협상은 한 시간이 걸렸습니다.

어휘 및 표현
publication 출판(물) ask if ~인지 묻다 join 함께 하다, 합류하다 go well 잘 진행되다 free 무료의 reserve ~을 예약하다 approve of ~에 찬성하다 submit ~을 제출하다 receipt 영수(증) totally 완전히, 전적으로 on board 동의하는, 한 배를 탄, 탑승한 negotiation 협상

Listen to a Conversation
4-5 대화를 들으시오.

> M: Hey, Megan, are you going to swing by the post office today?
> 안녕, 메건, 오늘 우체국에 잠깐 들를 예정이니?
>
> W: Yes, but I'm still waiting to receive documents from our legal team. They're taking longer than they promised, so I'll probably head out after lunch.
> 응, 하지만 여전히 우리 법무팀으로부터 문서를 받으려고 기다리는 중이야. 그쪽에서 약속한 것보다 더 오래 걸리고 있어서, 아마 점심 시간 후에 나갈 거야.
>
> M: I actually have a package to send as well. Do you think you could drop it off for me? I don't have time to deal with the long lines over there today.
> 나도 사실 보내야 하는 소포가 있어. 나 대신 갖다 줄 수 있니? 내가 오늘 거기 가서 긴 대기줄을 감당할 시간이 없어서.
>
> W: Well, I was assigned to go, and I'm free for most of the day, so sure. You can give me the package now.
> 저기, 내가 가는 것으로 배정되었고, 오늘 대부분 시간이 있으니까, 좋아. 지금 그 소포를 주면 돼.
>
> M: Thanks so much.
> 정말 고마워.

4 여자가 점심 식사 후 우체국에 가려는 이유는?
(A) 다른 팀 구성원들과 함께 갈 계획이다.
(B) 먼저 일부 문서를 받아야 한다.
(C) 우체국이 오직 예약만 받는다.
(D) 우체국이 특정 요일에 늦게 연다.

5 우체국에 가는 것에 대한 남자의 태도는?
(A) 그것에 대해 열성적이다.
(B) 그곳에서 기다리기엔 너무 바쁘다.
(C) 그것에 대한 경험이 많지 않다.
(D) 처음으로 혼자 가는 것을 기대하고 있다.

어휘 및 표현
swing by ~에 잠깐 들르다 receive ~을 받다 legal 법률과 관련된, 합법적인 take long 오래 걸리다 promise 약속하다 head out 밖으로 나가다, 밖으로 향하다 as well ~도, 또한 drop off ~을 갖다 놓다 deal with ~을 감당하다, ~에 대처하다 be assigned to do ~하도록 배정되다 reservation 예약 certain 특정한, 일정한 attitude 태도 enthusiastic 열성적인 look forward to -ing ~하기를 기대하다 by oneself 혼자, 스스로

6-7 대화를 들으시오.

M: So, are we still hiring for the graphic designer position?
자, 우리가 여전히 그래픽 디자이너 직책에 대해 채용 중인가요?

W: Yes, we are. The interview that was supposed to happen today fell through, so we're still looking.
네, 그렇습니다. 오늘 진행하기로 되어 있었던 면접이 무산되어서, 여전히 사람을 찾고 있습니다.

M: That's a bummer. I was excited to work with that candidate because she had a really strong portfolio.
아쉽네요. 저는 그 지원자와 함께 일하기를 기대했는데, 그분이 정말 뛰어난 포트폴리오를 지니고 있었거든요.

W: I know, right? Apparently, another company offered her a more competitive salary, so she decided to accept the offer.
그러시겠죠? 보니까, 다른 회사에서 그분에게 더 경쟁력 있는 연봉을 제안했기 때문에, 그 제안을 받아들이기로 결정하신 것 같아요.

M: Wow. I hope we can find someone fast because I really need a nice poster design for the huge corporate event my team is planning this summer.
와우. 저는 우리가 사람을 빨리 찾기를 바라는데, 저희 팀이 이번 여름에 계획 중인 대규모 기업 행사를 위해 멋진 포스터 디자인이 정말 필요하기 때문입니다.

6 화자들이 주로 논의하는 것은?
(A) 충원되지 않은 직책
(B) 한 가지 혁신적인 디자인
(C) 채용 과정에 대한 몇몇 변경 사항
(D) 한 지원서의 몇몇 특징

7 남자가 근무하고 있을 것 같은 회사 부서는?
(A) 인사
(B) 재무
(C) 그래픽 디자인
(D) 행사 기획

어휘 및 표현
hire 채용하다 be supposed to do ~하기로 되어 있다 fall through 무산되다 that's a bummer 아쉽네요, 안타깝네요 candidate 지원자, 후보자 portfolio 포트폴리오(구직 시 제출하는 자료집) apparently 보아하니, 듣자하니 competitive 경쟁력 있는 accept ~을 받아들이다 corporate 기업의

Listen to an Academic Talk
8-11 역사학 수업에서의 강연을 들으시오.

The Indus Valley, located in present-day Pakistan and northwest India, was home to one of the earliest urban civilizations in world history. This region was not just a collection of farming villages, but a network of carefully planned cities that flourished between

2600 and 1900 BCE. These cities were remarkable for their layout and infrastructure: they featured straight streets laid out on a grid, multi-storied houses made of uniform baked bricks, and advanced drainage systems that were far ahead of their time.

Agriculture along the Indus River supported wheat, barley, and cotton production, while craft industries produced beads, pottery, and textiles. Trade links extended as far as Mesopotamia, which we know because of the Indus seals discovered in cities like Uruk and Kish. These seals, made of soft stone, were likely used to mark goods or validate transactions between the two regions. Even to this day, the writing system of the Indus Valley remains a mystery, leaving many details of their culture unknown. The materials that do remain, however, make it clear that the Indus Valley supported one of the world's first complex societies. Next, we'll discuss how the Indus Valley civilization shaped the emergence of later cultures in South Asia.

현재의 파키스탄과 인도 북서부 지역에 위치한, 인더스 밸리는 세계사에서 가장 초기의 도시 문명 사회들 중 한 곳의 발상지였습니다. 이 지역은 단순히 농촌 마을들이 모여 있던 곳이 아니라, 기원전 2600년에서 1900년 사이에 번성했던 신중히 계획된 도시의 네트워크였습니다. 이 도시들은 그 배치와 기반 시설로 인해 주목할 만했으며, 균일하게 구워 낸 벽돌로 만든 격자 구조의 다층 주택들이 있는 곳에 펼쳐진 곧은 거리들, 그리고 당시에 한참 앞서 갔던 진보한 배수 시스템을 특징으로 했습니다.

인더스 강을 따라 농업은 밀과 보리, 그리고 면화 생산을 뒷받침했으며, 수공예 산업은 구슬과 도자기, 그리고 직물을 생산했습니다. 무역 연결망은 멀리 메소포타미아까지 이어져 있었으며, 이는 우리가 우루크와 키시 같은 도시에서 발견된 인더스 인장 때문에 알고 있습니다. 이 인장들은, 부드러운 돌로 만들어진 것으로서, 아마 상품을 표시하거나 그 두 지역들 사이의 거래를 인증하기 위해 사용되었을 것입니다. 심지어 오늘날에도, 인더스 밸리의 문자 체계는 여전히 불가사의로 남아 있어서, 그곳 문화의 많은 세부 요소가 알려지지 않은 상태입니다. 하지만, 분명히 남아 있는 물품들을 보면 인더스 밸리가 세계 최초의 복잡한 사회들 중 하나를 지탱했다는 사실이 명확해집니다. 다음으로, 인더스 밸리 문명이 어떻게 남아시아 지역에서 이후 문화들의 출현을 형성했는지 이야기해 보겠습니다.

8 인더스 밸리의 중요한 특징은?
(A) 풍요롭고 비옥한 농지로 알려져 있었다.
(B) 인도의 한 원주민 부족에 의해 확립되었다.
(C) 서로 연결된 도시들로 구성되어 있었다.
(D) 기반 시설이 바다의 영향을 크게 받았다.

9 화자의 말에 따르면, 다음 중 ~을 제외하고 모든 것이 인더스 밸리에 존재했다.
(A) 다층 주택
(B) 수공예품의 생산
(C) 다른 지역들과의 무역
(D) 상수도 시스템

10 화자가 우르크와 키시를 언급하는 이유는?
(A) 많은 사람들이 인더스 밸리에서 메소포타미아로 이주했음을 시사하기 위해
(B) 인더스 인장이 어떻게 아시아 전 지역에 걸쳐 사용되었는지 설명하기 위해
(C) 유명한 인더스 밸리 도시들의 예시를 제공하기 위해

(D) 인더스 밸리 무역로의 규모를 강조하기 위해

11 화자가 다음에 논의할 가능성이 가장 높은 것은?
(A) 인더스 밸리 문명이 남아시아 문화에 미친 영향
(B) 인더스 밸리 지역 내 새로운 무역로의 건설
(C) 인더스 강의 변모
(D) 메소포타미아 문명의 기원

어휘 및 표현

present-day 현재의　**urban** 도시의　**civilization** 문명 (사회)　**region** 지역　**flourish** 번성하다　**remarkable** 주목할 만한　**layout** 배치, 구획　**infrastructure** (사회) 기반 시설　**feature** ~을 특징으로 하다　**laid out** 펼쳐진　**grid** 격자 무늬　**multi-storied** 다층의　**uniform** 균일한, 획일적인　**advanced** 진보한, 발전된　**drainage** 배수　**far ahead of** ~을 한참 앞선　**craft industry** 수공예 산업　**trade links** 무역 연결망　**extend** 이어지다, 확장되다　**seal** 인장　**discover** ~을 발견하다　**made of** ~으로 만들어진　**mark** ~을 표시하다　**goods** 상품　**validate** ~을 인증하다　**transaction** 거래　**to this day** 오늘날에도　**details** 세부 요소, 상세 정보　**material** 물품, 재료　**remain** 남아 있다　**complex** 복잡한　**shape** ~을 형성하다　**emergence** 출현　**fertile** 비옥한　**establish** ~을 확립하다　**tribe** 부족　**interconnected** 서로 연결된　**influence** ~에 영향을 미치다　**illustrate** ~을 설명하다　**highlight** ~을 강조하다　**extent** 규모, 정도　**impact of A on B** A가 B에 미치는 영향　**transformation** 변모, 탈바꿈　**origin** 기원, 유래

12-15 문학 수업에서의 강연을 들으시오.

Stream of consciousness is a narrative method that aims to capture a character's thoughts as they naturally unfold, often in a loose, flowing, and sometimes fragmented way. Unlike traditional storytelling, this technique avoids clear structure and linear order, blending memories, emotions, and observations into a continuous stream that mirrors how the mind actually works. A well-known example is Virginia Woolf's novel *Mrs. Dalloway*. In this book, the characters' inner thoughts shift rapidly, such as recalling childhood moments while walking through London or jumping from one idea to another without warning. These mental transitions are presented without explanation or commentary, and this is a signature of the style. Stream of consciousness allows writers to explore the complexity of human thought, touching on themes like time, identity, and emotional depth. The lack of clear boundaries gives readers a more intimate and realistic view of the character's inner world, often making the experience feel personal and immersive. Next, we'll try mapping out a character's thoughts to see how this technique works in practice.

의식의 흐름은 등장인물의 생각이 자연스럽게 전개되는 과정에서 흔히 느슨하면서 물 흐르는 듯하게, 그리고 때로는 단편적인 방식으로 그 생각을 담아내는 것을 목표로 하는 서술 방법입니다. 전통적인 이야기 전달 방식과 달리, 이 기법은 명확한 구조와 선형적인 순서를 피하면서, 기억과 감정, 그리고 관찰 내용을 마음이 실제로 어떻게 작용하는지 비춰 주는 연속적인 흐름으로 어우러지게 합니다. 잘 알려진 예시가 버지니아 울프의 소설 <댈러웨이 부인>입니다. 이 책에서, 등장인물이 지닌 내면의 생각이 어린 시절의 순간들을 회상하는 것과 같이, 빠르게 변화하는 동안 런던 곳곳을 걸어 다니거나 예고 없이 한 가지 생각에서 다른 것으로 넘나들게 됩니다. 이런 심리적 전환은 설명이나 해설 없이 제시되며, 이것이 이 문체의 대표적인 특징입니다. 의식의 흐름은 작가들에게 인간의 생각이 지닌 복잡성을 탐구하면서, 시간과 정체성, 그리고 감정적 깊이 같은 주제들을 다룰 수 있게 해 줍니다.

명확한 경계의 부족이 독자들에게 등장인물의 내면 세계에 대해 더욱 친밀하고 현실적인 관점을 제공해 주어, 흔히 그 경험이 직접적이고 몰입적으로 느껴지도록 만들어 줍니다. 다음으로, 이 기법이 실제로 어떻게 작용하는지 알아 보기 위해 한 등장인물의 생각을 한번 구체적으로 정리해 보겠습니다.

12 강연의 주된 내용은?
(A) 고전 소설
(B) 이야기 전달 방식
(C) 감정에 관한 관찰
(D) 심리 과정에 관한 연구

13 화자가 소설 속 등장인물들이 지닌 내면의 생각을 언급한 이유는?
(A) 어린 시절의 기억이 소설 속에서 얼마나 중요한지 강조하기 위해
(B) 그 소설의 주제를 짚어 주기 위해
(C) 생각의 연속적인 흐름이 그 소설 속에서 어떻게 제시되는지 설명하기 위해
(D) 런던이 그 소설의 주된 배경임을 나타내기 위해

14 화자의 말에 따르면, 의식의 흐름이 지닌 대표적인 특징은?
(A) 흔치 않은 방식으로 등장인물의 추론 내용을 제시하는 것
(B) 생생한 심상을 이용해 과거의 사건들을 설명하는 것
(C) 내면의 대화를 담은 다수의 단락을 제공하는 것
(D) 추가적인 해설 없이 심리적 변화를 묘사하는 것

15 화자가 버지니아 울프 같은 작가들의 목표에 대해 암시하는 것은?
(A) 독서 경험을 몰입적으로 느끼도록 만드는 것
(B) 심리학이 어떻게 문학에 영향을 미치는지 관찰하는 것
(C) 혁신적인 서술 기법을 개발하는 것
(D) 생각을 불러일으키는 소설 작품을 만들어 내는 것

어휘 및 표현

stream of consciousness 의식의 흐름 **narrative method** 서술 방법 **aim to do** ~하는 것을 목표로 하다 **capture** (글, 그림, 사진 등으로) ~을 담아내다 **unfold** 전개되다 **loose** 느슨한 **flowing** 물 흐르는 듯한 **fragmented** 단편적인 **traditional** 전통적인 **linear order** 선형적인 순서 **blend A into B** A를 B와 어우러지게 하다 **observation** 관찰(한 것) **continuous stream** 연속적인 흐름 **mirror** ~을 비추다 **inner** 내면의 **shift** 변화하다, 바뀌다, 변화 **recall** ~을 회상하다 **transition** 전환 **present** ~을 제시하다 **explanation** 설명 **commentary** 해설 **signature** 대표적인 특징 **explore** ~을 탐구하다 **complexity** 복잡성 **touch on** ~을 다루다 **identity** 정체성 **lack** 부족 **boundary** 경계 **intimate** 친밀한 **immersive** 몰입하는 **map out** ~을 구체적으로 정리하다 **in practice** 실제로 **process** 과정 **emphasize** ~을 강조하다 **point out** ~을 짚어 주다, ~을 지적하다 **depict** ~을 설명하다, ~을 묘사하다 **primary** 주된 **reasoning** 추론, 추리 **unusual** 흔치 않은 **illustrate** ~을 설명하다, ~을 보여 주다 **vivid** 생생한 **imagery** 심상 **observe** ~을 관찰하다 **psychology** 심리학 **influence** ~에 영향을 미치다 **innovative** 혁신적인 **thought-provoking** 생각을 불러일으키는

Writing

정답 및 모범답안

Build a Sentence

1 Is this the most recent version of the poster?
2 Which building in the city are you planning to rent?
3 He was wondering if the tickets were sold out.
4 What type of art interests you the most?
5 I couldn't remember which issue was the most urgent.
6 Yes. She wanted to hear what I thought about the new trainee.
7 She showed me what I missed on the test.
8 Have you heard any news about when it will start?
9 On which website were you able to download the file?
10 We just learned where the files are usually kept.

Write an Email

Dear Manager,

I hope this message finds you well.

I am writing to provide feedback on our recent company dinner at Urban Kitchen. We had reserved the banquet room for about 20 people to celebrate our company's fifth anniversary and were excited to enjoy the evening together. While the elegant décor and calming music created a pleasant atmosphere, we experienced issues with the service. Our server was unaware of our reservation and made errors while taking our orders. The food, however, was delicious and enjoyable. I suggest additional training for your front-of-house staff to ensure that the service lives up to the reputation of your restaurant.

I look forward to your response.

Best regards,
Vanessa Lee

Write for an Academic Discussion

Even though Kevin makes a valid point regarding communication problems, I think the advantages of remote work will lead to more companies and employees adopting it in the future. First, remote work can reduce companies' operational costs, including office maintenance and utilities. It can also give companies access to a larger talent pool, allowing them to hire employees from anywhere, not just their local area. Second, it helps employees save money by reducing transportation expenses and allowing them to live away from expensive metropolitan areas. In addition, working from home can improve employees' work-life balance by giving them more control over their schedules. Therefore, companies should allow employees to work from home whenever possible, as it benefits both the organization and its workers.

해석/어휘

Build a Sentence

1-10 적절한 문장을 만드시오.

1 W: 네가 부탁한 파일이야.
　　M: 이 포스터가 최신 버전이니?

2 M: 나 내년에 빵집 열려고 해.
　　W: 도시에서 어떤 건물을 임차할 생각이야?

3 W: 폴이 네가 다녀온 음악 축제와 관련해 무엇을 물었니?
　　M: 티켓이 다 매진됐는지 궁금해하더라.

4 M: 나 미술 수업 신청했어.
　　W: 넌 어떤 유형의 미술에 제일 관심 있어?

5 W: 넌 IT 부서에서 어떤 도움이 필요했어?
　　M: 어떤 문제가 제일 급했는지 기억이 나지 않았어.

6 M: 너 미란다랑 점심 같이 먹었어?
　　W: 응, 신입사원에 대해 내 생각이 어떤지 듣고 싶어 했어.

7 M: 잰슨 선생님이 수업 끝날 때 뭐 보여주셨어?
　　W: 내가 시험에서 놓친 부분을 보여주셨어.

8 W: 아까 누가 그 기념식이 연기됐다고 하던데.
　　M: 언제 시작할지 소식 들은 거 있어?

9 W: 우리 교재를 무료로 온라인에서 찾았어.
　　W: 어느 사이트에서 파일을 받을 수 있었어?

10 M: 너와 제프는 왜 아직 양식 제출 안 했어?
　　 M: 이제야 서류가 보통 어디에 보관되는지 알았거든.

어휘 및 표현

wonder if ~인지 궁금하다　be sold out 매진이다　sign up for ~을 등록하다　department 부서　urgent 급한
new trainee 신입사원　postpone ~을 연기하다　textbook 교재　for free 무료로　submit ~을 제출하다

Write an Email

당신의 회사는 최근 특별한 행사를 기념하기 위해 한 레스토랑에서 저녁 만찬을 개최했다. 당신과 당신의 동료들은 음식은 만족스러웠으나 직원들의 서비스는 매우 불만족스러웠다. 당신은 회사를 대신하여 해당 레스토랑에 연락해야 한다.

레스토랑 매니저에게 이메일을 작성하시오.
이메일에서 다음을 수행하시오:

- 회사 기념 행사에 대해 서술하시오.
- 레스토랑의 장점과 단점을 설명하시오.
- 매니저가 향후 서비스를 개선할 수 있는 방안을 제안하시오.

완전한 문장으로 가능한 한 많이 작성하시오.

당신의 답변:

수신인: manager@urbankitchenrestaurant.com
제목: 레스토랑 서비스에 대한 피드백

매니저께,

저는 이 메시지가 당신께 잘 전달되길 바랍니다.

최근 어반 키친에서 진행한 회사 만찬에 대한 피드백을 드리기 위해 이메일을 씁니다. 저희는 회사 창립 5주년을 기념하기 위해 약 20명을 위한 연회실을 예약했으며, 함께 즐거운 저녁을 보낼 수 있을 것이라 기대했습니다. 우아한 인테리어와 차분한 음악이 편안한 분위기를 조성했지만, 서비스에서 문제를 겪었습니다. 담당 서버가 저희 예약 사실을 인지하지 못했으며 주문 접수 시 실수를 저질렀습니다. 다만, 음식은 맛있고 만족스러웠습니다. 레스토랑의 명성에 걸맞은 서비스를 제공하기 위해 프론트 직원들에 대한 추가 교육을 제안합니다.

당신의 답변을 기대하겠습니다.

안녕히 계세요,
바네사 리

(116 단어)

어휘 및 표현

banquet room 연회실 **celebrate** ~을 축하하다 **elegant** 우아한 **décor** 인테리어 **calming** 차분한 **pleasant** 편안한 **atmosphere** 분위기 **experience** 경험하다 **unaware of** ~을 인지하지 못하는 **reservation** 예약 **live up to** ~에 걸맞다 **reputation** 명성 **front-of-house staff** 손님 담당 업무 직원

Write for an Academic Discussion

교수가 경영학 수업을 진행 중이다. 교수의 질문에 답변하는 게시글을 작성하시오.

답변에서는 다음을 수행해야 한다:
- 본인의 의견을 제시하고 뒷받침하시오.
- 토론에 본인의 표현으로 기여하시오.

효과적인 답변은 최소 100단어 이상이어야 한다.

리 박사: 지난 몇 차례 수업 동안, 우리는 원격 근무 개념에 대해 논의해 왔습니다. 일부는 재택근무가 회사와 직원 모두에게 이익이 되므로 재택근무 직원 수가 증가할 것이라고 주장합니다. 다른 이들은 원격 근무 도입의 어려움은 보편적 관행이 되는 것을 막을 것이라고 믿습니다. 이에 대한 당신의 생각은 무엇입니까?

클레어: 제 생각에, 원격 근무가 더 보편화될 것입니다. 직원들은 재택 근무 시 생산성이 더 높다고 보고했습니다. 이는 회사에서는 동료들과의 의미 없는 대화 등 업무 시간을 빼앗는 방해 요소가 많기 때문일 수 있습니다.

케빈: 원격 근무에는 몇 가지 장점이 있지만, 의사소통 문제가 확산을 가로막을 것 같습니다. 제 경험상, 대면 회의가 온라인 회의보다 효과적입니다. 직접 만나면 논의에 훨씬 더 집중하기 쉽습니다.

케빈이 의사소통 문제에 대해 타당한 지적을 했지만, 저는 원격 근무의 장점 덕분에 앞으로 더 많은 기업과 직원들이 이를 채택할 것이라고 생각합니다. 첫째, 원격 근무는 사무실 유지 관리 및 공과금을 포함한 기업의 운영 비용을 절감할 수 있습니다. 또한 기업이 더 넓은 인재 풀에 접근할 수 있게 하여 지역 내뿐만 아니라 어디서나 직원을 채용할 수 있게 합니다. 둘째, 직원들은 교통비를 절감하고 비싼 대도시 지역에서 벗어나 거주할 수 있어 돈을 절약할 수 있습니다. 게다가, 재택근무는 직원들이 자신의 일정을 더 자유롭게 관리할 수 있게 함으로써 업무와 삶의 균형을 개선할 수 있습니다. 그러므로, 기업은 가능한 한 직원들이 재택근무를 할 수 있도록 허용해야 하며, 이는 조직과 근로자 모두에게 이익이 됩니다.

(123 단어)

어휘 및 표현

remote work 원격 근무 **working from home** 재택근무 **implement** ~을 시행하다, 도입하다 **widespread** 널리 퍼진 **distraction** 주의 산만 **engage in** ~에 관여하다 **meaningless** 무의미한 **in person** 직접 **face-to-face** 대면 **maintenance** 유지 관리 **utilities** 공과금 **talent** 인재 **expense** 비용 **metropolitan** 대도시의

TEST 1

Speaking

정답 및 모범답안

Listen and Repeat

1 The locker rooms are over there.
2 Towels are provided at the front desk.
3 It's a good idea to stretch before your workout.
4 You can fill your water bottle at the water dispenser.
5 Don't forget to cool down for at least five minutes after training.
6 Please return all borrowed equipment to its proper place after every use.
7 Check out the calendar for upcoming fitness classes, many of which are free of charge.

Take an Interview

8 *Thank you for taking part in this study. Today, I'd like to ask you some questions about social media. Which social media platform do you use the most?*

I am active on several social media platforms, but the one I use most often is Instagram. I find it to be the easiest platform to catch up on what my friends are doing and interact with them through posts and messages. I also enjoy watching short, entertaining videos that help me relax after a long day. Sometimes, I even shop through Instagram when I find interesting products. Overall, I find myself spending time on Instagram the most.

9 *I see. When you are using social media, do you prefer to browse or actively create your own posts?*

While I like to do both, my preference is browsing on social media rather than creating my own posts. This is because making posts takes a lot of effort and planning. One experience that comes to mind is when I posted my vacation photos on Instagram. I spent a long time selecting and editing the pictures and coming up with captions. In contrast, browsing is much more relaxing. All in all, I enjoy browsing on social media more than posting my own content.

10 *Interesting. Next, I'd like to get your opinion. In recent years, social media addiction has become a serious problem, especially among younger people. Do you think this issue will become even more serious in the future? Why or why not?*

It is likely that social media addiction will become even more serious among younger people in the future. The main reason is that since technology is now accessible to people at a younger age, many begin using social media very early. Because their brains are still developing, early exposure increases the risk of dependence later in life. Additionally, social media platforms are designed to keep users engaged, making younger people even more susceptible. In summary, I believe addiction to social media will continue to grow.

11 *Good points. I just have one more question. Some people believe that social media is essential for helping people stay connected. Do you agree or disagree with this idea? Explain why you think so.*

I disagree with the statement that social media is essential for people to keep in touch. While it has its merits, I believe it cannot replace meeting someone in person. An occasion I clearly remember is when I met a close friend after five years. We often talked through social media, but when we finally met, it felt much more meaningful. Talking face-to-face allowed us to share emotions that messages could not express. In conclusion, I think that real connections happen offline.

해석/어휘

Listen and Repeat

당신은 헬스장에서 회원들을 돕는 훈련을 받고 있다. 트레이너의 말을 듣고 따라 하시오. 오직 한 번만 따라 하시오.

1 탈의실은 저쪽에 있습니다.

2 수건은 안내 데스크에서 제공됩니다.

3 운동 전에 스트레칭을 하는 것이 좋습니다.

4 정수기에서 물병을 채울 수 있습니다.

5 운동 후에 최소 5분 이상 쿨다운하는 것을 잊지 마세요.

6 사용한 대여 장비는 매번 사용 후 제자리에 반납해 주세요.

7 다가오는 피트니스 수업 일정을 확인하세요. 많은 수업이 무료로 제공됩니다.

어휘 및 표현
locker room 탈의실 **workout** 운동 **water dispenser** 정수기, 급수기 **cool down** 쿨다운하다, 식히다 **proper place** 제자리

Take an Interview

당신은 소셜 미디어에 대한 연구 조사에 참여하기로 동의하였다. 당신은 연구원과 간단한 온라인 인터뷰를 진행하게 된다. 연구원이 몇 가지 질문을 할 것이다.

8 이 연구에 참여해 주셔서 감사합니다. 오늘, 저는 소셜 미디어에 관한 몇 가지 질문을 드리겠습니다. 가장 자주 사용하는 소셜 미디어 플랫폼은 무엇인가요?

저는 여러 소셜 미디어 플랫폼을 사용하지만, 그중에서 가장 자주 사용하는 것은 인스타그램입니다. 인스타그램은 친구들이 무엇을 하고 있는지 가장 쉽게 알아내고, 게시물이나 메시지를 통해 소통할 수 있는 플랫폼이라고 생각합니다. 또, 하루를 마치고 짧고 재미있는 영상을 보면서 휴식을 취하는 것도 즐깁니다. 가끔 흥미로운 상품을 발견하면 인스타그램을 통해 쇼핑을 하기도 합니다. 전반적으로, 저는 인스타그램에서

가장 많은 시간을 보내는 것 같습니다.

9 그렇군요. 소셜 미디어를 사용할 때 다른 사람의 게시물을 둘러보는 것과 능동적으로 자신의 게시물을 올리는 것 중 어떤 걸 더 선호하나요?

저는 두 가지 모두 좋아하지만, 제 게시물을 올리는 것보다 둘러보는 것을 더 선호합니다. 게시물을 만드는 데는 많은 노력과 계획이 필요하기 때문입니다. 생각나는 한 경험은, 제가 인스타그램에 여행 사진을 올렸을 때입니다. 사진을 고르고 편집하고 캡션을 생각하는 데 꽤 오랜 시간이 걸렸습니다. 반면, 둘러보는 것은 훨씬 더 편안합니다. 전체적으로, 저는 직접 게시물을 올리는 것보다 다른 사람들의 게시물을 보는 것을 더 즐깁니다.

10 흥미롭네요. 다음으로, 당신의 의견을 듣고 싶습니다. 최근 몇 년간 소셜 미디어 중독이 특히 젊은 세대 사이에서 심각한 문제로 떠오르고 있습니다. 앞으로 이 문제가 더 심각해질 것이라고 생각하나요? 이유는요?

저는 앞으로 젊은 세대 사이에서 소셜 미디어 중독이 더 심각해질 가능성이 높다고 생각합니다. 그 주된 이유는 요즘 기술 접근 연령이 점점 낮아지고 있어, 많은 아이들이 매우 어린 나이에 소셜 미디어를 사용하기 시작하기 때문입니다. 뇌가 아직 발달 중인 시기에 이런 플랫폼에 노출되면, 이후 의존 위험이 더 높아집니다. 게다가, 소셜 미디어 플랫폼 자체가 사용자들이 오래 머무르게끔 설계되어 있기 때문에 젊은 세대가 더욱 취약할 수밖에 없습니다. 요약하자면, 소셜 미디어 중독은 앞으로도 계속 증가할 것이라고 생각합니다.

11 좋은 지적이에요. 마지막으로 한 가지 질문만 더 하겠습니다. 어떤 사람들은 소셜 미디어가 사람들 간의 연결을 유지하는 데 꼭 필요하다고 믿습니다. 이에 대해 동의하나요, 아니면 반대하나요? 그 이유를 설명해주세요.

저는 사람들이 관계를 유지하는 데 소셜 미디어가 꼭 필요하다고 생각하지 않습니다. 소셜 미디어에도 장점은 있지만, 직접 만나는 것을 대체할 수는 없다고 믿습니다. 제가 분명히 기억하는 한 일화는, 5년 만에 친한 친구를 직접 만났을 때입니다. 우리는 소셜 미디어를 통해 자주 대화를 나눴지만, 실제로 만나니 훨씬 더 의미 있게 느껴졌습니다. 얼굴을 맞대고 이야기할 때는 메시지로는 전달되지 않는 감정을 공유할 수 있었기 때문입니다. 결론적으로, 진정한 연결은 온라인이 아니라 오프라인에서 이루어진다고 생각합니다.

어휘 및 표현

catch up on ~을 따라잡다, ~을 알아내다 post 게시물 come up with ~을 생각해내다, 내놓다 caption 캡션, 이미지 설명 addiction 중독 exposure 노출 dependence 의존 engaged 사로잡힌 susceptible 민감한, 취약한 merit 장점 in person 직접 emotion 감정

TEST 2
Reading Module 1

정답

Complete the Words
1-10 ple, n, king, erns, ars, ved, atic, ing, els, nces

Read in Daily Life
11-12 (B), (A)
13-15 (D), (C), (D)

Read an Academic Passage
16-20 (B), (B), (D), (C), (B)

해석/어휘

Complete the Words
1-10 다음 문단에서 빠진 글자를 채우시오.

> 밤하늘에 대한 초기의 관찰은 천문학의 토대를 마련해 주고, 인류가 우주를 이해해 온 방식을 형성해 주었다. 처음에, 사람들은 육안 추적 방식과 별들이 지닌 패턴에 의존했으며, 이는 행성 모형들을 이용한 체계적인 지도 제작으로 진화했다. 결국, 학자들이 천체 현상들에 대한 예측을 개선하고 현대 천체물리학의 기틀을 마련하는 과정에서 망원경 및 측정 기술의 발전이 이해를 가속화했다. 이러한 발전상은 행성의 움직임에 대한 지식을 깊이 있게 만들어 주고, 여러 문화에 걸친 아이디어들을 연결해 주었으며, 우주 탐사의 진화를 이끌어 주었다.

어휘 및 표현

observation 관찰 **lay the foundation for** ~의 토대를 마련하다 **astronomy** 천문학 **shape** ~을 형성하다 **cosmos** 우주 **initially** 처음에 **rely on** ~에 의존하다 **naked-eye** 육안의 **tracking** 추적, 파악 **evolve into** ~로 진화하다 **mapping** 지도 제작 **planetary** 행성의 **eventually** 결국, 마침내 **advance** 발전, 진보 **telescope** 망원경 **measurement** 측정 **accelerate** ~을 가속화하다 **scholar** 학자 **refine** ~을 개선하다 **prediction** 예측 **celestial** 천체의 **framework** 기틀, 뼈대 **astrophysics** 천체물리학 **deepen** ~을 깊이 있게 하다 **exploration** 탐사, 탐험

Read in Daily Life
11-12 이메일을 읽으시오.

> 제목: 추천서 요청
>
> 성 교수님께,
>
> 인턴십 프로그램에 필요한 추천서를 정중히 요청 드리기 위해 이메일을 씁니다. 교수님의 강의는 제가 강조할 수 있는 소중한 능력을 제게 제공해 주었다고 생각합니다. 제가 이미 제 성취에 대한 요약본 초안을 작성해 이 이메일에

첨부해 드렸습니다. 고려해 주셔서 감사 드립니다.

안녕히 계십시오.
애나 겔러

11 "이미 요약본 초안을 작성했습니다"라는 애나의 언급이 그녀의 태도와 관련해 시사하는 것은?
(A) 애나는 자신이 얼마나 뛰어난지 교수가 알기를 원한다.
(B) 애나는 교수의 시간을 배려해 주고 있다.
(C) 애나는 자신이 인턴십 프로그램에 합격할 것으로 생각한다.
(D) 애나는 교수의 강의에서 높은 학점을 받을 것으로 예상하고 있다.

12 애나가 요청하는 것은?
(A) 자신의 능력을 보여 주는 문서
(B) 인턴십 프로그램 일정표
(C) 교수의 작업물을 기사에 이용하기 위한 허락
(D) 자신의 이력서를 완성하는 데 대한 도움

어휘 및 표현

request 요청(서), ~을 요청하다 valuable 소중한 highlight ~을 강조하다 draft ~의 초안을 작성하다 summary 요약(본) achievement 성취, 업적 attach ~을 첨부하다 consideration 고려 attitude 태도 accomplished (기량 등이) 뛰어난 be considerate of ~을 배려하다 get accepted into ~에 합격하다 expect to do ~할 것으로 예상하다 grade 학점, 점수 describe ~을 설명하다, ~을 묘사하다 permission 허락 assistance with ~에 대한 도움 complete ~을 완성하다, ~을 완료하다 curriculum vitae 이력서

13-15 이메일을 읽으시오.

제목: 새로운 건강 워크숍 실시 - 10월 9일, 금요일

파커 씨께,

잘 지내시는지요. 10월 9일, 금요일, 오전 10시부터 오후 12시로 예정된 사상 첫 건강 워크숍과 관련해 알려 드리기 위해 이메일을 씁니다. 이 워크숍은 스트레스 관리 및 일과 삶의 균형을 증진하기 위해 고안된 우리 직원 참여 프로그램의 일환입니다.

참석이 권장되기는 하지만 선택적이므로, 일상 업무 활동은 지속될 것이라는 점에 유의하시기 바랍니다. 저희는 팀별로 그에 따라 일정을 계획하고 어떤 일시적인 업무 대체 필요성이든 서로 의사 소통하시기를 권해 드립니다. 일정 충돌 문제가 있으신 분들을 위해, 이 워크숍 녹화 영상이 이후에 이용 가능할 것입니다.

추가로, GC 헬스에서 오시는 강사들께서 이 시간들을 진행할 것이기 때문에, 직원들께서 이분들께 최대한의 존중과 정중함을 보여 드리기를 요청 드립니다. 우리 직원들의 행동이 우리 회사의 이미지를 대표한다는 사실을 잊지 마시기 바랍니다.

어떤 질문이든 있으시면, 555-1183번으로 인사팀에 연락 주시기 바랍니다.

안녕히 계십시오.
모튼 프로스트

13 워크숍의 목적은?
(A) 팀워크 능력을 향상시키는 것
(B) 회사 문화를 강화하는 것
(C) 직원 생산성을 증진하는 것
(D) 직원 건강을 향상시키는 것

14 건강 워크숍과 관련해 언급된 것은?
(A) 격월로 개최된다.
(B) 개인 물품 지참을 필요로 한다.
(C) 의무 참석이 아니다.
(D) 직원들은 완전히 무료이다.

15 누가 워크숍을 진행하는가?
(A) 모튼 프로스트 씨
(B) 인사팀
(C) 파커 씨
(D) 외부 강사들

어휘 및 표현

wellness 건강 **implementation** 실시, 시행 **do well** 잘 지내다 **engagement** 참여, 관여 **designed to do** ~하도록 고안된 **promote** ~을 증진하다; ~을 촉진하다(=boost) **note that** ~임에 유의하다 **attendance** 참석 **encouraged** 권장되는 **optional** 선택적인 **continue** 지속되다 **accordingly** 그에 따라 **communicate** 의사소통하다 **temporary** 일시적인, 임시의 **coverage** (업무 등의) 대체 **individual** 사람, 개인 **conflicting** 충돌하는, 상충하는 **available** 이용 가능한 **facilitate** (원활히) ~을 진행하다 **session** (특정 활동을 위한) 시간 **utmost** 최대의, 최고의 **respect** 존중, 존경 **cordiality** 정중함, 극진함 **behavior** 행동 **represent** ~을 대표하다, ~에 해당하다 **enhance** ~을 향상시키다, ~을 강화하다 **strengthen** ~을 강화하다 **improve** ~을 향상시키다 **hold** ~을 개최하다 **material** 물품, 자료, 재료 **mandatory** 의무적인 **completely** 완전히, 전적으로 **free** 무료의 **conduct** ~을 진행하다, ~을 수행하다

Read an Academic Passage
16-20 불교 사원

불교 사원은 여러 세기 동안 지어져 온 신성한 구조물이다. 이 구조물들은 고대의 영적 수행 및 불교 공동체의 문화적 가치에 대한 통찰력을 제공해 준다. 아시아 전역에서 발견되는, 이 사원들은 우뚝 솟은 탑과 정교한 조각술, 그리고 금색 불상으로 높이 평가받는다. 캄보디아의 앙코르 와트와 인도네시아의 보로부두르 사원은 전 세계의 여행객들 사이에서 가장 인기 있는 불교 성지들이다.

수도원이라고도 알려진, 불교 사원은 다양한 목적을 수반한다. 이곳은 수도승과 일반 신도들이 명상과 기도, 그리고 예불을 위해 모이는 곳이다. 또한 부처의 철학을 가르치고 도덕적 가치를 전파하는 중심지의 기능도 한다.

게다가, 흔히 그 공동체 내에서 평화와 측은지심, 그리고 헌신에 대한 상징으로서의 역할도 한다.

불교 사원의 건축 기법은 그 시대에 비해 대단히 발전되어 있었다. 건축업자들은 돌과 벽돌, 그리고 나무를 이용해, 흔히 그것들을 화려한 장식 디자인 및 정교한 예술품과 조합했다. 일부 사원은 부처의 삶 속에서 나온 이야기들을 전하는 벽화와 조각품들로 장식되어 있다. 특정 사원들이 일출 또는 일몰과 함께 하는 것과 같은, 태양계 행성 정렬을 나타내는 방식은 그 사원들의 방향이 의도적으로 계획되었음을 시사한다. 여러 지역에 걸쳐 나타나는 차이에도 불구하고, 불교 사원은 오래 지속되는 문화 유산을 지닌 명소로서 여전히 남아 있다.

16 첫 번째 문단의 단어 "esteemed"에 가장 가까운 의미는?
(A) 진보한, 발전된
(B) 명성 있는, 유명한
(C) 단호한, 굳게 결심한
(D) 구식의, 시대에 뒤진

17 앙코르 와트 및 보로부두르 사원과 관련해 언급된 것은?
(A) 금색 불상이 많이 있다.
(B) 해외 관광객을 가장 많이 끌어들인다.
(C) 명상 공간이 여러 세기 동안 이용되어 오고 있다.
(D) 탑 구조물들이 전 세계에서 가장 높다.

18 다음 중 ~을 제외하고 모든 것이 불교 사원과 관련해 사실이다.
(A) 평화와 측은지심, 그리고 헌신에 대한 상징으로서의 역할을 한다.
(B) 가르침의 중심지로서 운영되고 있다.
(C) 화려한 장식 디자인으로 장식되어 있다.
(D) 주로 공개 의식을 위해 이용되고 있다.

19 2 문단과 3 문단의 관계는?
(A) 3 문단이 2 문단에 언급된 도덕적 가치를 설명한다.
(B) 3 문단에 2 문단에 나열된 어려움에 대한 해결책을 제공한다.
(C) 3 문단이 어떻게 불교 사원들이 디자인되었는지를 이야기하는 반면, 2 문단은 그 시설들이 제공하는 기능을 이야기한다.
(D) 3 문단은 2 문단에서 이야기하는 불교 구조물들보다 더 새로운 유형의 불교 건축 양식에 관해 이야기한다.

20 글쓴이가 태양계 행성 정렬을 언급하는 이유는?
(A) 일부 불교 예술품이 왜 대단히 가치 있는 것인지 설명하기 위해
(B) 일부 불교 사원이 의도적으로 방향이 정해졌음을 나타내기 위해
(C) 부처의 삶에 있었던 한 가지 중요한 사건을 강조하기 위해
(D) 불교 구조물들의 이면에 존재하는 진보한 기술을 설명하기 위해

어휘 및 표현
temple 사원, 절 sacred 신성한 insight 통찰력 ancient 고대의 spiritual 영적인 practice 수행, 실행 be esteemed for ~으로 높이 평가받다 towering 우뚝 솟은 pagoda 탑 intricate 정교한 carving 조각술 statue 조각상 monastery 수도원 monk 수도승 layperson 일반 신도 meditation 명상 prayer 기도 ceremony

의식, 식 **function as** ~로서 기능하다 **philosophy** 철학 **moral value** 도덕적 가치 **serve as** ~로서의 역할을 하다 **compassion** 측은지심, 연민 **devotion** 헌신 **advanced** 발전된, 진보한 **combine A with B** A와 B를 조합하다 **ornate** 화려한 장식의 **detailed** 정교한, 상세한 **mural** 벽화 **sculpture** 조각품 **narrate** (이야기 등) ~을 전하다 **display** ~을 나타내다, ~을 보여 주다 **solar alignment** 태양계 행성 정렬 **orientation** 방향, 지향(점) **intentionally** 의도적으로(=deliberately) **variation** 차이, 변형(된 형태) **landmark** 명소 **enduring** 오래 지속되는 **heritage** 유산 **solution** 해결책 **facility** 시설(물) **architecture** 건축 (양식) **valuable** 가치 있는, 소중한 **indicate that** ~임을 나타내다 **highlight** ~을 강조하다 **describe** ~을 설명하다, ~을 묘사하다

Reading Module 2

정답

Complete the Words
1-10 ably, al, ects, ets, res, ts, reme, ke, able, ying

Read an Academic Passage
11-15 (B), (D), (D), (C), (B)

해석/어휘

Complete the Words

1-10 다음 문단에서 빠진 글자를 채우시오.

> 목성은 태양계에서 가장 큰 행성으로서, 소용돌이치는 구름 및 거대 폭풍과 함께, 대부분 수소와 헬륨으로 구성되어 있다. 그 놀라울 정도로 강력한 중력의 끌어당기는 힘은 근처의 행성들에게 영향을 미치고 지나가는 혜성들을 붙잡아 두지만, 그 극심한 환경은 그곳을 살 수 없는 곳으로 만든다. 목성을 연구함으로써, 천문학자들은, 예를 들어, 거대 가스 행성이 어떻게 형성되는지, 그 자기장이 어떻게 발전하는지, 그리고 심층 기류가 어떻게 대적점 같은 특징들을 만들어 내는지와 같은 행성 형성 과정을 이해할 수 있다.

어휘 및 표현

planet 행성 **solar system** 태양계 **made of** ~으로 구성된, ~으로 만들어진 **hydrogen** 수소 **swirling** 소용돌이치는 **massive** 거대한 **remarkably** 놀라울 정도로, 주목할 만하게 **gravitational** 중력의 **pull** 끌어당기는 힘 **affect** ~에 영향을 미치다 **capture** ~을 붙잡다 **comet** 혜성 **extreme** 극심한, 극한의 **condition** 환경, 조건, 상태 **uninhabitable** 살 수 없는, 거주할 수 없는 **astronomer** 천문학자 **formation** 형성 (과정) **gas giant** 거대 가스 행성 **magnetic field** 자기장 **atmospheric current** (대기의) 기류 **feature** 특징 **Great Red Spot** (목성의) 대적점

Read an Academic Passage

11-15 마라톤 달리기

> 도심 속 경주와 자선 행사, 그리고 국제 대회를 포함해, 마라톤 달리기가 지구력 스포츠의 인기 있는 유형으로서 점점 더 인정받고 있다. 장거리 경주는 선수를 신체적 한계로 밀어붙이면서, 개인적 성취와 전 세계적인 동료애에 대한 기회를 제공하고 있다. 지역 사회 마라톤은 건강한 생활 방식을 장려하는 한편, 엘리트 선수 행사는 전 세계에서 최고의 선수들을 끌어들인다. 이런 경주들은 향상된 심폐 지구력과 뛰어난 성취감 같은, 중요한 건강 및 동기 부여 이점들을 제공해 준다.
>
> 하지만, 마라톤 달리기에 문제가 없는 것은 아니다. 훈련하는 데 수 개월의 준비 과정을 요구하기 때문에, 엄격한 일정 및 생활 방식의 변화를 필요로 한다. 경주자는 혹사와 탈수, 그리고 탈진으로 인한 부상 위험을 감수하게 되며, 이는 진전을 방해할 수 있다. 게다가, 대회에 참가하는 경우, 비록 많은 이들이 여전히 참가를 하나의 보람 있는 목표로 여기고 있지만, 이동 비용 및 참가비가 신참자들을 좌절시킬지도 모른다.

다양한 핵심 파트너들이 마라톤과 관련된 부상의 발생을 줄이기 위해 노력하고 있다. 예를 들어, 트레이너들은 부상을 방지하기 위해 내재된 회복 기간과 함께 개인 맞춤형 달리기 계획을 고안하고 있다. 스포츠 용품 회사들은 운동 능력과 안전을 향상시켜 주는, 쿠션 처리된 신발과 수분 보충용 팩 같은, 운동 장비 분야에서 발전을 이뤄 왔다. 더 많은 지방 정부들과 후원사들도 지역 사회 경주대회를 후원하고 있으며, 안전하게 마라톤에 참가하는 방법에 관해 사람들을 교육하기 위한 조치를 취하고 있다.

11 다음 중 마라톤 달리기의 건강상 이점으로 지문에 언급된 것은?
(A) 부상 발생 가능성을 줄인다.
(B) 심폐지구력을 증진시킨다.
(C) 쉽게 시작할 수 있는 스포츠이다.
(D) 사람들에게 건강에 더 좋은 음식을 먹게 만들 수 있다.

12 지문의 단어 "sense"에 가장 가까운 의미는?
(A) 인식, 의식
(B) 지혜
(C) 영리함
(D) 감각, 느낌

13 마라톤 달리기와 연관되어 있는 문제는?
(A) 더 낮은 체력 수준
(B) 제한적인 수면 시간
(C) 비싼 훈련 비용
(D) 엄격한 생활 방식 관리

14 트레이너들이 부상 문제를 다루는 방법은?
(A) 새로운 유형의 운동 장비를 개발함으로써
(B) 신속한 회복을 위한 팁을 제공함으로써
(C) 개인 맞춤형 달리기 계획을 고안함으로써
(D) 신참자들보다는 오직 최고의 운동 선수들만 상대함으로써

15 글쓴이가 핵심 파트너들을 언급하는 목적은?
(A) 마라톤 달리기의 접근 가능성을 강조하기 위해
(B) 마라톤 달리기가 지닌 문제들에 대한 여러 해결책을 설명하기 위해
(C) 마라톤 업계에서 활동 중인 다양한 사람들과 단체들을 확인해 주기 위해
(D) 사람들에게 지역 사회 마라톤에 참가하도록 권하기 위해

어휘 및 표현

charity 자선 (활동) competition (경기 등의) 대회 gain recognition 인정받다 endurance 지구력 athlete 운동 선수 physical limit 신체적 한계 achievement 성취, 업적(=accomplishment) camaraderie 동료애 attract ~을 끌어들이다 significant 중요한, 상당한 motivational 동기를 부여하는 benefit 이점, 혜택 improve ~을 향상시키다 cardiovascular endurance 심폐 지구력 challenge 문제, 도전, 과제 demand ~을 요구하다 require ~을 필요로 하다 strict 엄격한 risk ~에 대한 위험을 감수하다 injury 부상 overuse 혹사, 과용 dehydration 탈수 exhaustion 탈진 undermine ~을 방해하다, ~을 약화시키다 progress 진전, 진척

participate in ~에 참가하다 **discourage** ~을 좌절시키다 **rewarding** 보람 있는 **reduce** ~을 줄이다, ~을 감소시키다 **occurrence** 발생 **A-related** A와 관련된 **personalized** 개인에게 맞춰진 **built-in** 내재된, 내장된 **recovery** 회복, 복구 **prevent** ~을 방지하다 **make advances** 발전을 이루다 **gear** 장비 **hydration** 수분 보충 **local** 지방의, 현지의 **take steps** 조치를 취하다 **how to do** ~하는 방법 **likelihood** 가능성 **boost** ~을 증진하다 **pick up** 시작하다 **compel A to do** (억지로) A에게 ~하게 만들다 **stamina** 체력 **limited** 제한적인 **address** (문제 등) ~을 다루다, ~을 처리하다 **rather than** ~ 보다는, ~가 아니라 **emphasize** ~을 강조하다 **accessibility** 접근 가능성, 이용 가능성 **demonstrate** ~을 설명하다, ~을 보여 주다 **solution** 해결책 **identify** ~을 확인하다 **organization** 단체, 조직(체) **active** 활동하는 **encourage A to do** A에게 ~하도록 권하다

TEST 2
Listening Module 1

정답

Listen and Choose a Response
1-10 (B), (B), (B), (C), (C), (A), (D), (B), (D), (D)

Listen to a Conversation
11-12 (A), (D)
13-14 (A), (B)
15-16 (C), (D)

Listen to an Announcement
17-18 (A), (D)
19-20 (B), (A)

Listen to an Academic Talk
21-24 (C), (A), (D), (B)
25-28 (C), (C), (C), (A)

스크립트/해석/어휘

Listen and Choose a Response

1-8 가장 적절한 응답을 고르시오.

1 Did you really miss your flight?
너 정말 항공편을 놓친 거야?

(A) 미안, 우리가 할 수 있는 게 없어.
(B) 나 정말로 끔찍한 교통 체증에 갇혀 있었어.
(C) 비행기에 문제가 있는 게 틀림없어.
(D) 분실물 신고서를 제출하자.

2 Who can tell me the password for this computer?
누가 이 컴퓨터 비밀번호 좀 알려 줄 수 있니?

(A) 두 곳의 방 모두 열려 있어.
(B) 제니퍼가 아이디어 있을 거야.
(C) 첫 번째 것.
(D) 브렌트가 테스트를 통과했어.

3 How do you make the screen brighter?
화면을 어떻게 더 밝게 만들지?

(A) 밖이 너무 어두워.

(B) 자동으로 조정될 거야.
(C) 새로운 날짜를 선택하자.
(D) 난 녹색을 좋아해.

4 Can I give you my thoughts on that design?
그 디자인에 대한 내 생각을 말해도 될까?

(A) 응, 우리는 지금 그들에게 물어봐야 해.
(B) 그건 결정되지 않은 것 같아.
(C) 물론이지, 얘기해 봐.
(D) 그래픽 디자이너에게 물어봐.

5 We may have to cancel the reservation.
우리는 그 예약을 취소해야 할 수도 있어.

(A) 나를 위해 예약해 줘서 고마워.
(B) 나는 제시간에 딱 맞춰서 도착했어.
(C) 틀림없이 더 나은 해결책이 있을 거야.
(D) 난 보통 오전 시간대를 선호해.

6 The conference hall doors are all locked.
컨퍼런스 홀 출입문들이 모두 잠겨 있어.

(A) 내가 관리실에 연락해 볼게.
(B) 컨퍼런스 센터 근처에 있어.
(C) 자동문이 더 흔해.
(D) 다 마치면 방을 잠가 줘.

7 Did you have time to update the slides?
슬라이드들을 업데이트할 시간이 있었니?

(A) 나는 다른 곳에 가기로 정했어.
(B) 우리는 오늘 점심 식사 후에 회의가 있어.
(C) 연설자가 더 나을 수도 있었어.
(D) 내가 다른 프로젝트로 바빴어.

8 Is the café serving breakfast now?
그 카페가 지금 아침 식사를 제공하고 있니?

(A) 그곳은 이 지역에서 내가 가장 좋아하는 곳이야.
(B) 오늘은 너무 늦었어.
(C) 나는 현금으로 결제했어.
(D) 나는 커피를 마시지 않아.

9 Why haven't you left yet?
너 왜 아직 안 갔어?

(A) 내 인터넷이 느려.
(B) 겨우 몇 개만 남아 있었어.
(C) 10시까지 도착하도록 해 볼게.
(D) 몇 가지 일들 좀 마무리하는 중이야.

10 Isn't there a park nearby?
　　근처에 공원이 하나 있지 않니?
(A) 치열한 경쟁이었어.
(B) 우리 주차장이 바로 지금 비어 있어.
(C) 내가 그것을 이미 확인했다고 꽤 확신해.
(D) 산책하러 갈래?

어휘 및 표현

miss ~을 놓치다 get stuck with ~에 갇혀 있다 traffic jam 교통 체증 issue 문제, 사안 file a report 신고서를 제출하다 missing 분실한, 없는, 빠진 pass (시험 등) ~을 통과하다 adjust 조정되다, 조절되다 choose ~을 선택하다 thought 생각 undecided 결정되지 않은 go ahead (앞선 말에 대해) 어서 하세요 cancel ~을 취소하다 reservation 예약 appointment 예약, 약속 on time 제시간에, 제때 solution 해결책 prefer ~을 선호하다 contact ~에게 연락하다 common 흔한 could have p.p. ~할 수도 있었다 be tied up with ~로 바쁘다, ~에 묶여 있다 close competition 치열한 경쟁 stroll 산책, 산책하다, 거닐다

Listen to a Conversation

11-12 대화를 들으시오.

> M: I'm excited to paint the living room this weekend. Which color should we decide on?
> 이번 주말에 거실에 페인트칠을 하게 되어서 기대돼. 어느 색으로 결정해야 할까?
>
> W: How about light blue? I want to make the room feel bright, but not in an overwhelming way.
> 밝은 청색은 어때? 거실이 밝은 느낌이 들게, 하지만 압도적이지는 않은 방식으로 만들고 싶어.
>
> M: OK. I've heard blue can be tricky to match with furniture. We should test a small patch first.
> 좋아. 청색이 가구와 어울리기 까다로울 수 있다는 얘기를 들은 적이 있어. 우선 작은 패치로 테스트해야 될 것 같아.
>
> W: Definitely. I'll let you pick which wall to start with.
> 당연하지. 어느 벽으로 시작할지 네가 골라 봐.

11 화자들이 주로 논의하는 것은?
(A) 자신들의 주택 개조 공사 프로젝트
(B) 자신들이 가장 좋아하는 도색용 색상
(C) 아파트 둘러보기
(D) 다가오는 미술 축제

12 여자가 거실에 하고 싶어 하는 것은?

(A) 가구를 재배치하는 일
(B) 새로운 조명을 설치하는 일
(C) 벽을 흰색으로 칠하는 일
(D) 공간을 밝게 만드는 일

어휘 및 표현

decide on ~을 결정하다 how about ~? ~는 어때요? overwhelming 압도적인 tricky 까다로운 match with ~와 어울리다, ~와 맞추다 definitely (강한 긍정) 물론이지, 당연하지 pick ~을 고르다 renovation 개조, 보수 upcoming 다가오는, 곧 있을 rearrange ~을 재배치하다 install ~을 설치하다 brighten ~을 밝게 하다

13-14 대화를 들으시오.

> W: Are you still coming to the book club on Wednesday evening?
> 여전히 수요일 저녁에 독서 동아리에 오는 거야?
>
> M: I wish I could, but my cousin is arriving that night. I promised I'd pick him up from the airport.
> 그럴 수 있다면 좋겠지만, 내 사촌이 그날 밤에 도착해. 내가 공항으로 데리러 간다고 약속했거든.
>
> W: That's a pity. I heard the discussion is going to be really entertaining.
> 아쉽다. 토론 시간이 정말 즐거울 거라고 들었거든.
>
> M: I know. I've been eager to talk about that novel for weeks.
> 그러니까. 몇 주 동안 그 소설에 관해서 얘기하기를 간절히 원했거든.
>
> W: I can jot down notes for you during the meeting and share them afterward.
> 내가 널 위해 그 모임 중에 내용을 받아 적어서 나중에 공유해 줄 수 있어.
>
> M: Thanks. That would help me stay in the loop.
> 고마워. 그렇게 해 주면 내가 계속 정보를 유지하는 데 도움이 될 거야.

13 남자가 독서 동아리에 참석할 수 없는 이유는?
(A) 사촌을 차로 태워 줘야 한다.
(B) 초과 근무할 계획이다.
(C) 다른 나라에 도착할 예정이다.
(D) 할당된 소설을 읽지 않았다.

14 여자가 남자를 위해 하려는 것은?
(A) 녹화하는 일
(B) 메모하는 일
(C) 자신의 아이디어를 공유하는 일
(D) 일정을 변경하는 일

어휘 및 표현

arrive 도착하다 promise (that) ~라고 약속하다 pick up ~을 차로 데리러 가다 that's a pity 아쉬워, 안타까워 entertaining 즐겁게 하는 be eager to do ~하기를 간절히 원하다 jot down ~을 적어 놓다 share ~을 공유하다

afterward 나중에, 이후에 stay in the loop 계속 정보를 유지하다 attend ~에 참석하다 give a ride 차를 태워 주다 touch down 도착하다, 착륙하다 assign ~을 배정하다

15-16 대화를 들으시오.

> M: Are you attending the charity banquet tonight?
> 오늘밤에 자선 연회에 참석하니?
>
> W: Yes, I am. I just took a look at the dinner menu.
> 응. 해. 방금 저녁 식사 메뉴를 살펴 봤어.
>
> M: I saw that, too. Any thoughts on it?
> 나도 확인해 봤어. 어떻게 생각해?
>
> W: Well, the overall selection seems very fancy. I'm especially excited to try all the desserts.
> 음, 전반적인 선택 대상이 아주 고급스러워 보여. 나는 특히 디저트를 전부 한번 먹어 보는 게 기대돼.
>
> M: Same here. I'm also a big dessert lover.
> 마찬가지야. 나도 디저트를 아주 좋아하거든.

15 화자들이 논의하고 있는 행사는?
(A) 회사 전체를 대상으로 하는 기념 행사
(B) 저녁 자선 콘서트
(C) 자선 연회 만찬
(D) 자선 제과제품 세일

16 메뉴에 대해 여자가 생각했던 것은?
(A) 전반적으로 맛있어 보인다.
(B) 제공되는 것이 다양하지 않다.
(C) 더 많은 디저트 선택 대상을 포함해야 한다.
(D) 고급스러운 선택 대상이 있다.

어휘 및 표현

attend ~에 참석하다 charity 자선 (단체) banquet 연회 any thoughts on ~? ~에 대해 어떻게 생각해? overall 전반적인, 전반적으로 selection 선택 (가능한 대상) fancy 고급스러운, 근사한 companywide 회사 전체의 celebration 기념 행사, 축하 행사 offering 제공되는 것 diverse 다양한 include ~을 포함하다

Listen to an Announcement

17-18 학교 라디오에서 공지사항을 들으시오.

> Attention all students. The campus fitness center has officially reopened after a full equipment upgrade. To celebrate, we're offering free access tomorrow only from 7 A.M. to 7 P.M. All new membership registrations for gym classes and wellness programs will be discounted by five percent for one day only. This'll be the perfect way to kickstart

your fitness goals this semester. And after your workout, don't forget to explore our new relaxation lounge and use the massage chairs, which are completely free of charge!

모든 학생들에게 알립니다. 교내 피트니스 센터가 전체적인 장비 업그레이드 끝에 정식으로 재개장했습니다. 이를 기념하기 위해, 내일 오전 7시부터 오후 7시에 한 해 무료 이용 서비스를 제공합니다. 체육관 강좌 및 건강 프로그램에 대한 모든 신규 회원 등록은 단 하루 동안 5퍼센트 할인될 것입니다. 이는 이번 학기에 여러분의 건강 관련 목표를 시작하기에 완벽한 방법이 될 것입니다. 그리고 운동 후에는, 잊지 마시고 새로운 휴식용 라운지도 살펴보시고 마사지 의자들도 사용해 보세요. 이는 완전히 무료입니다!

17 공지의 주제는?
(A) 피트니스 센터에서 열리는 특별 일일 행사
(B) 손상된 교내 체육관의 복구
(C) 레크리에이션 센터에서 열리는 스포츠 토너먼트
(D) 새로운 운동 팀의 출범

18 학생들에게 하도록 권장되는 것은?
(A) 휴식용 라운지에서 낮잠을 자는 일
(B) 단체 운동 시간에 참가하는 일
(C) 일일 요가 강좌에 등록하는 일
(D) 몇몇 새로운 마사지 의자를 시험해 보는 일

어휘 및 표현

officially 정식으로, 공식적으로 equipment 장비 celebrate 기념하다, 축하하다 free 무료의 access 이용, 접근 registration 등록 wellness 건강 kickstart ~을 시작하다 semester 학기 workout 운동 explore ~을 살펴보다 relaxation 휴식 completely 완전히, 전적으로 free of charge 무료인

19-20 대학교 동아리 모임에서 공지사항을 들으시오.

Welcome, everyone. Today, we'll be talking about our spring music concert. We'll discuss which pieces would be great to perform in the courtyard next Saturday. Please suggest a song if you have any ideas.

환영합니다, 여러분. 오늘은, 우리 봄철 음악 콘서트에 관해 이야기해 볼 예정입니다. 어느 작품이 다음 주 토요일에 뜰에서 공연하기 아주 좋을 것인지 논의해 보겠습니다. 어떤 아이디어든 있으시면 곡을 제안해 주시기 바랍니다.

19 공지의 주제는?
(A) 유명인의 특별 공연
(B) 계절 음악 공연
(C) 봄철 원예 축제
(D) 영화 작품의 사운드트랙

20 학생들에게 하도록 권장되는 것은?
(A) 연주할 작품을 추천하는 일
(B) 자원봉사자로 등록하는 일

(C) 오케스트라 동아리에 기부하는 일
(D) 오디션용 동영상을 준비하는 일

어휘 및 표현
piece (글, 그림, 음악 등의) 작품 perform ~을 공연하다, ~을 연주하다 suggest ~을 제안하다 celebrity 유명인
production 제작(된 작품) sign up 등록하다, 신청하다 volunteer 자원봉사자 donate 기부하다, 기증하다

Listen to an Academic Talk
21-24 경영학 수업에서의 강연을 들으시오.

> Today, we're exploring the concept of greenwashing, a term used to describe when companies exaggerate or misrepresent their environmental efforts. Greenwashing happens when a company wants to appear eco-friendly without actually making significant changes to its practices. This usually involves promoting minor green initiatives or using environmentally positive language while continuing harmful production methods, giving the impression of sustainability to appeal to customers.
>
> A notable example is the fast fashion industry. Many clothing brands launch "sustainable" lines or advertise recycled fabrics, but the majority of their operations still rely on resource-intensive production and low-cost labor in developing countries. Over time, customers are becoming more skeptical of such claims, and brands that are caught exaggerating face public criticism. Another example is large corporations labeling products as "eco-friendly" while the actual environmental impact remains high, such as using slightly recycled packaging or claiming carbon neutrality without third-party verification. These tactics can mislead buyers and put pressure on genuinely sustainable competitors.
>
> Greenwashing challenges businesses to reflect on their messaging and actual practices. Established companies may rely on appearances, assuming consumers won't notice anything misleading, until regulators or social media scrutiny reveals the truth. Understanding greenwashing helps companies protect their reputation and maintain long-term credibility. Next, we'll review several case studies of companies that successfully shifted from greenwashing to authentic sustainability initiatives.
>
> 오늘, 우리는 그린워싱이라는 개념을 살펴 볼 텐데, 이는 회사들이 자사의 환경 관련 노력들을 과장하거나 잘못 표현하는 경우를 묘사하는 데 쓰이는 용어입니다. 그린워싱은 회사가 실제로는 자사의 관행에 대해 중요한 변화를 일으키지 않은 채로 환경 친화적인 것처럼 보이기를 원하는 경우에 나타납니다. 이는 일반적으로 작은 규모의 친환경 계획들을 홍보하거나 환경적으로 긍정적인 언어를 사용하면서 유해한 생산 방법을 지속해, 고객들의 관심을 끌기 위해 지속 가능성에 대한 인상을 심어 주는 일을 수반합니다.
>
> 한 가지 주목할 만한 예시가 패스트 패션 업계입니다. 많은 의류 브랜드가 "지속 가능한" 제품 라인을 출시하거나 재활용 섬유를 광고하지만, 대다수의 회사 운영은 여전히 자원 집약적 생산 및 개발 도상국의 저가 노동력에 의존하고 있습니다. 시간이 흐르면서, 고객들은 이러한 주장에 대해 더욱 회의적인 상태가 되어 가고 있으며, 과장

광고로 적발되는 브랜드들은 대중의 비난에 직면하고 있습니다. 또 다른 예시는 약간 재활용된 포장재를 이용하거나 제3자의 인증 없이 탄소 중립성을 주장하는 것과 같이, 제품을 "환경 친화적"이고 실제 환경적 영향력이 여전히 높은 상태인 것으로 라벨 표기하는 대기업들입니다. 이러한 전략들은 구매자들을 오도하고 진정으로 지속 가능한 경쟁사들에게 압박감을 줄 수 있습니다.

그린워싱은 기업들에게 자사의 메시지 전달과 실제 관행을 심사숙고하도록 요구합니다. 기존의 회사들은 규제 기관이나 소셜 미디어의 검증이 진실을 드러낼 때까지, 오도하는 어떤 것이든 소비자들이 알아차리지 못할 것이라고 생각하면서, 겉으로 보이는 것에 의존할 수 있습니다. 그린워싱을 이해하는 것이 명성을 보호하고 장기적인 신뢰성을 유지하도록 회사들에게 도움을 줍니다. 다음으로, 성공적으로 그린워싱에서 진정한 지속 가능성 계획으로 변화한 회사들에 대한 여러 가지 사례 연구 내용을 살펴 보겠습니다.

21 강연의 주제는?
(A) 친환경 마케팅의 정의
(B) 지속 가능한 성장의 필요성
(C) 그린워싱의 개념
(D) 환경 친화적인 소재의 발전

22 강연에 따르면, 그린워싱의 한 가지 특징은?
(A) 환경적으로 긍정적인 언어를 활용한다.
(B) 지속 가능한 생산 방법을 포함한다.
(C) 중립적인 회사 이미지를 확립해 준다.
(D) 정부가 주도하는 친환경 계획에 대한 참여를 수반한다.

23 화자가 패스트 패션 업계를 언급한 이유는?
(A) 의류 생산에 수반되는 저가 노동력을 강조하기 위해
(B) 일반인들이 왜 특정 의류 회사들을 불매해야 하는지 증명하기 위해
(C) 신제품에 재활용 섬유를 이용해야 하는 필요성에 의문을 제기하기 위해
(D) 과장된 주장을 펼치는 것이 어떻게 브랜드에 역효과를 낼 수 있는지 보여 주기 위해

24 기존의 회사들과 관련해 추론할 수 있는 것은?
(A) 자사의 브랜드 이미지를 홍보하기 위해 소셜 미디어에 의존한다.
(B) 소비자들이 오도하는 메시지를 알아차리지 못할 것이라고 생각한다.
(C) 점검을 실시할 규제 기관을 고용한다.
(D) 환경 친화적인 곳이 되어 자사의 명성을 보호한다.

어휘 및 표현

explore ~을 살펴 보다 greenwashing 그린워싱(기업이나 단체가 실제와 달리 홍보 등을 통해 친환경 이미지를 내세움) term 용어 describe ~을 묘사하다, ~을 설명하다 exaggerate ~을 과장하다 misrepresent ~을 잘못 표현하다 eco-friendly 환경 친화적인 practice 관행, 관례 involve ~을 수반하다 promote ~을 홍보하다 initiative 계획 positive 긍정적인 continue ~을 지속하다 impression 인상, 느낌 sustainability 지속 가능성 appeal to ~의 관심을 끌다 notable 주목할 만한 the majority of 대다수의 rely on ~에 의존하다 resource-intensive 자원 집약적인 skeptical of ~에 대해 회의적인 be caught -ing ~하는 것이 적발되다 face ~에 직면하다 criticism 비난, 비판 label ~을 라벨 표기하다 impact 영향(력) carbon neutrality 탄소 중립성 third-party 제3자의 verification 인증 tactic 전략 mislead ~을 오도하다 genuinely 진정으로 competitor 경쟁사 challenge A to do A에게 ~하도록 요구하다   reflect on ~을 심사숙고하다   established 기존의, 확립된   assume (that) ~라고 생각하다   regulator 규제 기관   scrutiny 검증, 정밀 조사   reveal ~을 드러내다   reputation 명성   credibility 신뢰성   shift ~을 변경하다, 변화하다   authentic 진정한, 진짜인   utilize ~을 활용하다   incorporate ~을 포함하다   neutral 중립적인   participate in ~에 참여하다   green 친환경의   underline ~을 강조하다   boycott 구매를 거부하다, 불매하다   backfire on ~에 역효과를 낳다   inspection 점검, 검사   established 정착하여 안정된, 기존의

25-28 심리학 수업에서의 강연을 들으시오.

Social facilitation describes how people's performance can shift depending on whether they're alone or being observed. This concept, studied by psychologists like Robert Zajonc, suggests that the presence of others can either boost or hinder how well someone completes a task. Typically, simple or well-practiced activities improve under observation, while complex or unfamiliar ones may suffer. For example, imagine a person who enjoys sketching. They might draw more confidently when friends are around but feel nervous and make mistakes during a formal art competition. The difference in performance here reflects the influence of social context and the pressure people feel when they're being watched.

This phenomenon also influences group decision-making. When individuals are part of a team, they may feel compelled to align with group norms or expectations. To avoid standing out or causing conflict, they might suppress their own opinions or follow the majority. Studying social facilitation helps us understand how specific environments might shape someone's behavior, motivation, and performance in any given moment. Next, we'll do some role-playing exercises to explore how group dynamics influence an individual's choices and actions.

사회적 촉진은 사람들의 수행 능력이 혼자 있는지, 아니면 관찰되는 지에 따라 어떻게 달라질 수 있는지 설명합니다. 이 개념은, 로버트 자이언스 같은 심리학자들에 의해 연구된 것으로서, 타인의 존재가 일을 얼마나 잘 완수하는지를 촉진하거나 방해할 수 있음을 시사합니다. 일반적으로, 단순하거나 잘 숙련된 활동들은 관찰 중에 향상되지만, 복잡하거나 익숙하지 않은 것들은 악화될 수 있습니다. 예를 들어, 스케치하는 것을 즐기는 사람을 상상해 보세요. 친구들이 함께 있을 때는 더욱 자신감 있게 그릴지도 모르지만, 정식 미술 대회 중에는 긴장감을 느끼거나 실수할 수도 있습니다. 여기서 수행 능력의 차이는 관찰되고 있을 때 사회적 맥락 및 사람들이 느끼는 압박감의 영향을 반영합니다.

이러한 현상은 집단 의사 결정에도 영향을 미칩니다. 사람들이 팀의 일부일 때, 집단의 기준이나 기대치와 방향성이 일치해야 한다는 의무감을 느낄 수 있습니다. 돋보이거나 갈등을 초래하는 것을 피하기 위해, 자신의 의견을 억누르거나 대다수를 따를지도 모릅니다. 사회적 촉진을 연구하면 어떻게 특정 환경이 모든 주어진 순간에 누군가의 행동과 동기 부여, 그리고 수행 능력을 형성할 수 있을지 이해하는 데 도움이 됩니다. 다음으로, 집단 역학이 어떻게 사람의 선택과 행동에 영향을 미치는지 살펴 볼 수 있도록 몇몇 역할극 연습을 해 보겠습니다.

25 강연의 주제는?
(A) 사람들이 어떻게 타인에 대해 빠른 판단을 내리는가
(B) 사람들이 갈등이 생길 때 어떻게 대화를 진행해야 하는가
(C) 사람들이 보는 사람들이 있거나 없을 때 어떻게 다르게 행동하는가

(D) 공개 연설 능력을 향상시키는 방법

26   화자가 스케치를 즐기는 사람을 언급한 이유는?
(A) 동료의 적당한 압박감이 주는 이점을 보여 주기 위해
(B) 긴장하는 것이 자연스러운 반응임을 나타내기 위해
(C) 사회적 촉진의 예시를 제공하기 위해
(D) 뇌에 좋은 운동을 강조하기 위해

27   화자에 따르면, 사람들이 갈등을 초래하는 것을 피하기 위해 때때로 하는 것은?
(A) 다른 문화들을 이해하려 노력하는 일
(B) 사람들 앞에서 사회적 문제들에 관해 이야기하는 것을 삼가는 일
(C) 타인에게 동조하기 위해 자신의 의견을 억누르는 일
(D) 오직 한쪽 편에 대해서만 동의하는 것을 거부하는 일

28   화자가 다음에 소개하려는 것은?
(A) 사회적 촉진을 설명하기 위한 역할극 연습
(B) 사회적 촉진에 관한 다큐멘터리
(C) 사회적 촉진과 관련된 문제들을 해결하는 방법들
(D) 사회적 촉진의 흔한 유형들

어휘 및 표현

social facilitation 사회적 촉진(타인의 존재가 개인의 행동에 영향을 미치는 심리적 현상)   **describe** ~을 설명하다   **shift** 달라지다, 바뀌다   **depending on** ~에 따라 (다른), ~에 좌우되는   **observe** ~을 관찰하다   **presence** 존재(감)   **boost** ~을 촉진하다   **hinder** ~을 방해하다   **well-practiced** 잘 숙련된   **improve** 향상되다, ~을 향상시키다   **complex** 복잡한   **unfamiliar** 익숙하지 않은   **suffer** 악화되다   **nervous** 긴장한   **reflect** ~을 반영하다   **influence** 영향(력), ~에 영향을 미치다   **context** 맥락   **phenomenon** 현상   **feel compelled** 의무감을 느끼다   **align with** ~와 방향성이 일치하다   **norm** 기준, 표준   **avoid -ing** ~하는 것을 피하다   **stand out** 돋보이다, 두드러지다   **cause** ~을 초래하다   **conflict** 갈등   **suppress** ~을 억누르다(=repress)   **the majority** 대다수   **specific** 특정한, 구체적인   **motivation** 동기 부여   **role-playing** 역할극   **explore** ~을 살펴 보다   **dynamics** 역학   **judgment** 판단   **facilitate** ~을 원활히 진행하다, ~을 촉진하다   **arise** 발생하다   **audience** 보는 사람들   **benefit** 이점, 혜택   **moderate** 적당한   **peer** 동료, 또래   **highlight** ~을 강조하다   **refrain from -ing** ~하는 것을 삼가다   **in public** 사람들 앞에서   **go along with** ~에 동조하다, ~와 어울리다   **refuse to do** ~하기를 거부하다   **solve** ~을 해결하다   **related to** ~와 관련된

TEST 2
Listening Module 2

정답

Listen and Choose a Response
1-3   (C), (A), (D)

Listen to a Conversation
4-5   (A), (D)
6-7   (B), (C)

Listen to an Academic Talk
8-11   (C), (D), (B), (A)
12-15   (A), (B), (C), (B)

스크립트/해석/어휘

Listen and Choose a Response

1-3   가장 적절한 응답을 고르시오.

1   Are you going to the banquet tonight?
오늘 밤 연회에 갈 거야?

(A) 응, 매일 밤 7시에.
(B) 물론이지, 그 은행은 늦게까지 계속 문을 열어.
(C) 내일 마감 기한인 과제가 있어.
(D) 무대 한 가운데에.

2   Would you prefer to walk or take the bus to the warehouse?
창고에 걸어서 가고 싶으세요, 아니면 버스를 타고 가시겠요?

(A) 여기서 꽤 멀리 있지 않나요?
(B) 물론이죠, 그 창고에 가 본 적 있어요.
(C) 오전 10시 버스표 두 장 주세요.
(D) 저는 저녁에 산책하는 걸 선호해요.

3   Who will edit the article?
누가 그 기사를 편집할 거죠?

(A) 에이미가 아주 흥미로운 글이라고 얘기했어요.
(B) 새로운 칼럼이 곧 실릴 겁니다.
(C) 그 기사는 지역 내 신생 기술 업체에 관한 겁니다.
(D) 리 씨가 그 일을 하는 우리 담당자입니다.

어휘 및 표현

banquet 연회   **paper** 과제(물), 논문, 보고서   **due** ~가 마감 기한인   **prefer to do** ~하는 것을 선호하다   **edit** ~을 편집하다   **engaging** 흥미로운   **piece** 글, 기사   **local** 지역의, 현지의   **start-up** 신생 업체

Listen to a Conversation

4-5 대화를 들으시오.

> M: I'm considering getting into hiking to get my mind off work. Do you hike much?
> 일 생각은 잊고 머리 좀 식히려고 등산 시작하는 걸 고려하고 있어. 넌 등산 많이 가니?
>
> W: I do. It's a great way to exercise and spend time outdoors. You should start with shorter, easier trails first.
> 응. 운동하면서 야외에서 시간 보내기 아주 좋은 방법이야. 더 짧고 더 쉬운 등산로에서 먼저 시작해 봐.
>
> M: That makes sense. Any other tips?
> 무슨 말인지 이해돼. 다른 팁이 또 있니?
>
> W: Yes, make sure to hit the trails early to avoid the big crowds.
> 응, 사람이 붐비는 걸 피할 수 있게 반드시 일찍 등산하러 나서야 해.
>
> M: Thanks, that's a good idea. The weather looks great this weekend. I'm already excited.
> 고마워, 좋은 생각이네. 날씨가 이번 주말에 아주 좋은 것 같아. 벌써 기대돼.

4 남자가 등산을 시작하고 싶다고 말하는 이유는?
(A) 일에서 벗어나 정신적인 휴식을 취하기 위해
(B) 멋진 자연 사진을 촬영하기 위해
(C) 동료 직원들과 즐거운 시간을 보내기 위해
(D) 경치 좋은 전망을 즐기기 위해

5 여자가 남자에게 하도록 권하는 것은?
(A) 미리 날씨를 확인하는 일
(B) 등산 모임에 가입하는 일
(C) 물병을 챙겨 가는 일
(D) 오전에 출발하는 일

어휘 및 표현
get into ~을 시작하다, ~에 빠져 들다   way to do ~하는 방법   exercise 운동하다   trail 등산로, 산길   make sense 이해가 되다, 앞뒤가 맞다   make sure to do 반드시 ~하도록 하다   hit the trail 등산하러 나서다   avoid ~을 피하다   crowd 붐비는 사람들, 인파   break (짧은) 휴식   coworker 동료 (직원)   in advance 미리, 사전에

6-7 대화를 들으시오.

> M: Hey, Sharon, have you listened to the new album by RK Band yet?
> 안녕, 샤론, 혹시 RK 밴드의 새 앨범 들어 본 적 있어?
>
> W: Not yet. I've seen some comments online, though. Some people are saying it's their best work yet, but others totally disagree. Have you listened to it?
> 아직 못 들어 봤어. 근데, 온라인에서 몇몇 의견은 확인해 봤어. 어떤 사람들은 지금까지 중에서 그들이 만든 최고의 작품이라고 말하지만, 다른 사람들은 완전히 반대하고 있어. 넌 들어 봤어?

M: Yes, I went through the whole thing yesterday. I actually liked how distinct each track was. The last two were a bit disappointing though. It felt like they were cut short.
응, 어제 전체적으로 쭉 다 들었어. 난 사실 각 트랙이 얼마나 뚜렷이 다른지가 마음에 들었어. 근데, 마지막 두 곡은 좀 실망스러웠어. 곡들이 갑자기 끝나는 것 같은 느낌이었거든.

W: Oh, it seems like it's worth checking out then. I'll give it a listen this weekend while I'm working on my art project.
아, 그럼 확인해 볼 만한 가치가 있는 것 같네. 이번 주말에 내 미술 프로젝트에 대한 작업을 하면서 한번 들어 봐야겠다.

6 여자가 앨범과 관련해 암시하는 것은?
(A) 많은 음악 차트에서 1위에 오르고 있다.
(B) 그에 대한 온라인상의 반응은 다양하다.
(C) 밴드가 직접 제작했다.
(D) 상을 받아야 한다.

7 앨범과 관련해 남자를 실망시키는 것은?
(A) 너무 비쌌다.
(B) 명확한 장르를 담고 있지 않았다.
(C) 일부 곡들이 충분히 길지 않았다.
(D) 박자가 느렸다.

어휘 및 표현
comment 의견, 발언 though (문장 끝이나 중간에서) 하지만, 그런데 totally 완전히, 전적으로 disagree 반대하다 go through ~을 쭉 살펴 보다 distinct 뚜렷이 다른, 독특한 be cut short 갑자기 끝나다 worth -ing ~할 만한 가치가 있는 give a listen 한번 들어 보다 top ~에서 1위에 오르다 reaction 반응 varied 다양한 tempo 박자, 속도

Listen to an Academic Talk
8-11 역사학 수업에서의 강연을 들으시오.

Today we'll explore the Pony Express, a brief but legendary mail delivery system that connected the eastern United States with the expanding frontier in the west. The Pony Express was not a single rider's journey, but a relay of horsemen carrying messages from station to station across nearly two thousand miles of rough terrain. Established in 1860, it became well known for its remarkable speed, since letters that once took weeks, or even months, by stagecoach could arrive in a little over a week. Yet it wasn't only personal mail that was being sent. Government reports, newspapers, and packages that were crucial for business and politics were also delivered at record times.

The Pony Express also demonstrated how important communication was for uniting a growing nation. It connected settlers and leaders across long distances and showed that information could move faster than ever before. For example, the news of Abraham Lincoln's presidential election reached California by this service, which strengthened ties between regions during a tense period. Still, the system's decline came quickly with the spread of the telegraph, which could transmit messages almost instantly. Although it lasted only eighteen months, the Pony Express remains symbolic of the determination and innovation required in linking communities across a nation. Next, we'll examine a map of its routes and stations.

오늘, 우리는 포니 익스프레스를 살펴 볼 텐데, 이는 간단하지만 전설적인 우편물 배달 시스템으로서, 미국 동부 지역과 경계가 확장되던 서부 경계 지역을 연결해 주었습니다. 포니 익스프레스는 말을 타는 단 한 사람의 여정이 아니라, 거의 2천 마일에 달하는 험난한 지형을 가로질러 역에서 역으로 말을 타고 메시지를 전달했던 사람들의 릴레이였습니다. 1860년에 확립된, 이 시스템은 놀랄 만한 그 속도로 잘 알려지게 되었는데, 한때 역마차로 몇 주, 또는 심지어 몇 달씩 걸렸던 편지가 일주일보다 조금 더 걸리는 시간 만에 도착할 수 있었기 때문이었습니다. 하지만 발송된 것은 개인 우편물만이 아니었습니다. 비즈니스와 정치에 있어 아주 중요했던 정부 보고서와 신문, 그리고 소포들도 기록적인 시간으로 배달되었습니다.

포니 익스프레스는 의사 소통이 성장하는 국가를 통합하는 데 있어 얼마나 중요한지도 보여 주었습니다. 이는 장거리에 걸쳐 정착민들과 지도자들을 연결해 주었고, 정보가 그 어느 때보다 더 신속히 이동할 수 있다는 사실을 보여 주었습니다. 예를 들어, 에이브러햄 링컨의 대통령 선거 당선 소식이 이 서비스를 통해 캘리포니아에 이르렀는데, 이는 긴장된 기간 중에 지역들 사이에서 유대감을 강화해 주었습니다. 그럼에도 불구하고, 이 시스템의 쇠퇴는 거의 즉시 메시지를 전송할 수 있었던, 전보의 확산과 함께 빠르게 다가왔습니다. 겨우 18개월 동안만 지속되기는 했지만, 포니 익스프레스는 국가 전체에 걸쳐 지역 사회들을 연결하는 데 필요했던 결단력과 혁신을 상징하는 존재로 남아 있습니다. 다음으로, 그 경로와 역들이 있는 지도를 살펴 보겠습니다.

8 강연의 주제는?
(A) 미국 우편국의 유래
(B) 말이 이끄는 마차의 진화
(C) 우편물 배달 시스템의 유산
(D) 종이에서 디지털 통신으로의 전환

9 강연에 따르면, 포니 익스프레스를 잘 알려지게 만들어 준 측면은?
(A) 인력
(B) 비용
(C) 가격
(D) 속도

10 화자가 에이브러햄 링컨의 당선을 언급한 이유는?
(A) 전보가 왜 시간이 흐를수록 중요해졌는지 설명하기 위해
(B) 포니 익스트레스가 어떻게 지역들을 통합하는 데 도움을 주었는지 설명하기 위해
(C) 고품질 서비스를 위한 포니 익스프레스의 공헌을 강조하기 위해
(D) 1860년대에 있었던 주요 사건을 확인해 주기 위해

11 포니 익스프레스가 역사에 미친 영향과 관련해 추론할 수 있는 것은?
(A) 전국에 걸친 의사 소통에 있어 결단력과 혁신을 대표했다.
(B) 서부 지역들이 경제적으로 팽창하는 데 도움을 주었다.
(C) 다른 인근 국가들에 의해 채택되었다.

(D) 주와 주를 잇는 전화선의 설치에 영향을 주었다.

어휘 및 표현
Pony Express 포니 익스프레스(19세기 미국에서 조랑말을 이용한 우편물을 배달했던 시스템) **brief** 간단한, 짧은 **legendary** 전설적인 **expand** 확장되다, 팽창하다 **frontier** 경계 (지역) **relay** 릴레이, 전달, 중계 **terrain** 지형 **establish** ~을 확립하다 **remarkable** 놀랄 만한, 주목할 만한 **crucial** 아주 중요한 **politics** 정치(학) **demonstrate** ~을 보여 주다 **unite** ~을 통합하다(=unify) **settler** 정착민 **than ever before** 그 어느 때보다 **presidential election** 대통령 선거 **reach** ~에 이르다, ~에 도달하다 **strengthen** ~을 강화하다 **tie** 유대(감) **tense** 긴장된 **decline** 쇠퇴, 하락 **telegraph** 전보 **transmit** ~을 전송하다 **instantly** 즉시 **last** 지속되다 **symbolic** 상징하는 **determination** 결단력(=willpower) **innovation** 혁신 **link** ~을 연결하다 **examine** ~을 살펴 보다 **origin** 유래, 기원 **evolution** 진화, 발전 **legacy** 유산 **transition** 전환 **aspect** 측면, 양상 **prominent** 중요한, 유명한 **portray** ~을 설명하다, ~을 묘사하다 **underscore** ~을 강조하다 **commitment** 공헌, 헌신 **identify** ~을 확인하다 **represent** ~을 대표하다, ~에 해당하다 **adopt** ~을 채택하다 **influence** ~에 영향을 미치다 **interstate** 주와 주를 잇는

12-15 역사학 수업에서의 강연을 들으시오.

Tiwanaku is an ancient civilization located in present-day Bolivia near Lake Titicaca. Even though its site is now in a state of ruins, it was once presumed to be a ceremonial and political center, spanning about 2 square miles at its peak. In fact, the people of Tiwanaku may have had a different name for their city, but it is unknown because they had no written language.

Massive stone structures can be found throughout the site, but over the decades, many parts have been damaged from looting or improper excavation. One reconstructed area is the Semi-Subterranean Temple, a sunken platform decorated with carved stone heads and several pillars protruding from the walls. Although many of its detailed features are not in their most original form, archaeologists believe that the courtyard was used for rituals and astronomical observations.

In Tiwanaku, elites, the general public, and even pilgrims all came to the site to take part in religious ceremonies that worshipped gods related to nature and the sky. This spiritual life was fundamental to Tiwanaku society's survival in the high-altitude Andes Mountains. Next, we will look at another pre-Colombian civilization that developed in the Andean region before the Spanish arrived.

티와나쿠는 티티카카 호수 근처에 현재의 볼리비아에 위치했던 고대 문명이었습니다. 비록 그 부지가 지금은 폐허 상태에 있기는 하지만, 한때 의식 및 정치의 중심지로 여겨졌으며, 절정기에는 약 2 평방 마일에 걸쳐 있었습니다. 사실, 티와나쿠 사람들은 자신들의 도시에 대해 다른 이름을 지니고 있었을 수도 있는데, 이들이 문자 언어가 없었기 때문에 알려져 있지 않습니다.

이 부지 전역에서 거대 석조 구조물들이 발견될 수 있지만, 수십 년 동안에 걸쳐, 많은 부분들이 약탈 또는 부적절한 발굴 작업으로 인해 손상되어 왔습니다. 복원된 구역 한 곳이 '반지하 신전'인데, 이곳은 돌로 조각된 사람 머리와 벽마다 돌출되어 있는 여러 기둥으로 장식된 지면보다 낮은 광장입니다. 그 세부 특징들 중 많은 것이 가장 원형의 형태로 있지는 않지만, 고고학자들은 그 광장이 종교 의식과 천문학적 관찰에 이용되었다고 생각합니다.

티와나쿠에서는, 엘리트 계층과 일반 대중, 그리고 심지어 순례자들도 모두 이 부지로 와서 자연 및 하늘과 관련된 신들을 숭배하는 종교적인 의식에 참여했습니다. 이 영적인 삶은 고도가 높은 안데스 산맥 지역에 위치한 티와나쿠 사회의 생존에 있어 필수적이었습니다. 다음으로, 스페인 사람들이 도착하기 전에 안데스 지역에서 발달한 콜럼버스 시대 이전의 또 다른 문명을 살펴 보겠습니다.

12 강연의 주제는?
(A) 한 고대 유적지가 지닌 중요성
(B) 도시들이 티티카카 호수 근처에서 생겨난 이유
(C) 티와나쿠 사람들에 의해 개발된 건설 방식
(D) 천체의 위치를 바탕으로 한 종교적인 의식들

13 화자가 "티와나쿠"라는 이름과 관련해 말하는 것은?
(A) 한 비문에 새겨진 경전에서 옮겨 적은 것이다.
(B) 문자의 부족으로 인해 글로 기록되지 못했다.
(C) 포르투갈어에서 나온 것이다.
(D) 현재의 볼리비아 주민들에 의해 확립되었다.

14 화자가 '반지하 신전'과 관련해 지적하는 것은?
(A) 관광객들 사이에서 가장 인기 있는 구역이다.
(B) 전에 수백 개의 석조 기둥으로 둘러싸여 있었다.
(C) 많은 변화를 거쳐 왔다.
(D) 그 장식물이 다양한 민족 공동체를 표현한다.

15 화자가 티와나쿠 종교와 관련해 암시하는 것은?
(A) 단일신 숭배와 관련되어 있었다.
(B) 모든 사회 계층에 속한 사람들에 의해 행해졌다.
(C) 티와나쿠 문화에서 작은 역할을 했다.
(D) 오늘날에도 여전히 행해지는 종교 의식을 포함했다.

어휘 및 표현

ancient 고대의 civilization 문명 (사회) state 상태 ruins 폐허, 유적(지) be presumed to do ~하는 것으로 여겨지다(추정되다) ceremonial 의식의, 예식의 political 정치의 span (거리, 기간 등) ~에 걸쳐 있다, ~에 걸쳐 이어지다 peak 절정(기), 전성기 massive 거대한 structure 구조(물) site 부지, 현장 decade 10년 looting 약탈 improper 부적절한 excavation 발굴, 굴착 reconstruct ~을 복원하다, ~을 재건하다 sunken 지면보다 낮은, 가라앉은 carved 조각된 pillar 기둥 protrude from ~에서 돌출되다 detailed 세부적인 feature 특징 archaeologist 고고학자 ritual 종교 의식 astronomical 천문학의 observation 관찰 pilgrim 순례자 take part in ~에 참여하다 religious 종교적인 worship ~을 숭배하다 related to ~와 관련된 spiritual 영적인 fundamental 필수적인, 근본적인 high-altitude 고도가 높은 pre-Colombian 콜럼버스 시대 이전의 emerge 출현하다 method 방식 based on ~을 바탕으로 하는 celestial body 천체 transcribe ~을 옮겨 적다 scripture 경전 monument 기념비(적인 것) undocumented 글로 기록되지 못한 due to ~로 인해 lack 부족 establish ~을 확립하다 undergo ~을 거치다, ~을 겪다 represent ~을 표현하다, ~에 해당하다 ethnic 민족의 involve ~와 관련되다, ~을 수반하다 practice ~을 실천하다, 행하다 play a minor role in ~에 있어 작은 역할을 하다 include ~을 포함하다

TEST 2

Writing

정답 및 모범답안

Build a Sentence

1 Did any of the guests give a speech?
2 He wanted to ask if I plan to attend the seminar.
3 Why have you decided to move away from town?
4 Who told you that the show was canceled?
5 They told me what their favorite features were.
6 Can we find out if they relocated their office first?
7 Do you know if there will be any guest speakers?
8 Can you tell me if the professor gave any new assignments?
9 She wanted to see whom I would work best with.
10 Is that the one where trained animals appear on screen?

Write an Email

Hello Carl,

I hope you are doing well.

I am writing to apologize for the noise coming from my house recently. The noise was due to a family reunion I was hosting. With young children visiting and everyone socializing, I did not realize how loud it had become. I understand how this may have been disruptive, and I am truly sorry for any inconvenience caused. My family will be staying for one more week, and to prevent further disturbance, I have arranged for them to stay at a nearby hotel. I hope this will resolve any inconvenience. Please let me know if there is anything else I can do.

I hope that you have a wonderful day.

Best regards,
Emily

Write for an Academic Discussion

While I understand Bella's point about greater opportunities, I am of the opinion that urbanization creates serious problems. Rapidly growing cities can harm the environment through the overuse of natural resources, such as water and energy. They can also increase greenhouse gas emissions, which contribute to air pollution and climate change. Additionally, overcrowding can make daily life more difficult for residents. High demand for housing often drives up prices, making it harder for people to find affordable places to live. A larger urban population also places a greater burden on infrastructure, particularly the transportation system, leading to traffic congestion and longer commutes. To conclude, the concentration of people in cities gives rise to a variety of challenges.

해석/어휘

Build a Sentence

1-10 적절한 문장을 만드시오.

1 W: 지난주 결혼식 진짜 재밌었어.
   M: 손님 중에 누가 연설했어?

2 M: 왜 교수님이 수업 끝나고 너한테 얘기하고 싶어 했어?
   W: 세미나에 참석할 계획 있는지 물어보시려고 했대.

3 W: 나 곧 새 아파트로 이사가.
   M: 왜 마을을 떠나기로 결정한 거야?

4 W: 토크쇼 소식 들었어.
   M: 그 쇼 취소됐다고 누가 말해줬어?

5 W: 제품 검수자들이 세션 끝나고 뭐라고 했어?
   M: 자신들이 제일 마음에 드는 기능이 무엇인지 말해 줬어.

6 W: 이 소포 바로 보내야 해.
   W: 먼저 사무실 이전했는지 알아볼 수 있어?

7 W: 학교에서 특별 세미나 준비하는 것 같아.
   M: 초청 연사가 있을지 아니?

8 M: 넌 오늘 수업에서 놓친 게 별로 없어.
   W: 교수님이 새 과제 내주셨는지 알려줄래?

9 W: 가브리엘라는 멘토 과제에 대해 뭐라고 했어?
   M: 내가 누구랑 가장 잘 맞게 일할 수 있는지 보고 싶대.

10 W: 〈와일드 라이드〉가 서커스 관련 영화래.
   M: 훈련된 동물들이 나오는 영화가 그거 맞지?

어휘 및 표현

give a speech 연설하다 feature 특징, 기능 package 소포, 꾸러미 relocate 이전하다 assignment 과제

Write an Email

당신은 최근에 가족을 집에 초대했다. 옆집 이웃인 칼이 집에서 나는 소음에 대해 불만을 제기하는 메시지를 보냈다. 당신은 사과하고 다시는 그런 일이 없을 것이라고 안심시키길 원한다.

칼에게 이메일을 작성하시오. 이메일에서 다음을 수행하시오:

- 소음에 대한 이유를 설명하시오.
- 당신의 이웃에게 사과하시오.
- 당신이 어떠한 행동을 취할지 서술하시오.

완전한 문장으로 가능한 한 많이 작성하시오.

당신의 답변:

수신인: 칼
제목: 소음에 대한 사과

칼에게,

잘 지내시죠.

최근 저희 집에서 발생한 소음에 대해 사과하기 위해 이메일을 씁니다. 소음은 제가 주최한 가족 모임때문이었어요. 어린 아이들이 방문하고 모두가 어울리다 보니 소음이 얼마나 커졌는지 깨닫지 못했네요. 이로 인해 얼마나 지장을 주었는지 알고 있으며, 야기된 어떠한 불편에 대해서도 진심으로 사과드려요. 가족들은 앞으로 일주일 더 머무를 예정인데, 추가적인 소란을 방지하기 위해, 근처 호텔에 숙박하도록 마련했어요. 이로 인해 어떠한 불편도 해소되길 바랍니다. 제가 할 다른 것이 있다면 알려 주세요.

좋은 하루 되시길 바랍니다.

안녕히 계세요.
에밀리

(120 단어)

어휘 및 표현

apologize 사과하다　**reassure** ~을 안심시키다　**take an action** 행동을 취하다　**family reunion** 가족 모임　**host** ~을 주최하다　**socialize** 어울리다　**disruptive** 지장을 주는　**inconvenience** 불편　**disturbance** 소란, 방해　**arrange** 마련하다　**resolve** ~을 해결하다

Write for an Academic Discussion

교수가 인문 지리학 수업을 진행 중이다. 교수의 질문에 답변하는 게시글을 작성하시오.

답변에서는 다음을 수행해야 한다:
- 본인의 의견을 제시하고 뒷받침하시오.
- 토론에 본인의 표현으로 기여하시오.

효과적인 답변은 최소 100단어 이상이어야 한다.

로드리고 박사: 다음 주, 우리는 도시화를 논의할 예정인데, 도시화란 사람들이 도시로 이동하고 도시 지역의 인구가 증가하는 것을 의미합니다. 일부는 더 많은 사람들이 도시에 거주하면 생활 수준이 향상된다고 주장하는 반면, 다른 이들은 다양한 문제를 야기한다고 믿습니다. 이 문제에 대해 여러분의 관점은 무엇입니까? 그 이유는 무엇입니까?

벨라: 저는 도시에 살기 위해 더 많은 사람들이 오는 것은 좋은 일이라고 생각합니다. 도시는 일자리와 교육 기회가 더 풍부한 것으로 알려져 있습니다. 사람들이 도시로 이주하면, 자녀를 더 우수한 교사진이 있는 학교에 보낼 수 있습니다. 또한, 시골보다 도시에서 훨씬 더 많은 취업 기회를 얻을 수 있습니다.

제이콥: 저는 도시에 더 많은 사람이 사는 것이 좋은 일이라고 생각하지 않습니다. 도시는 인구 밀도가 높아 사람들이 서로 가까이 지내는 경우가 많습니다. 이로 인해 질병이 빠르게 확산되기 쉬워져 유행병 위험이 증가하고 공중 보건에 더 큰 위협이 됩니다.

벨라의 더 많은 기회에 대한 주장은 이해되지만, 저는 도시화가 심각한 문제를 야기한다고 생각합니다. 급속히 성장하는 도시는 물과 에너지 같은 천연자원의 과도한 사용으로 환경을 훼손할 수 있습니다. 또한 온실가스 배출을 증가시켜, 대기 오염과 기후 변화에 기여하기도 합니다. 더불어, 과밀화는 주민들의 일상생활을 더욱 어렵게 만듭니다. 높은 주택 수요는 가격을 끌어 올려, 사람들이 살기 좋은 가격대의 주거지를 찾기 어렵게 만듭니다. 더 많은 도시 인구는 또한 교통 시스템을 비롯한 인프라에 더 큰 부담을 가해, 교통 체증과 통근 시간 증가로 이어집니다. 결론적으로, 도시로의 인구 집중은 다양한 문제를 야기합니다.

(117 단어)

어휘 및 표현

human geography 인문 지리학 **urbanization** 도시화 **population** 인구 **living standard** 생활 수준 **a variety of** 다양한 **perspective** 관점 **opportunity** 기회 **densely** 인구가 밀집한, 빽빽한 **close proximity** 인접, 아주 가까움 **outbreak** 유행병의 발발 **be of the opinion that** ~라고 생각하다 **rapidly** 급속히 **overuse** 과도한 사용 **greenhouse gas emissions** 온실가스 배출 **pollution** 오염 **climate change** 기후 변화 **overcrowding** 과밀화 **resident** 주민 **drive up** ~을 끌어 올리다 **affordable** 알맞은 **place a burden** 부담을 가하다 **traffic congestion** 교통 체증 **concentration** 집중 **challenge** 문제

TEST 2
Speaking

정답 및 모범답안

Listen and Repeat

1 Welcome to the university library.
2 Our library has a wide selection of books.
3 Newspapers and magazines are located over here.
4 Over here is where you can borrow and return books.
5 You can use the computer to search the library's database.
6 The printer is currently being repaired and is not available for use.
7 If you need help locating a resource, please go to the counter for assistance.

Take an Interview

1 *Thank you for taking the time to speak with me about careers. First, what are the most common career paths that people you know tend to choose? For example, do they work in education, media, hospitality, or other fields?*

I would say that most of my family members work in healthcare. For example, both of my parents are doctors, and many of my extended family members work in hospitals as nurses or pharmacists. Among my friends, the most common career path seems to be education, as many are studying to become teachers. Careers in technology, like programming or IT, are also fairly popular. To sum up, the majority of people around me tend to choose careers in healthcare, education, and technology.

2 *Interesting. Do you think it is better to change careers or to stay in one career for a long time? Why?*

I tend to think it is more beneficial to change careers at least once or twice. This is because moving between different companies or industries is a good way to expand your professional network. You can meet and work with a wide range of colleagues, supervisors, and industry experts, and you can learn a lot from these experiences. The connections you make can also be very helpful later in your career. Overall, I believe changing careers can offer more opportunities for professional growth.

3 *Interesting. Next, I'd like to get your opinion. Where I live, more people are choosing to work shorter hours for less pay. What is your opinion on this trend? Do you think it is better to earn less but have more free time, or to work longer hours for higher pay?*

In my opinion, it is better to earn less but have more free time. One reason is that extra free time allows people to relax and unwind after a stressful day at work, and it also helps prevent burnout. Another reason is that it provides opportunities to focus on personal growth, such as pursuing hobbies, traveling, or spending time with loved ones, which all contribute to a person's overall well-being. For these reasons, I believe that working shorter hours despite the lower pay has more benefits.

4 *Good points. I just have one more question. Some people believe that AI will replace many jobs in the future. Do you agree or disagree? Explain why you think so.*

I agree with the statement that AI will replace many jobs in the future. In fact, this phenomenon is already happening on a large scale in various industries. Because AI technology is advancing rapidly while the cost of it is also decreasing, many jobs are being taken over by AI. For example, positions in manufacturing, customer service, and even some creative fields, like writing and graphic design, are being affected. In conclusion, I predict that even more jobs will be replaced by AI in the future.

해석/어휘

Listen and Repeat

당신은 대학교 도서관에서 학생들을 돕는 연수를 받고 있다. 트레이너의 말을 듣고 따라 하시오. 오직 한 번만 따라 하시오.

1 대학교 도서관에 오신 것을 환영합니다.

2 우리 도서관에는 다양한 종류의 책이 있습니다.

3 신문과 잡지는 이쪽에 있습니다.

4 이곳에서 책을 대출하거나 반납할 수 있습니다.

5 컴퓨터를 이용해 도서관 데이터베이스를 검색할 수 있습니다.

6 프린터는 현재 수리 중이라 사용하실 수 없습니다.

7 자료의 위치를 찾는 데 도움이 필요하시면 안내 데스크로 가서 도움을 받으세요.

어휘 및 표현
a wide selection of 다양한 종류의 locate ~의 위치를 찾다 resource 자료 assistance 도움

Take an Interview

당신은 경력에 대한 연구 조사에 참여하기로 동의하였다. 당신은 연구원과 간단한 온라인 인터뷰를 진행하게 된다. 연구원이 몇 가지 질문을 할 것이다.

1 저와 경력에 대해 이야기할 시간을 내주셔서 감사합니다. 먼저, 당신이 아는 사람들은 주로 어떤 직업 경로를 선택하나요? 예를 들어, 교육, 미디어, 서비스업 등 어떤 분야에서 일하나요?

제 가족 대부분은 의료 분야에서 일한다고 할 수 있습니다. 예를 들어, 부모님 두 분 모두 의사이시고, 친척들 중에는 간호사나 약사로 병원에서 일하는 분들이 많습니다. 제 친구들 중에서는 교육 분야를 선택하는 경우가 가장 흔한데, 교사가 되기 위해 공부 중인 친구들이 많습니다. 또한 프로그래밍이나 IT 같은 기술 분야도 꽤 인기가 있습니다. 요약하자면, 제 주변 사람들 다수는 의료, 교육, 기술 분야의 직업을 선택하는 편입니다.

2 흥미롭네요. 그럼, 직업을 바꾸는 것이 좋다고 생각하나요, 아니면 한 직업에 오래 머무는 것이 좋다고 생각

하나요? 이유는요?

저는 적어도 한두 번은 직업을 바꾸는 것이 더 유익하다고 생각하는 편입니다. 그 이유는, 서로 다른 회사나 산업을 오가며 일하는 것이 전문적인 인맥을 넓히는 좋은 방법이기 때문입니다. 그 과정에서 다양한 동료, 상사, 업계 전문가들과 만나고 협력하면서 많은 것을 배울 수 있습니다. 이렇게 쌓은 인맥은 나중에 경력 발전에도 큰 도움이 될 수 있습니다. 전반적으로, 저는 직업을 바꾸는 것이 더 많은 성장 기회를 제공한다고 믿습니다.

3 흥미롭네요. 다음으로, 당신의 의견을 듣고 싶습니다. 제가 사는 곳에서는 적은 급여를 받더라도 근무 시간을 줄이려는 사람들이 늘고 있습니다. 이런 추세에 대해 어떻게 생각하나요? 더 많은 여가를 위해 수입을 줄이는 게 낫다고 생각하나요, 아니면 더 많은 돈을 벌기 위해 오래 일하는 게 낫다고 생각하나요?

제 생각에는, 적게 벌더라도 여가 시간이 더 많은 것이 낫습니다. 그 이유 중 하나는, 여가 시간이 많으면 직장에서의 스트레스 많은 하루를 끝내고 쉬면서 긴장을 풀 수 있어 번아웃을 예방할 수 있기 때문입니다. 또 다른 이유는, 취미 생활을 하거나 여행을 가거나 가족 및 친구들과 시간을 보내는 등 개인의 성장을 위한 시간을 가질 수 있기 때문입니다. 이러한 활동들은 모두 전반적인 행복을 높이는 데 도움이 됩니다. 이런 이유들로, 저는 급여가 조금 적더라도 근무 시간을 줄이는 것이 더 많은 이점을 준다고 생각합니다.

4 좋은 지적이에요. 마지막으로 한 가지 질문만 더 하겠습니다. 어떤 사람들은 인공지능(AI)이 앞으로 많은 일자리를 대체할 것이라고 믿습니다. 이에 대해 동의하나요, 아니면 반대하나요? 그 이유를 설명해주세요.

저는 AI가 앞으로 많은 일자리를 대체할 것이라는 의견에 동의합니다. 사실, 이런 현상은 이미 여러 산업에서 대규모로 일어나고 있습니다. AI 기술은 빠른 속도로 발전하고 있으며, 그 비용 또한 점점 낮아지고 있기 때문에 많은 직종이 AI로 대체되고 있습니다. 예를 들어, 제조업, 고객 서비스, 그리고 글쓰기나 그래픽 디자인 같은 일부 창의적 분야에서도 영향을 받고 있습니다. 결론적으로, 앞으로 더 많은 일자리가 AI에 의해 대체될 것이라고 예측합니다.

어휘 및 표현

career path 직업 경로　**healthcare** 의료　**extended family member** 친척　**pharmacist** 약사　**fairly** 꽤　**the majority of** ~의 다수　**professional network** 전문적 인맥　**a wide range of** 다양한　**colleague** 동료　**supervisor** 상사　**expert** 전문가　**relax and unwind** 쉬면서 긴장을 풀다　**burnout** 번아웃, 기력 소모　**contribute to** ~에 기여하다　**well-being** 안녕, 행복, 건강　**on a large scale** 대규모로

TEST 3
Reading Module 1

정답

Complete the Words
1-10   ow, eps, ration, ping, nd, ese, tions, so, o, ferent
11-20   rms, rgy, dered, inable, sil, ause, o, se, ural, r

Read in Daily Life
21-22   (B), (A)
23-25   (C), (C), (B)
26-28   (D), (C), (B)

Read an Academic Passage
29-33   (B), (C), (B), (A), (A)

해석/어휘

Complete the Words

1-10 다음 문단에서 빠진 글자를 채우시오.

> 요리법은 음식을 만드는 과정을 안내하는 지침이다. 요리법은 자르기, 섞기, 굽기 등 준비 과정의 다양한 단계를 보여준다. 이러한 단계별 지침 또한 맛이나 식감 같은 다양한 선호도에 맞게 달라질 수도 있다. 전통적, 현대적, 퓨전 버전 등 여러 유형이 존재한다. 요리와 요리법(요리가 만들어지는 과정)에 대한 연구는 각 문화의 음식 전통과 다양한 지역에서 맛이 어떻게 발전해 왔는지를 우리에게 알려줄 수 있다.

어휘 및 표현

recipe 요리법, 조리법 instructions 지시, 안내 guide ~을 안내하다, 이끌다 meal 식사, 음식 preparation 준비, 조리 과정 chopping 썰기, 자르기 mixing 섞기, 혼합하기 baking 굽기 step-by-step 단계별의, 순차적인 directions 지침, 방법 preference 선호, 기호 flavor 맛, 풍미 texture 식감, 질감 traditional 전통적인 fusion 퓨전, 혼합 culinary 요리의, 조리의 art 기법, 기술 evolve 발전하다, 진화하다

11-20 다음 문단에서 빠진 글자를 채우시오.

> 전 세계적으로 에너지 수요가 계속 증가함에 따라 태양, 바람, 물과 같은 재생 가능한 에너지원에 대한 관심이 높아지고 있다. 이러한 형태의 에너지는 천연자원을 고갈시키거나 대기를 오염시키지 않기 때문에 화석 연료보다 더 지속 가능하다고 여겨진다. 예를 들어, 태양광 패널은 광전 효과로 알려진 과정을 이용하여 태양빛을 전기로 변환한다. 한편, 풍력 터빈은 움직이는 공기의 운동 에너지를 포착하여 사용할 수 있는 전력으로 바꾼다.

어휘 및 표현

demand 수요 renewable 재생 가능한 source 자원, 원천 power 전력, 힘 sustainable 지속 가능한 fossil fuel 화석 연료 natural resource 천연 자원 pollute ~을 오염시키다 atmosphere 대기 solar panel 태양광

패널 convert 변환하다 photovoltaic effect 광전 효과 wind turbine 풍력 터빈 capture ~을 포착하다, 잡다
kinetic energy 운동 에너지 transform 바꾸다

Read in Daily Life

21-22 이메일을 읽으시오.

날짜: 6월 3일
제목: 예약 도서 수령

친애하는 그린 씨께,

고객님께서 예약하신 도서 『항해의 역사』는 6월 8일 오전 9시부터 11시 사이에 하퍼 도서관 안내 데스크에서 수령하실 수 있습니다. 도서는 카드 소지자에게만 대여가 가능하므로, 도서를 수령하러 오실 때는 반드시 도서관 카드를 지참해주시기 바랍니다.

안녕히 계세요.
로라 하퍼 드림

---

21 그린 씨가 책을 가장 일찍 수령할 수 있는 시간은?
(A) 오전 8시
(B) 오전 9시
(C) 오전 10시
(D) 오전 11시

22 그린 씨가 도서관 카드를 반드시 가져와야 하는 이유는?
(A) 본인 확인을 위해
(B) 요금을 지불하기 위해
(C) 더 많은 책을 대출하기 위해
(D) 예약을 연장하기 위해

어휘 및 표현
subject 제목 reserved 예약된 pickup 수령 reminder 알림, 상기시키는 말 seafaring 항해 available 이용 가능한, 준비된 front desk 안내 데스크 library 도서관 collect ~을 수령하다, 모으다 item 물품, 항목 release ~을 인도하다, 내보내다 cardholder 카드 소지자 confirm ~을 확인하다 identity 신원 fee 요금 borrow ~을 빌리다, 대출하다 reservation 예약

23-25 이메일을 읽으시오.

날짜: 4월 5일
제목: 직원 워크숍

친애하는 발데즈 씨께,

존슨 오피스 솔루션즈의 연례 전문성 개발 워크숍이 5월 2일 금요일 오전 9시에 정확히 이스톤 에비뉴의 회의실에서

시작될 예정입니다. 모든 팀 리더는 반드시 참석하여 그룹 활동을 지원해야 합니다. 귀하의 팀 훈련 보고서가 행사 이틀 전까지 업데이트되어 업로드되었는지 확인해 주시기 바랍니다. 워크숍은 하루 대부분 동안 진행될 것으로 예상되므로, 리버사이드 카페에서 참석자들에게 점심이 제공될 예정입니다.

첨부된 직원 명단을 검토하시고 귀하의 팀원 중 누가 워크숍에 참석할 것인지 확인해 주세요. 최종 명단은 코르테즈 씨에게 보내주시기 바랍니다. 또한 5월 3일 오전에는 팀 리더들이 전날 행사에 대한 피드백 세션에 참석해야 하므로 고객 통화 일정을 잡지 않도록 부탁드립니다.

안녕히 계세요.
엠마 존슨 드림

23 존슨 씨가 발데즈 씨에게 이메일을 보낸 이유는?
(A) 그녀가 활동을 이끄는 것을 돕기 위해
(B) 그녀에게 훈련 보고서를 업데이트하라고 상기시키기 위해
(C) 다가오는 행사에 대해 알리기 위해
(D) 절차 수정에 대한 그녀의 의견을 요청하기 위해

24 발데즈 씨가 코르테즈 씨에게 연락해야 하는 이유는?
(A) 공급 목록을 요청하기 위해
(B) 행사 활동을 제안하기 위해
(C) 행사 참석자를 확인하기 위해
(D) 고객 통화 일정을 공유하기 위해

25 5월 3일 오전에 대해 시사하는 것은?
(A) 워크숍의 마지막 활동들이 진행될 것이다.
(B) 발데즈 씨가 워크숍에 대한 자신의 의견을 제공할 것이다.
(C) 직원들이 리버사이드 카페에서 점심을 제공받을 것이다.
(D) 발데즈 씨가 회사 고객들로부터 피드백을 수집할 것이다.

어휘 및 표현
staff 직원 workshop 워크숍, 연수 annual 연례의 professional 전문적인 development 개발, 성장 conference hall 회의실 attend ~에 참석하다 training 훈련, 교육 event 행사 attendee 참석자 review ~을 검토하다 attached 첨부된 employee list 직원 명단 schedule ~ 일정을 잡다 client call 고객 통화 session 세션, 시간 regarding ~에 대한 previous 이전의

26-28 문자 메시지 대화를 읽으시오.

짐 니콜슨 (오후 2:00)	안녕하세요 여러분, 프로그램 업데이트 마감이 내일이라는 점을 다시 한 번 알려드립니다. 제출 전에 모든 테스트를 마무리해 주세요.
샘 킴 (오후 2:05)	알겠습니다. 새 버전이 얼마나 직관적일지 조금 걱정했는데, 포커스 그룹의 피드백이 정말 힘을 주네요!
유진 비쇼프 (오후 2:10)	좋은 소식이네요, 샘. 제가 원활하게 작동하는지 확인하기 위해 여러 기기에서 점검을 진행하겠습니다.

| 크레이그 모리 (오후 2:15) | 만일 큰 문제들이 발생하면, 제가 도와드릴 수 있습니다. 이메일을 꼼꼼히 확인하고 있을게요. |
| 짐 니콜슨 (오후 2:20) | 고마워요, 크레이그. 완성도 높고 신뢰할 수 있는 업데이트를 목표로 합시다. |

26 유진의 책임은?
(A) 모든 테스트 요구 사항을 최종 확정하는 것
(B) 모든 테스트 항목을 체크하는 것
(C) 포커스 그룹의 피드백을 분석하는 것
(D) 다양한 기기에 안정성 테스트

27 크레이그가 도울 방법은?
(A) 동료들에게 연락함으로써
(B) 신뢰할 수 있는 업데이트에 대해 이메일을 보냄으로써
(C) 어떠한 비상사태를 처리함으로써
(D) 포커스 그룹을 지원함으로써

28 업데이트된 프로그램에 대해 추론할 수 있는 것은?
(A) 회사의 가장 성공적인 제품이다.
(B) 사용하기 쉽다.
(C) 부정적인 평가를 받았다.
(D) 모든 기기에서 작동한다.

어휘 및 표현

reminder 알림, 상기시키는 말 update 업데이트, 수정 사항 testing 테스트, 시험 intuitive 직관적인 focus group 포커스 그룹 (소규모 조사 집단) encouraging 격려의, 힘을 주는 run 진행하다, 운영하다 check 확인, 점검 across 전체에 걸쳐, 온 device 기기 seamlessly 원활하게, 매끄럽게 pop up 발생하다, 나오다 aim ~을 목표로 하다 polished 완성된 reliable 신뢰할 수 있는 requirement 요구 사항 check off 체크 표시하다 testing box 테스트 박스 항목 analyze ~을 분석하다 colleague 동료 emergency 비상사태 function 작동하다

Read an Academic Passage
29-33 사막 식물의 광합성 적응

사막 식물은 강렬한 햇빛, 고온, 제한된 수분 등 극한 환경에 직면한다. 생존을 위해 많은 사막 식물은 광합성—식물이 햇빛, 이산화탄소, 물을 에너지와 산소로 전환하는 과정—에 특화된 적응 방식을 발달시켜왔다.

주요 적응 방식 중 하나는 크레슐산 대사(CAM) 광합성 경로이다. 대부분의 식물이 낮에 기공이라 불리는 잎의 아주 작은 구멍을 열어 이산화탄소를 흡수하는 것과 달리, CAM 식물은 밤에 기공을 연다. 밤에는 기온이 더 낮기에 이러한 타이밍은 증발로 인한 수분 손실을 줄인다. 흡수된 이산화탄소는 저장되었다가 낮에 광합성에 사용된다.

또 다른 전략은 C4 광합성 경로로, 이 경로에서 사막 식물들은 이산화탄소를 포획하는 더 효율적인 방법을 진화시켰다. 광합성에 이산화탄소를 직접 사용하는 대신, 먼저 특수 세포에 농축시켜 강한 햇빛과 고온에서도 효율적으로 광합성을 지속할 수 있게 한다. 이 적응은 다른 식물들이 금방 시들어 버리는 뜨겁고 건조한 환경에서 사막 식물들이 번성하도록 돕는다.

이러한 광합성 적응은 개별 종의 생존을 돕는 동시에 생태계 전체를 형성한다. 사막 식물은 식생 피복을 유지함으로써 토양 침식을 방지하고 다양한 야생동물을 지원한다. 과학자들은 이 식물들이 에너지와 수분 사용을 어떻게 효율적으로 관리하는지 이해하기 위해 계속해서 연구하고 있다. 이 연구에서 얻은 통찰은 향후 가뭄에 강한 작물 개발에 기여할 수 있을 것으로 보인다.

29 지문의 단어 "convert"에 가장 가까운 의미는?
(A) 저장하다
(B) 변환하다
(C) 흡수하다
(D) 제거하다

30 지문에 따르면, CAM 광합성의 주요 장점은?
(A) 물의 증발 속도를 증가시킨다.
(B) 식물이 더 많은 햇빛을 흡수할 수 있게 한다.
(C) 밤에 활동함으로써 수분 손실을 줄인다.
(D) 식물이 이산화탄소를 생성하는 것을 방지한다.

31 C4 경로가 CAM 경로와 다른 점은?
(A) 전적으로 야간 광합성에 의존한다.
(B) 식물이 강렬한 햇빛 아래서 효율적으로 기능할 수 있게 한다.
(C) 서늘한 환경에서만 발생한다.
(D) 이산화탄소를 며칠 동안 저장한다.

32 2 문단과 3 문단의 관계는?
(A) 2 문단은 한 종류의 시스템을 소개하고, 3 문단은 다른 시스템을 기술한다.
(B) 2 문단은 주장을 제시하고, 3 문단은 이를 반박한다.
(C) 2 문단은 문제를 설명하고, 3 문단은 해결책을 제시한다.
(D) 2 문단은 이론을 제시하고, 3 문단은 뒷받침하는 근거를 제공한다.

33 글쓴이가 마지막 문단에서 가뭄에 강한 작물 개발을 언급한 이유는?
(A) 사막 식물이 인간에게 어떻게 도움이 될 수 있는지 설명하기 위해
(B) 사막 식물과 작물의 영양가를 비교하기 위해
(C) 기후 변화의 위험성을 강조하기 위해
(D) 사막 식물의 화학적 구조를 설명하기 위해

어휘 및 표현

photosynthesis 광합성 adaptation 적응 extreme 극한 intense 강렬한 specialized 특화된 process 과정 convert ~을 전환하다 carbon dioxide 이산화탄소 oxygen 산소 acid 산, 산성 metabolism 대사, 신진대사 pathway 경로 pore 구멍 stomata 기공(stoma)의 복수형 absorb ~을 흡수하다 timing 타이밍, 시기 선택 evaporation 증발 strategy 전략 evolve ~을 진화시키다, 발달시키다 capture ~을 잡다, 포획하다 concentrate ~을 농축시키다, 집중시키다 photosynthesize 광합성하다 thrive 번성하다 wilt 시들다, 지치다 shape ~을 형성하다 ecosystem 생태계 vegetation cover 식생 피복(땅에 식물이 덮여 있는 정도나 상태) soil erosion 토양 침식 wildlife 야생동물 insight 통찰 contribute to ~에 기여하다 drought-resistant 가뭄에 강한 crop 작물 state ~을 말하다 refute ~을 반박하다 theory 이론 evidence 근거 nutritional value 영양가

Reading Module 2

> 정답

Complete the Words

1-10   nicate, al, sical, nd, rds, own, eir, ial, ten, ch

Read an Academic Passage

11-15   (C), (D), (C), (B), (B)

> 해석/어휘

Complete the Words

1-10   다음 문단에서 빠진 글자를 채우시오.

> 펭귄은 날지 못하는 새로, 콜로니라고 불리는 집단 속에서 번성한다. 이들은 음성 신호, 몸짓, 그리고 접촉을 통해 소통한다. 이 새들은 강한 사회적 유대로 잘 알려져 있으며, 위험한 순간에 서로를 자주 도와준다. 이들은 먹이터와 안전한 둥지 장소를 기억할 수 있는데, 이는 혹독한 기후 속에서 생존하는 데 도움이 된다. 이러한 회복력 있는 동물은 생태계에서 중요한 역할을 하며, 물고기 개체 수를 조절하고, 영양분 순환을 돕고, 해양 생물 다양성을 유지하는 데 기여한다.

어휘 및 표현

flightless 날지 못하는 **thrive** 번성하다, 잘 자라다 **colony** 집단, 군락 **communicate** 소통하다 **vocal** 음성의, 소리의 **physical** 신체적 **social bond** 사회적 유대 **danger** 위험 **feeding ground** 먹이터 **nesting area** 둥지 장소 **harsh climate** 혹독한 기후 **resilient** 회복력 있는 **crucial** 결정적인, 매우 중요한 **ecosystem** 생태계 **cycle** 순환하다 **nutrient** 영양분 **marine** 해양의 **biodiversity** 생물 다양성

Read an Academic Passage

11-15   문자 체계의 역사

> 문자의 발명은 지식을 저장하고 세대 간에 전달할 수 있게 함으로써 인류 문명을 변화시켰다. 초기 문자 체계에는 사물을 단순한 이미지로 나타낸 그림 문자가 포함되어 있었다. 시간이 지나면서 이러한 체계는 소리와 개념을 나타내는 기호로 발전하였고, 이는 알파벳과 표어 문자 체계의 기반을 놓았다. 문자는 행정, 교역, 그리고 문화적 정체성의 보존에 중요한 역할을 했다.
>
> 언어학적 연구에 따르면, 문자 체계는 지리적 환경, 사용 가능한 재료, 그리고 사회적 필요에 의해 형성되어 왔다. 예를 들어, 쐐기 문자는 점토판에 새겨졌고, 이집트의 상형 문자는 돌에 조각되거나 파피루스에 채색되었다. 각 문자 체계는 언어적 특징뿐만 아니라 그것을 만든 사회가 가진 자원도 반영했다.
>
> 오늘날 학자들은 문자 체계의 발전을 연구하여 의사소통이 인류의 진보를 어떻게 형성했는지를 이해하려고 한다. 그들은 알파벳이 문화적 접촉을 통해 어떻게 퍼졌는지, 문자 체계가 새로운 언어에 어떻게 적응했는지, 그리고 문해력이 사회 구조를 어떻게 변화시켰는지를 살펴본다. 문자의 진화를 이해하는 것은 교육의 성장, 관료제의 등장, 그리고 대륙 간 아이디어의 전달을 설명하는 데 도움이 된다.

11 지문의 단어 "foundation"에 가장 가까운 의미는?
(A) 제한
(B) 설립, 확립
(C) 기초, 기반
(D) 번역

12 초기 문자 체계는 ~을 제외하고 다음 중 모든 것에 기여했다.
(A) 문화 보존
(B) 행정 목적
(C) 교역 활동
(D) 종교 행사

13 2 문단에 따르면, 초기 문자 체계의 형태에 영향을 준 것은?
(A) 계절적 날씨
(B) 정치적 지도력
(C) 지역 자재
(D) 농업의 확산

14 2 문단과 3 문단의 관계는?
(A) 3 문단은 2 문단의 역사적 사례들과 모순된다.
(B) 3 문단은 2 문단에서 언급된 문자 체계의 문화적 영향에 대해 자세히 설명한다.
(C) 3 문단은 2 문단에서 소개된 지리적 중요성을 일축한다.
(D) 3 문단은 현대 알파벳에만 초점을 맞추는 반면, 2 문단은 고대 문자 체계에 대해 설명한다.

15 현재 학자들이 탐구하고 있는 것은?
(A) 알파벳과 종교 사이의 연결
(B) 문자 체계가 새로운 언어에 적응하는 방식
(C) 교역이 기존 체계를 대체하는 데에 미친 역할
(D) 기후가 문해율에 미친 영향

어휘 및 표현

invention 발명 writing 문자, 글쓰기 transform ~을 변화시키다 civilization 문명 store ~을 저장하다 transmit ~을 전달하다 script 문자 체계 pictograph 그림 문자 represent ~을 나타내다 evolve 발전하다, 진화하다 symbol 기호 sound 소리 foundation 기초 logographic 표어의(단어를 나타내는) crucial 결정적인, 매우 중요한 administration 행정 trade 무역, 교역 preservation 보존 cultural identity 문화적 정체성 linguistic 언어학적인 geography 지리 material 재료, 자재 societal 사회적인 cuneiform 쐐기 문자 inscribe ~을 새기다 clay tablet 점토판 hieroglyph 상형 문자(고대 이집트에서 사용) papyrus 파피루스 carve ~을 조각하다, 새기다 feature 특징 scholar 학자 shape ~을 형성하다 progress 진보 adapt to ~에 적응하다 literacy 문해력, 읽고 쓸 줄 아는 능력 social structure 사회 구조 evolution 발전, 진화 bureaucracy 관료제 spread 확산 agriculture 농업 contradict ~와 모순되다, ~을 반박하다 elaborate 자세히 설명하다, 상술하다 dismiss ~을 일축하다, 묵살하다 explore ~을 탐구하다 religion 종교

TEST 3
Listening Module 1

정답

Listen and Choose a Response

1-8 (A), (A), (B), (A), (D), (B), (A), (D)

Listen to a Conversation

9-10 (C), (C)
11-12 (A), (B)

Listen to an Announcement

13-14 (A), (A)
15-16 (C), (D)

Listen to an Academic Talk

17-20 (B), (C), (A), (B)

스크립트/해석/어휘

Listen and Choose a Response

1-8 가장 적절한 응답을 고르시오.

1 Why won't this printer start?
왜 이 프린터가 작동하지 않지?

(A) 전원선이 느슨하네.
(B) 창문이 열려 있어.
(C) 복도 불이 켜져 있어.
(D) 난 보고서를 이미 제출했어.

2 I can't attend the workshop tomorrow.
나 내일 워크숍에 참석할 수 없어.

(A) 그럼 다른 날짜를 알아보자.
(B) 지난번엔 일찍 도착했어?
(C) 내 일정에도 없었어.
(D) 어제 늦게 회의가 있었어.

3 The student art fair is scheduled for next Friday evening.
학생 미술 전시회는 다음 주 금요일 저녁으로 예정되어 있어.

(A) 그거 내가 들어줄게.
(B) 누가 전시품을 심사하는지 알아?
(C) 구내식당은 보통 일찍 문을 닫아.

(D) 내 친구는 달리기를 잘해.

4 What time should I meet David at the bus station?
내가 데이빗을 버스 정류장에서 몇 시에 만나야 하지?

(A) 내가 처리할게—너는 안 가도 돼.
(B) 그는 창가 자리를 좋아해.
(C) 정류장 카페가 막 다시 문을 열었어.
(D) 공사 때문에 입구가 막혔어.

5 Doesn't the pharmacy stay open late on Thursdays?
약국은 목요일에 늦게까지 열지 않나?

(A) 난 안 가는 게 좋겠어.
(B) 아니, 시간이 너무 오래 걸려.
(C) 공원 바로 옆에 있어.
(D) 응, 맞아.

6 Did you bring the travel documents?
여행 서류 가져왔어?

(A) 버스 타는 게 더 빨라.
(B) 초록색 폴더 안에 있어.
(C) 아무거나 괜찮아.
(D) 응, 나도 방금 도착했어.

7 Wait, the theater performance isn't tomorrow night, is it?
잠깐만, 연극 공연이 내일 밤은 아니지, 그렇지?

(A) 아니, 오늘 밤이야.
(B) 아니, 난 참석 못 해.
(C) 응, 정말 가고 싶어.
(D) 응, 그들이 맞아.

8 I'm not free later this afternoon.
난 오늘 오후 늦게는 시간이 안 돼.

(A) 나 이미 여기 있어.
(B) 보통 좀 오래 걸려.
(C) 그건 의도한 게 아니었어.
(D) 알겠어.

어휘 및 표현

power cable 전원선 loose 느슨한, 꽉 끼여있지 않은 hallway 복도 fair 전시회, 박람회 judge ~을 심사하다
exhibit 전시품 cafeteria 구내식당, 카페테리아 handle ~을 처리하다 construction 공사 block ~을 막다
entrance 입구 pharmacy 약국 theater performance 연극 공연 intentional 의도적인

Listen to a Conversation

9-10 대화를 들으시오.

> M: My phone keeps shutting down on its own. It freezes and restarts constantly.
> 내 휴대폰이 자꾸 혼자 꺼져. 멈췄다가 계속 재시작돼.
>
> W: That must be annoying. Did you try updating the software or running a scan?
> 정말 짜증나겠네. 소프트웨어 업데이트나 스캔은 해봤어?
>
> M: Yes, both. It didn't solve the problem. I may need to take it to a repair shop.
> 응, 둘 다 해봤어. 문제 해결이 안 됐어. 수리점에 맡겨야 할 것 같아.
>
> W: That's a smart idea. They'll be able to figure out the cause.
> 좋은 생각이야. 거기서 원인을 알아낼 수 있을 거야.
>
> M: I'll stop by this afternoon.
> 오늘 오후에 들를게.

9 남자가 겪고 있는 휴대폰 문제는?
(A) 화면이 깨졌다.
(B) 전원이 켜지지 않는다.
(C) 계속 재부팅된다.
(D) 충전 속도가 매우 느리다.

10 남자가 나중에 할 가능성이 가장 높은 일은?
(A) 새 기기를 구매한다
(B) 소프트웨어를 업데이트한다
(C) 수리 센터를 방문한다
(D) 여자의 휴대폰을 사용한다

어휘 및 표현

shut down 정지하다, 꺼지다 on one's own 혼자, 스스로 freeze 멈추다 restart 다시 시작하다 constantly 계속, 끊임없이 annoying 짜증나는, 성가신 run a scan 스캔하다, 스캔 검사를 실행하다 repair 수리 figure out ~을 알아내다 cause 원인 stop by 들르다 cracked 깨진 charge 충전하다 purchase ~을 구매하다

11-12 대화를 들으시오.

> M: Are you heading to the print shop today?
> 오늘 인쇄소에 갈 거야?
>
> W: I stopped by there this morning. Why?
> 오늘 아침에 잠깐 들렀어. 왜?
>
> M: I just realized I promised to bring handouts for tomorrow's presentation, and I won't have a chance to get them printed tonight.
> 내가 내일 발표용 유인물을 가져오기로 약속한 걸 이제야 기억했는데, 오늘 밤엔 인쇄할 기회가 없을 것 같아.

> W: That's fine. I had some copies made already when I went yesterday.
> 괜찮아. 내가 어제 갔을 때 이미 몇 부 복사해 놨어.

11 남자가 언급한 문제는?
(A) 발표 자료를 가지고 있지 않다.
(B) 회의 장소 확인을 잊었다.
(C) 업무 행사용 메모를 잃어버렸다.
(D) 인쇄소 주소를 찾을 수 없다.

12 여자가 "이미 몇 부 복사해 놨어"라고 말할 때 암시하는 것은?
(A) 그녀는 내일 인쇄소에 다시 가지 않을 것이다.
(B) 그녀는 남자에게 줄 만큼 충분한 인쇄물을 가지고 있다.
(C) 인쇄소가 최근에 장비를 업그레이드했다.
(D) 남자는 발표 준비를 미뤄도 된다.

어휘 및 표현
head to ~에 가다 handout 유인물 materials 자료 imply ~을 암시하다 postpone ~을 미루다, 연기하다

Listen to an Announcement
13-14 대학교 동아리 모임에서 공지사항을 들으시오.

> Welcome to the photography club's monthly gathering! Before we begin today's activities, I want to remind everyone about the rules for our upcoming photo exhibition. This year's theme is city life, and all submissions must be sent in by October 30 to be featured at the event. We hope that all of you submit your best work for the event!
>
> 사진 동아리 월례 모임에 오신 것을 환영합니다! 오늘 활동을 시작하기 전에, 다가오는 사진 전시회 규칙에 대해 모두에게 상기시키고자 합니다. 올해의 주제는 도시 생활이며, 모든 출품작은 10월 30일까지 제출되어야 행사에 전시될 수 있습니다. 여러분 모두가 최고의 작품을 제출해 주시길 바랍니다!

13 화자가 도시 생활을 언급한 이유는?
(A) 그것이 전시회의 주제이다.
(B) 특별 게스트가 그것에 대해 이야기할 것이다.
(C) 오늘 강의의 주제이다.
(D) 일부 동아리 회원들은 이 도시가 처음이다.

14 화자가 참가자들에게 권장하는 행동은?
(A) 마감일까지 작품을 제출하는 일
(B) 작년 사진을 검토하는 일
(C) 채용 공고에 지원하는 일
(D) 특별 강좌에 등록하는 일

어휘 및 표현
gathering 모임 exhibition 전시회 be featured 나오다, 특징으로 나타나다 theme 주제 lecture 강의

job opening 채용 공고 sign up for ~에 등록하다

15-16 대학교 행사에서 공지사항을 들으시오.

> Attention, everyone. Just a reminder that the university's annual charity auction will be held tomorrow at 5:00 P.M. at the student center. All the money raised will go straight to supporting local causes. Come hang out, make a difference, and be part of something awesome!
>
> 여러분, 주목해 주세요. 대학의 연례 자선 경매가 내일 저녁 5시에 학생회관에서 개최될 예정임을 알려드립니다. 모금된 모든 금액은 지역 사회를 지원하는 데 직접 사용됩니다. 함께 어울리고, 변화를 만들어 보세요. 그리고 아주 멋진 일의 일부가 되어 보세요!

15 공지의 주요 주제는?
(A) 기부 캠페인
(B) 신입생 오리엔테이션
(C) 다가오는 자선 경매 행사
(D) 새로운 대학 행사

16 화자가 청중이 하기를 기대하는 것은?
(A) 행사에 자원봉사로 참여하는 일
(B) 온라인으로 기부하는 일
(C) 유학생을 지원하는 일
(D) 행사에 참석하는 일

어휘 및 표현

charity 자선 **auction** 경매 **local** 지역의 **cause** 조직, 사회, 대의, 운동 **hang out** 시간을 보내다 **awesome** 아주 멋진 **donation** 기부 **drive** 운동, 캠페인 **volunteer** 자원봉사하다 **international student** 유학생

Listen to an Academic Talk

17-20 천문학 수업에서의 강연을 들으시오.

> Neutrinos are incredibly small particles that almost never interact with anything. That's why they're so hard to detect. Even though we can't see or feel them, trillions of neutrinos pass through our bodies every second without us noticing. Scientists didn't spot neutrinos directly. Instead, they observed unusual energy patterns during nuclear reactions, which suggested the existence of neutrinos. To catch them, researchers built huge detectors deep underground. These detectors are filled with water or special liquids that help spot the rare moments when a neutrino does interact. Learning about neutrinos helps us understand how the Sun produces energy and how the universe has changed over time. Computer simulations show that without neutrinos, stars wouldn't act the same—and galaxies might not have formed the way they did. Now that we know neutrinos exist, the big question is: what are they made of? Let's take a look at some of the main ideas scientists are exploring.

중성미자는 믿을 수 없을 만큼 작은 입자로, 거의 아무것과도 상호작용하지 않습니다. 그래서 중성미자를 탐지하기가 매우 어렵습니다. 우리가 볼 수도 느낄 수도 없지만, 매초 수조 개의 중성미자가 우리는 알아차리지도 못한 채 우리 몸을 지나가고 있습니다. 과학자들은 중성미자를 직접 발견한 것이 아닙니다. 대신, 핵 반응 중에 나타나는 특이한 에너지 패턴을 관찰했고, 그것이 중성미자의 존재를 암시했습니다. 이를 포착하기 위해 연구자들은 지하 깊은 곳에 거대한 탐지기를 만들었습니다. 이 탐지기들은 물이나 특수한 액체로 채워져 있어, 중성미자가 드물게 상호작용하는 순간을 포착할 수 있게 해줍니다. 중성미자에 대해 배우는 것은 태양이 어떻게 에너지를 생성하는지, 그리고 우주가 시간이 지나며 어떻게 변화했는지를 이해하는 데 도움이 됩니다. 컴퓨터 시뮬레이션에 따르면, 중성미자가 없다면 별들은 지금과 같은 방식으로 작동하지 않았을 것이며, 은하들도 지금과 같은 형태로 형성되지 않았을 것입니다. 이제 우리는 중성미자의 존재를 알게 되었고, 다음으로 중요한 질문은 이것입니다: 중성미자는 무엇으로 이루어져 있을까요? 과학자들이 탐구하고 있는 주요 이론들을 살펴보겠습니다.

17 강연의 주요 주제는?
(A) 핵 에너지가 생성되는 방식
(B) 관측하기엔 너무 작은 입자들
(C) 지하 장치의 개발
(D) 인체에서 발견되는 다양한 화학물질

18 교수에 따르면, 과학자들이 중성미자를 처음 확인한 방법은?
(A) 별의 온도를 측정함으로써
(B) 태양 내 입자 수를 계산함으로써
(C) 에너지 수준의 예상치 못한 변화를 관찰함으로써
(D) 지면에서 반사된 빛을 분석함으로써

19 교수가 컴퓨터 시뮬레이션을 언급한 이유는?
(A) 중성미자가 우주의 진화에 영향을 준다는 주장을 뒷받침하기 위해
(B) 별에서 핵 반응이 어떻게 측정되는지를 설명하기 위해
(C) 전통 물리학 이론의 문제점을 설명하기 위해
(D) 탐지기에서 수집된 데이터가 어떻게 저장되는지를 보여주기 위해

20 교수가 다음에 이야기할 가능성이 가장 높은 것은?
(A) 입자 탐지기를 만드는 방법
(B) 중성미자의 구조에 대한 가설들
(C) 중성미자를 의학에 활용할 수 있는 방법
(D) 우주에서 중성미자가 이동하는 속도

어휘 및 표현

neutrino 중성미자, 중성미립자 particle 입자 interact 상호작용하다 detect 탐지하다 spot ~을 발견하다
nuclear reaction 핵 반응 suggest ~을 암시하다 existence 존재 detector 탐지기 liquid 액체 rare 드문
galaxy 은하 form 형성하다 be made of ~로 이루어지다 explore ~을 탐구하다 observe ~을 관찰하다
chemical 화학물질 temperature 온도 cosmic 우주의 measure ~을 측정하다 illustrate ~을 설명하다
traditional 전통의, 기존의 physics 물리학 theory 이론 method 방법 structure 구조 medicine 의학
travel 이동하다 space 우주

TEST 3
Listening Module 2

정답

Listen and Choose a Response
1-3   (A), (C), (C)

Listen to a Conversation
4-5   (B), (A)
6-7   (C), (D)

Listen to an Academic Talk
8-11   (B), (A), (A), (B)
12-15   (D), (B), (A), (C)

스크립트/해석/어휘

Listen and Choose a Response

1-3   가장 적절한 응답을 고르시오.

1   Who's in charge of updating the presentation slides?
　　누가 발표 슬라이드 업데이트 담당이지?

(A) 그건 내 담당이야.
(B) 내가 해.
(C) 많은 차질이 있었어.
(D) 모든 것이 순조롭게 진행되고 있어.

2   Why was yesterday's meeting called off?
　　왜 어제 회의가 취소되었지?

(A) 두 시간 전에 일어났어.
(B) 많은 참가자들.
(C) 대신 연기되었어.
(D) 다른 날짜를 정하자.

3   Could you look over my history essay?
　　내 역사 에세이를 빠르게 살펴봐 줄 수 있니?

(A) 너의 피드백을 정말 듣고 싶어.
(B) 넌 정말 친절하구나.
(C) 어떤 부분이 걱정되니?
(D) 그건 별로 중요하지 않아.

어휘 및 표현

in charge of ~의 담당인   **setback** 차질   **proceed** 진행되다   **smoothly** 순조롭게   **call off** ~을 취소하다

participant 참가자 **postpone** ~을 연기하다, 미루다 **look over** ~을 빠르게 살펴보다 **generous** 친절한, 관대한

Listen to a Conversation
4-5 대화를 들으시오.

M: Did you already hand in the sports equipment we borrowed from the gym?
우리가 체육관에서 빌린 운동 장비, 이미 반납했어?.

W: I thought we could keep it for the whole month.
한 달 동안 가지고 있어도 되는 줄 알았는데.

M: No, the new policy allows only a two-week loan period. Didn't they tell you that when you picked up the equipment?
아니야. 새로운 정책에 따르면 대여 기간은 2주뿐이야. 장비 가져갈 때 그 얘기 못 들었어?

W: Nobody mentioned it. Oh, then it has to be returned tomorrow!
아무도 말 안 해줬어. 오, 그럼 내일까지 반납해야겠네!

M: That's right.
맞아.

W: I'll drop it off today, just to be safe.
오늘 갖다 줄게, 안전하게 말이야.

---

4 여자가 놀란 정보는?
(A) 체육관이 다른 건물로 이사했다.
(B) 대여 기간이 더 짧아졌다.
(C) 체육관이 휴일 동안 문을 닫는다.
(D) 체육관 운영 시간이 연장되었다.

5 여자가 아마도 다음에 할 것은?
(A) 장비를 반납한다
(B) 체육관 직원에게 전화한다
(C) 연체료를 낸다
(D) 다른 물건을 빌린다

어휘 및 표현
hand in ~을 반납하다 **borrow** ~을 빌리다 **policy** 정책 **allow** ~을 허용하다 **loan** 대여 **pick up** ~을 가져가다 **drop off** ~을 갖다 놓다 **extend** ~을 연장하다 **overdue fee** 연체료

6-7 대화를 들으시오.

W: Are you going to the book fair this Friday?
이번 금요일에 도서 박람회에 갈 거야?

M: Of course! I like checking out what new books have come out.
물론이지! 어떤 새로운 책들이 나왔는지 보는 걸 좋아하거든.

W: Well, I've heard there will be author readings and book signings.
작가 낭독회랑 사인회도 있을 거라고 들었어.

M: That's great! I'll print out the event schedule.
멋지다! 행사 일정표를 출력해 갈게.

W: Perfect! Let's meet up there around 10 A.M.
완벽해! 그럼 오전 10시에 거기서 만나자.

6 화자들이 이야기하고 있는 행사는?
(A) 음식 축제
(B) 공예 박람회
(C) 도서 박람회
(D) 미술 전시회

7 남자가 행사에 가져가려고 계획한 것은?
(A) 책
(B) 노트북 컴퓨터
(C) 카메라
(D) 일정표

어휘 및 표현

fair 박람회 check out 확인하다, 보다 author reading 작가 낭독회 signing 사인회 print out 출력하다 meet up (약속을 하여) 만나다 craft 공예

Listen to an Academic Talk
8-11 디자인 수업에서의 강연을 들으시오.

Bio-inspired design means learning from nature to solve human problems. Scientists and engineers look at how animals and plants work, then use those ideas to create better tools, buildings, and technologies. One famous example is Velcro. A Swiss engineer saw how sticky seeds from plants clung to his dog's fur and used that idea to invent Velcro. Another example comes from termites. These insects build large mounds with smart ventilation systems that keep the inside cool. Architects studied these mounds to design buildings that use less energy for heating and cooling. Nature also helps us improve renewable energy. For example, butterfly wings trap light very well. Engineers are testing solar panels with coatings that work the same way to catch more sunlight. Some drones are even shaped like birds to fly more smoothly. By learning from nature, we can create designs that are more efficient and better for the environment.

생체 모방 디자인이란 자연으로부터 배워 인간의 문제를 해결하는 것을 의미합니다. 과학자들과 엔지니어들은 동물과 식물이 어떻게 작동하는지를 관찰한 후, 그 아이디어를 활용해 더 나은 도구, 건물, 기술을 만듭니다. 유명한 예로는 벨크로가 있습니다. 한 스위스 엔지니어가 식물에서 나온 끈적한 씨앗이 자신의 개의 털에 달라붙는 것을 보고 그 아이디어를 활용해 벨크로를 발명했습니다. 또 다른 예는 흰개미에서 나옵니다. 이 곤충들은 내부를

시원하게 유지하는 똑똑한 환기 시스템이 있는 큰 흙더미를 만듭니다. 건축가들은 이러한 흙더미를 연구하여 난방과 냉방에 적은 에너지를 사용하는 건물을 설계했습니다. 자연은 또한 재생 가능 에너지를 개선하는 데 도움을 줍니다. 예를 들어, 나비의 날개는 빛을 매우 잘 모아 둡니다. 엔지니어들은 더 많은 햇빛을 포착하기 위해 같은 방식으로 작동하는 코팅을 적용한 태양광 패널을 실험하고 있습니다. 일부 드론은 새처럼 생겨 더 부드럽게 날 수 있습니다. 자연으로부터 배움으로써, 우리는 더 효율적이고 환경에 더 좋은 디자인을 만들 수 있습니다.

8 강의의 주요 초점은?
(A) 동물이 포식자를 피하는 방법
(B) 자연이 인간의 발명에 영감을 주는 방식
(C) 재생 가능 에너지의 발전
(D) 동물 행동의 진화

9 교수가 개를 언급하는 이유는?
(A) 발명이 자연의 메커니즘을 모방한 방식을 보여주기 위해
(B) 동물의 움직임을 드론과 비교하기 위해
(C) 식물이 동물 행동에 영향을 주는 방식을 설명하기 위해
(D) 반려동물과 인간의 협력을 설명하기 위해

10 교수가 흰개미 흙더미에 대해 강조하는 것은?
(A) 내부 온도가 일정하게 유지된다.
(B) 흰개미는 때때로 건물을 손상시킨다.
(C) 건설에 매우 적은 에너지가 필요하다.
(D) 포식자로부터 동물을 보호한다.

11 교수가 태양광 패널에 대해 암시하는 것은?
(A) 소음이 곤충을 방해할 수 있다.
(B) 나비 날개의 디자인에서 영감을 받았을 수 있다.
(C) 높은 건물에 설치하기가 더 쉽다.
(D) 재활용 재료로 만들어진다.

어휘 및 표현

bio-inspired 생명체에서 영감을 받은 sticky 끈적끈적한 seed 씨앗 cling to ~에 들러붙다 fur 털 invent ~을 발명하다 termite 흰개미 mound 흙더미 ventilation 환기 architect 건축가 heating 난방 cooling 냉방 renewable 재생 가능한 trap ~을 가두다, 모아 두다 efficient 효율적인 predator 포식자 inspire ~에 영감을 주다 advance 발전 evolution 진화, 발전 constant 일정한, 끊임없는, 변함없는 temperature 온도 damage ~을 손상시키다 disturb ~을 방해하다 install 설치하다

12-15 영화학 수업에서의 강연을 들으시오.

I'd like to talk to you about one of the most prominent and influential documentary filmmakers of all time, Ken Burns. Burns has been making films and television miniseries for around four decades now, and his first documentary feature, *Brooklyn Bridge*, released in 1981, was nominated for an Academy Award. When the bridge opened in 1883, it was seen as a symbol of American advancement and engineering prowess, and Burns manages to convey that feeling perfectly in his film. *The Civil War*, a television documentary miniseries, ended up winning more than 40 awards—Grammy Awards, Emmy Awards, you name it—and it still stands as one of the biggest successes of his career. But, it's worth noting that it had its fair share of critics, too. A lot of historians took exception to Burns's focus on the battles of the American Civil War rather than the issues that caused them, or their repercussions. Another documentary series, *Baseball*, is a comprehensive look at "America's pastime" and the way it has shaped, and been shaped by our culture over many years. On that note, I'm also looking forward to his upcoming film about the boxer Muhammad Ali. But that's just because those topics are close to my heart.

오늘 저는 역사상 가장 중요하면서 영향력이 컸던 다큐멘터리 영화감독들 중 한 명인 켄 번즈에 관해 이야기하고자 합니다. 번즈는 지금까지 약 40년 동안 영화와 텔레비전 미니시리즈들을 만들어 왔으며, 1981년에 개봉한 첫 번째 다큐멘터리 장편 영화 〈브루클린 다리〉는 아카데미상 후보로 지명되었습니다. 그 다리가 1883년에 개통되었을 때, 미국의 발전상과 토목 공사 기술력에 대한 하나의 상징으로 여겨졌으며, 번즈는 자신의 영화에서 그러한 느낌을 완벽하게 구현해 내고 있습니다. TV 다큐멘터리 미니시리즈인 〈남북전쟁〉은 결과적으로 그래미상과 에미상을 비롯해 40개가 넘는 온갖 상을 받게 되었으며, 여전히 그의 경력에서 가장 큰 성공작 중 하나로 우뚝 서 있습니다. 하지만, 이 작품이 비평가들로부터 그에 합당한 대가를 치렀다는 점도 주목해 볼 만한 가치가 있습니다. 많은 역사가들이 미국 남북전쟁의 전투들을 초래한 문제점들이나 그 후의 영향보다는 오히려 전투들에 초점을 맞춘 번즈에게 이의를 제기했습니다. 또 다른 다큐멘터리 시리즈, 〈베이스볼〉은 "미국의 국민 오락"을 포괄적으로 바라보면서 그것이 오랜 기간에 걸쳐 어떻게 우리 문화를 형성시켜 왔는지 그리고 반대로 어떻게 우리 문화에 의해 그것이 형성되어 왔는지를 모두 보여줍니다. 말 나온 김에, 저는 곧 공개될 복서 무하마드 알리에 관한 그의 영화도 고대하고 있습니다. 하지만 이는 단지 그러한 주제들이 제 마음에 와닿기 때문입니다.

12 강연의 주된 목적은?
(A) 여러 감독들의 영화 제작 방식을 비교하기 위해
(B) 한 유명 다큐멘터리의 문화적 영향을 강조하기 위해
(C) 왜 켄 번즈가 작품에 대해 인정받지 못했는지 설명하기 위해
(D) 한 유명 다큐멘터리 제작자의 여러 작품을 논의하기 위해

13 화자의 말에 따르면, 〈브루클린 다리〉의 장점들 중 하나는?
(A) 번즈의 영화 제작 접근법이 시간이 흐름에 따라 얼마나 크게 변화했는지 보여준다.
(B) 미국의 독창성과 발전상에 대한 느낌을 효과적으로 묘사하고 있다.
(C) 해당 다리 건설에 참여한 사람들의 개인적인 삶에 초점을 맞추고 있다.
(D) 저예산 고품질 영화 제작의 한 가지 예시에 해당된다.

14 화자의 말에 따르면, 〈남북전쟁〉이 일부 역사가들에게 평이 좋지 않은 이유는?
(A) 전쟁의 결과를 설명하는 데 충분한 시간을 쏟지 못했다.
(B) 주요 군사적 충돌 중에 발생된 핵심 사건들을 잘못 전했다.
(C) 관람객들의 관심을 사로잡기 위해 특수 효과에 지나치게 의존했다.
(D) 전쟁에 참여한 특정 집단에 대해 명백한 편향을 드러냈다.

15 화자가 다큐멘터리 영화에 대한 자신의 취향과 관련해 암시하는 것은?
(A) 취향이 문화적 변화에 의해 직접적으로 영향받아 왔다.
(B) 취향이 시간이 흐를수록 크게 변화되어 왔다.
(C) 스포츠와 관련된 다큐멘터리를 선호한다.
(D) 전쟁과 역사에 관한 영화에 대해 만족하지 않는 경향이 있다.

어휘 및 표현
prominent 중요한, 주목할 만한 feature 장편 영화 be nominated for ~에 대한 후보로 지명되다 prowess 기술력, 기량 convey ~을 전달하다 note that ~라는 점에 주목하다 have one's fair share 합당한 대가를 치르다, ~을 당연히 받아 들이다 take exception to ~에 이의를 제기하다 repercussion 반향, 영향 comprehensive 포괄적인, 종합적인 pastime 오락 on that note 말 나온 김에 director 감독 recognition 인정 renowned 유명한 portray ~을 그리다, 묘사하다 ingenuity 독창성 serve as ~에 해당되다, ~의 역할을 하다 consequence 결과 misrepresent ~을 잘못 전하다 military 군사적인 conflict 충돌 obvious 분명한, 명백한 bias 편견, 편향 taste 취향 preference 선호 dissatisfied 만족하지 않는

TEST 3 Writing

정답 및 모범답안

Build a Sentence

1. Unfortunately, I did not receive an invitation.
2. Have you heard that alligators live in the lake?
3. I asked her when our exact deadline was.
4. He needed to confirm what I included in my application.
5. The tools you purchased are scheduled to arrive on Wednesday.
6. He wanted to know if I went anywhere exciting.
7. She works faster than all of the other employees we've hired.
8. The mall next to the train station sells all types of formal attire.
9. When do you expect to finish the project?
10. They were curious about why I planned to start a business.

Write an Email

Dear Mr. Nadal,

I hope this message finds you well.

I am writing to request the cancellation of my gym membership. I joined Powerhouse Gym two weeks ago and signed up for the Silver Pass, which grants me unlimited access for one year. Unfortunately, I recently experienced a sharp pain in my leg while running, and my doctor has advised me to rest and avoid exercising for the next couple of months. Since I am unsure when I will be able to return to your gym, I would appreciate it if you could cancel my membership and ensure that I am no longer charged. Once my leg gets better, I hope to rejoin your gym.

I look forward to your response.

Best regards,
Hazel Kim

Write for an Academic Discussion

While I understand Jane's point about sanitation, I believe medical advancements have been the main factor behind the increase in life expectancy. First, diagnostic technologies, such as MRI and CT scans, enable doctors to identify illnesses at a much earlier stage than before. This allows treatment to begin before illnesses become serious, greatly improving the chances of recovery for patients. Second, advances in surgical techniques, including robot-assisted procedures and the use of lasers, have made operations not only more precise but also much safer, allowing patients to recover more quickly and with fewer complications. These medical breakthroughs mean that conditions that were once considered fatal can now be treated effectively. In conclusion, medical advancements have been crucial in extending lifespans.

해석/어휘

Build a Sentence

1-10 적절한 문장을 만드시오.

1 W: 워크숍에 올 거니?
　　M: 아쉽게도 초대장을 못 받았어.

2 M: 다음 달에 낚시 가는 거 너무 기대돼.
　　W: 그 호수에 악어 산다는 얘기 들었어?

3 W: 아다니 박사님께 뭘 알고 싶었던 거야?
　　M: 마감일이 정확히 언제인지 여쭤봤어.

4 W: 워렌 교수님이 왜 전화하신 거야?
　　M: 내가 지원서에 무엇을 포함했는지 확인하실 필요가 있으셨어.

5 W: 소포는 언제 도착해?
　　W: 네가 주문한 공구는 수요일에 도착할 예정이야.

6 W: 다니엘이 너한테 무엇을 물어봤어?
　　M: 내가 어디 재밌는 곳을 다녀왔는지 알길 원했어.

7 W: 리아가 왜 승진한 거야?
　　M: 그녀는 우리가 고용한 직원들 중에 제일 빨리 일해.

8 W: 그 정장 어디서 샀어?
　　M: 기차역 옆에 있는 쇼핑몰에서 모든 종류의 정장을 다 팔아.

9 W: 내 최종 과제의 주제를 바꿀까 생각 중이야.
　　W: 그 프로젝트를 언제쯤 끝낼 것 같아?

10 W: 주노와 헥터가 세션 끝나고 뭘 물어봤어?
　　M: 내가 왜 창업하려는지 궁금해했어.

어휘 및 표현

invitation 초대장　alligator 악어　application 지원서　package 소포　promotion 승진　suit 정장　formal attire 정장　assignment 과제　session 세션, 특정 시간

Write an Email

당신은 최근에 새로운 헬스장에 가입했다. 당신은 건강상의 문제로 인해 회원권을 취소하려고 헬스장 주인인 나달 씨에게 연락해야 한다. 당신은 건강이 나아지면 다시 돌아오기를 희망한다.

나달 씨에게 이메일을 작성하시오. 이메일에서 다음을 수행하시오:

- 어떤 회원권을 가지고 있는지 언급하시오.
- 회원권을 취소해야 하는 이유를 설명하시오.
- 이후에 어떻게 처리되기를 원하는지 서술하시오.

완전한 문장으로 가능한 한 많이 작성하시오.

당신의 답변:

수신인: 나달 씨
제목: 헬스장 회원권 취소

나달 씨께,

저는 이 메시지가 당신께 잘 전달되길 바랍니다.

저는 헬스장 회원권 취소를 요청드리고자 이메일을 씁니다. 저는 2주 전에 Powerhouse Gym에 가입했고, 1년 동안 무제한 이용이 가능한 Silver Pass를 등록했습니다. 불행하게도, 최근 달리기를 하던 중 다리에 심한 통증을 느꼈고, 의사는 제게 앞으로 몇 달간 운동을 피하고 휴식을 취하라고 권했습니다. 언제 다시 헬스장에 갈 수 있을지 확실하지 않기 때문에, 회원권을 취소해주시고 더 이상 요금이 청구되지 않도록 조치해주시면 감사하겠습니다. 다리가 회복되면, 당신의 헬스장에 다시 등록하고 싶습니다.

당신의 답변을 기대하겠습니다.

안녕히 계세요,
헤이즐 김

(125 단어)

어휘 및 표현

cancellation 취소 **sign up for** ~에 등록하다 **grant A B** A에게 B를 부여하다 **sharp pain** 심한 통증 **advise A to B** A에게 B하도록 권하다

Write for an Academic Discussion

교수가 사회학 수업을 진행 중이다. 교수의 질문에 답변하는 게시글을 작성하시오.

답변에서는 다음을 수행해야 한다:

- 본인의 의견을 제시하고 뒷받침하시오.
- 토론에 본인의 표현으로 기여하시오.

효과적인 답변은 최소 100단어 이상이어야 한다.

존스 박사: 우리가 수업 시간에 논의했듯이, 평균 기대 수명이 지난 몇 세기 동안 전 세계적으로 증가해왔으며, 앞으로도 계속 상승할 것으로 예상됩니다. 어떤 사람들은 위생 개선이 주요 요인이었다고 믿는 반면, 다른 사람들은 의학의 발전이 더 큰 영향을 미쳤다고 생각합니다. 당신은 어떤 관점에 동의하며, 그 이유는 무엇입니까?

제인: 저는 위생 개선이 사람들이 더 오래 사는 데 중요한 역할을 했다고 생각합니다. 예전에는, 사람들이 쓰레기를 거리로 버렸고, 정수되지 않은 물로 인해 많은 사람들이 병에 걸렸습니다. 우리는 지금 하수도 시스템과 깨끗한 물에 쉽게 접근할 수 있는 훨씬 더 위생적인 환경에서 살고 있습니다.

샘: 저는 의학의 발전이 기대 수명이 증가한 가장 큰 이유라고 믿습니다. 이제 우리는 예전에는 치명적이었을 질병들을 치료할 수 있습니다. 과거에는 팬데믹이 되었을 수도 있는 질병도 이제는 간단한 백신으로 예방할 수 있어, 더 오래 사는 데 기여하고 있습니다.

저는 제인의 위생에 대한 의견을 이해하지만, 저는 의학의 발전이 기대 수명이 증가한 주된 요인이라고 생각합니다. 첫째, MRI나 CT 스캔과 같은 진단 기술은 의사들이 질병을 이전보다 훨씬 더 이른 단계에서 발견할 수 있게 해줍니다. 이는 질병이 심각해지기 전에 치료를 시작할 수 있게 해주며, 환자가 회복될 가능성을 크게 높여줍니다. 둘째, 로봇을 활용한 수술이나 레이저 사용 등 외과 기술의 발전은 수술을 더욱 정밀하고 안전하게 만들어, 환자들이 더 빠르게 회복하고 합병증도 줄어들게 해줍니다. 이러한 의학적 혁신들은 과거에는 치명적이었던 질병들도 이제는 효과적으로 치료될 수 있음을 의미합니다. 결론적으로, 의학의 발전은 기대 수명을 연장하는 데 결정적인 역할을 해왔습니다.

(120 단어)

어휘 및 표현

life expectancy 기대 수명 **sanitation** 위생 **medical advancement** 의학의 발전 **influential** 영향 있는 **unpurified** 정수되지 않은, 정화되지 않은 **sanitary** 위생적인 **sewer** 하수(도) **fatal** 치명적인 **pandemic** 팬데믹, 대규모 유행병 **contribute to** ~에 기여하다 **lifespan** 수명 **diagnostic** 진단의 **identify** ~을 발견하다, 알아보다, 확인하다 **treatment** 치료 **recovery** 회복 **surgical** 수술의, 외과의 **procedure** 수술, 절차 **operation** 수술 **complication** 합병증 **breakthrough** (획기적인) 발전 **crucial** 결정적인, 중대한

TEST 3

Speaking

정답 및 모범답안

Listen and Repeat

1 Welcome to the park visitor center.
2 The main trail begins near the ranger station.
3 Our picnic area offers a place to enjoy snacks.
4 Let me show you our camping grounds located nearby.
5 Visit the observation deck to enjoy stunning views of the area.
6 We recommend checking the bulletin board to learn about guided tours and events.
7 Before starting your hike, secure your belongings and make sure your phone is charged.

Take an Interview

1 *Thank you for speaking with me. Today, I'd like to ask you some questions about your commuting habits. First, how do your friends or family usually commute to school or work? For example, by car, subway, or other ways?*

Actually, my family and most of my friends use public transportation to commute to work or school. My parents go to work by bus, which takes them about an hour each day, depending on traffic conditions. My friends mostly take the subway to university, as there is a station just a short walk away from campus. Those who live very close by usually walk or ride a bicycle instead. To sum up, most people I know use public transportation to commute.

2 *Thank you. When you commute, do you prefer to relax and not do anything, or to do something, like read, listen to music, or work?*

Between the two, my preference is to do something on my way to university. To give a personal example, I take my commute time as an opportunity to improve my English by memorizing vocabulary or listening to podcasts to practice my listening skills. Other times, when I am tired after studying, I simply listen to music or watch videos on my phone. If I do nothing, I feel bored and feel like I'm wasting my time. Overall, I prefer using my commute productively.

3 *Interesting. Next, I'd like to get your opinion. In recent years, there has been a trend toward walking or cycling instead of using vehicles to reduce carbon emissions. Do you think that in the future, more people will adopt these habits? Why or why not?*

There is a chance that walking or cycling will become commonplace in the coming years. One reason is that cities are improving infrastructure, such as building better sidewalks and dedicated bicycle lanes. Another reason is that people are becoming more eco-conscious, and many are choosing these habits to reduce their carbon footprint. However, it is undeniable that vehicles will not be completely replaced, as they are still needed for various purposes. In conclusion, walking and cycling will likely increase, but vehicles will remain essential.

4 *Good points. I just have one more question. Some people believe that living close to school or work to reduce one's commute time is important for improving quality of life. Do you agree or disagree? Explain why you think so.*

I tend to agree that spending less time commuting to school or work significantly improves your quality of life. The main reason is that the less time spent traveling, the more time and energy are available for other activities. For instance, people can go to the gym or take a walk, which benefits their health. They can also spend more quality time with family and friends. For this reason, living closer to school or work can make daily life more enjoyable and less stressful.

> 해석/어휘

Listen and Repeat
당신은 공원 방문객들을 맞이하는 연수를 받고 있다. 트레이너의 말을 듣고 따라 하시오. 오직 한 번만 따라 하시오.

1 공원 방문객 센터에 오신 것을 환영합니다.

2 주요 산책로는 공원 관리소 근처에서 시작됩니다.

3 저희 피크닉 공간은 간식을 즐기실 수 있는 장소를 제공합니다.

4 근처에 위치한 캠핑장을 안내해드리겠습니다.

5 전망대를 방문하시면 이 지역의 멋진 풍경을 감상하실 수 있습니다.

6 가이드 투어나 행사 정보를 얻기 위해 안내 게시판을 확인하시길 권장합니다.

7 하이킹을 시작하기 전, 소지품을 잘 챙기시고 휴대폰이 충전되어 있는지 확인하세요.

어휘 및 표현
trail 산책로 **ranger station** 공원 관리소 **stunning view** 멋진 풍경 **bulletin board** 게시판 **belongings** 소지품

Take an Interview
당신은 통근·통학 습관에 대한 연구 조사에 참여하기로 동의하였다. 당신은 연구원과 간단한 온라인 인터뷰를 진행하게 된다. 연구원이 몇 가지 질문을 할 것이다.

1 저와 말씀을 나눠 주셔서 감사합니다. 오늘, 저는 당신의 통근·통학 습관에 대한 몇 가지 질문을 드리겠습니다. 먼저, 당신의 가족이나 친구들은 보통 어떤 방식으로 학교나 직장에 통근하나요? 예를 들어 자동차, 지하철, 또는 다른 방법이 있을까요?

사실, 저희 가족과 대부분의 친구들은 대중교통을 이용해 학교나 직장에 갑니다. 부모님은 버스를 타고 출근

하시는데, 교통 상황에 따라 하루에 약 한 시간이 걸립니다. 친구들은 대부분 지하철을 타고 대학에 가는데, 캠퍼스에서 도보로 가까운 거리에 지하철역이 있기 때문입니다. 아주 가까운 곳에 사는 사람들은 보통 걸어서 가거나 자전거를 타고 갑니다. 요약하자면, 제가 아는 대부분의 사람들은 대중교통을 이용해 통근합니다.

2 감사합니다. 당신은 통근·통학 시에, 아무것도 하지 않고 쉬는 걸 선호하나요, 아니면 책을 읽거나 음악을 듣거나 일을 하는 등 무언가를 하는 걸 선호하나요?

둘 중에서, 제가 선호하는 것은 통학 중에 무엇인가를 하는 것입니다. 개인적인 예를 들자면, 저는 통학 시간을 영어 실력을 향상시키는 기회로 활용합니다. 단어를 외우거나 팟캐스트를 들으며 듣기 연습을 하기도 하죠. 때로는, 공부 후 피곤할 때, 그냥 음악을 듣거나 휴대폰으로 영상을 보기도 합니다. 아무것도 하지 않으면, 지루하고 시간을 낭비하는 기분이 들어요. 전반적으로, 저는 통학 시간을 생산적으로 활용하는 걸 좋아합니다.

3 흥미롭네요. 다음으로, 당신의 의견을 듣고 싶습니다. 최근에, 탄소 배출을 줄이기 위해 차량 대신 걷거나 자전거를 타는 경향이 생기고 있습니다. 당신은 앞으로 더 많은 사람들이 이런 습관을 받아들일 거라고 생각하나요? 이유는요?

앞으로 걷기나 자전거 타기가 일반화될 가능성이 있습니다. 첫 번째 이유는 도시들이 인도를 개선하거나 자전거 전용 도로를 만드는 등 기반 시설을 개선하고 있기 때문입니다. 두 번째 이유는 사람들이 환경에 대한 의식이 높아지고 있어서, 많은 이들이 탄소 발자국을 줄이기 위해 이런 습관을 선택합니다. 하지만, 차량이 완전히 대체되기는 어렵다는 점도 분명한데, 여전히 다양한 용도로 필요하니까요. 결론적으로, 걷기와 자전거 타기는 증가할 가능성이 크지만, 차량은 여전히 필수적인 존재로 남을 것입니다.

4 좋은 지적이에요. 마지막으로 한 가지 질문만 더 하겠습니다. 어떤 사람들은 통근 시간을 줄이기 위해 학교나 직장 근처에 사는 것이 삶의 질을 높이는 데 중요하다고 믿습니다. 이에 대해 동의하나요, 아니면 반대하나요? 그 이유를 설명해주세요.

저는 통학 또는 통근하는 시간을 줄이는 것이 삶의 질을 크게 향상시킨다고 생각하는 편입니다. 가장 큰 이유는 이동 시간이 줄어들수록 다른 활동에 쓸 수 있는 시간과 에너지가 더 많아지기 때문입니다. 예를 들어, 사람들이 헬스장에 가거나 산책을 할 수 있는데, 이는 건강에 도움이 됩니다. 또한 가족이나 친구들과 더 많이 귀중한 시간을 보낼 수 있죠. 이런 이유로, 학교나 직장 가까이에 사는 것은 일상생활을 더 즐겁고 덜 스트레스 받게 만들어줍니다.

어휘 및 표현

commuting habit 통근·통학 습관 **public transportation** 대중 교통 **productively** 생산적으로 **carbon emissions** 탄소 배출 **adopt** ~을 받아들이다, 채택하다 **commonplace** 일반화되는, 아주 흔한 **sidewalk** 보도 **dedicated bicycle lane** 자전거 전용 도로 **eco-conscious** 환경을 생각하는 **carbon footprint** 탄소 발자국 **quality time** 귀중한 시간